T5-AFK-806

SOVIET FAR EASTERN POLICY

1931–1945

SOVIET FAR EASTERN POLICY

1931–1945

By HARRIET L. MOORE

HOWARD FERTIG

NEW YORK · 1973

Howard Fertig, Inc. Edition 1973
Published by arrangement with Princeton University Press

Library of Congress Cataloging in Publication Data
Moore, Harriet Lucy, 1912-
Soviet Far Eastern policy, 1931-1945.
Reprint of the ed. published by Princeton University Press, Princeton, N. J., in series: Institute of Pacific relations, I. P. R. inquiry series.
Includes bibliographical references.
1. East (Far East)—Foreign relations—Russia.
2. Russia—Foreign relations—East (Far East)
I. Title. II. Series: Institute of Pacific Relations.
I. P. R. inquiry series.
DS518.7.M66 1973 327.47'05 76-80573

Printed in the United States of America
by Noble Offset Printers, Inc.

INTRODUCTION

To many Americans, perhaps to most Americans, the policy of the Soviet Union toward China and Japan has been an enigma. The particular aspect of Soviet Asiatic policy which is of most interest to Americans concerns Soviet entry into the war against Japan. So long as the Soviet policy as a whole is considered enigmatic, neither this nor any other aspect of it can be rationally analyzed.

We must, then, deal first with a definition: the difference between an enigma and a problem. An enigma is an unintelligible riddle, which can perhaps be guessed but cannot be solved. A problem, on the other hand, is a complex of known and unknown factors, which can be analyzed by determining the known and unknown factors, and eventually solved by working from the known to the unknown.

To a certain extent the foreign policy of every country is a problem. Rarely can the average American say that he knows all the factors even in America's own foreign policy. It is normal, when analyzing foreign policy, to run across factors which are like x's in an equation. Usually, even the expert is forced to admit that he does not understand all of these x-factors. The best that he can do is to work out the equation or problem in such a way that it becomes comprehensible as a whole, even if some of the details remain puzzling or only partially understood. A working hypothesis or working solution can then be stated, by assigning tentative or approximate values to the x-factors.

If we can reduce Soviet policy from the total incomprehensibility of an enigma to a level at which it becomes, like the policies of other countries, comprehensible in general outline even though many details remain obscure, we shall have gone a long way. Miss Moore has accomplished just this. By careful compilation of the record, and by frequent cross-reference to the unfolding of Soviet policy in Europe, the ups and downs of Soviet-American relations, and the overall course of events, she first breaks down the enigmatic into the problematic. Then, by grouping the identifiable factors, she opens the way to a rational consideration of the x-factors.

Miss Moore's work is timely and important, because we are entering on a new phase of history. The Soviet Union, by virtue of its large share in the Victory in Europe and the commanding position it holds in Asia, has a great deal more power than the old Russia ever had. America has also attained a greater sum of power, and a wider outreach of strength, than ever before. By all the accepted standards, America is the only country which is even more powerful than the Soviet Union. American-Soviet relations must therefore rank as more important than relations between any other two countries in the world.

In these relations America, because of her greater power, has the greater initiative—if she will take it and use it. Where Soviet policy is all-important is in its capacity to react to the American initiative, or to take the initiative if America should let it go by default.

As an analysis of the record, and as a guide to the alternatives of the present and the potentialities of the future, Miss Moore's work is unique in English. She has done a notable service to the interest of the people of America.

The Walter Hines Page School of International Relations
The Johns Hopkins University

OWEN LATTIMORE

CONTENTS

APPENDICES

*This recent text is given in a Supplement beginning on p. 265.

PREFACE

IN THE LAST decade preoccupation with the Soviet Union in Europe has obscured the fact that the U.S.S.R. is also a potent power in Asia. Russia alone of the great western powers came to the Far East overland and has a long land frontier in the East. Its federation includes five oriental republics in Central Asia and indeed more than half its lands lie in Asia, thus involving it in Far Eastern conflicts whenever and wherever they arise. The Russo-Japanese War, Japanese intervention in Siberia, cooperation with Sun Yat-Sen's revolution are but landmarks in a long and difficult history of Far Eastern relations, both Tsarist and Soviet. Though less familiar to Americans, this Far Eastern history has left as deep an impress on Russian thinking as has its European history. From 1931 to 1941 it was not in Europe but on Russia's eastern border—the longest highly fortified border in the world—that the Soviets expected war from day to day. Their neutrality in the East has been one not of indifference but one of dangerous tension, repeatedly threatened by skirmishes, both diplomatic and military.

Soviet attitudes toward the Far Eastern conflict have not been too easily accessible to Americans because much of the material has appeared only in Russian. In addition, the lack of effective international cooperation prior to Pearl Harbor meant that the Soviet Union for the most part was acting alone and often the details of its policies escaped our attention.

Today, turning from victory in Europe to the problem of victory in the Pacific, it is clear enough that for the future security of the Far East the Soviet Union will be a necessary factor. Its exclusion from the Washington Conference and Nine-Power Agreements concerning the Pacific may well have been the fatal flaw in the security machinery developed after the last war, and it goes without saying that this will not be repeated.

Looking back over the years to 1931 when the Far Eastern war began, no contrast is greater than in the position of the Soviet Union then and now. Today it is an integral part of a great world alliance to destroy aggressive powers and keep the peace. It possesses one of the greatest armed forces in all history, along with the industrial base essential to its maintenance and supply. Its new economic, social and political order has withstood the severest test to which a nation can be put and has evidently emerged stronger and more stable than ever before. The economic and strategic development of Siberia, Central Asia and the Soviet Far East have been stepped up to meet the menace in the East. The Soviet Union today is undoubtedly one of the great powers of the Pacific.

Whether or not its power is brought to bear on the serious problems of the day in the Far East is a matter of grave concern to all countries of the Pacific basin. In retrospect, the record as the Soviets have written it would answer the question in the affirmative. Not only is it plain that for the U.S.S.R. peace and security in the East have always been a question of national defense; to this end, Moscow has through the years, since Litvinov first formulated the phrase "peace is indivisible," advocated international machinery in the East as well as the West, machinery backed by requisite force.

The reader of this short study will not find the full story of the Soviet Union as a Far Eastern power. That story will not be written until archives are opened, not only in Moscow, but in China, Japan and the western capitals. What is attempted in this book is to bring to the American reader an account of what the Soviet Union said and did in the Far

East from 1931 until 1945. It gives approximately the picture which the Soviet people themselves have of this part of the world scene, for the study is compiled almost exclusively from Soviet sources. In addition, the appendices include translations of Soviet editorial comments on the most important developments. As far as possible, the account of actual events has been checked against non-Soviet sources but the author has not been able to make use of materials in Chinese or Japanese. Although it has not been possible to give adequate space to European events whose impact on Soviet Far Eastern policies has been so great, it will be obvious to the reader that Soviet relations at one end of its vast domain cannot but be of vital importance to its relations at the other. It is also outside the scope of this study to give an account of Soviet internal developments, especially the building up of its economy in the East which may be important to the future of Asia as a source of trade, military strength, and political example to the other nations of the Far East.

The author is indebted to the International Secretariat of the Institute of Pacific Relations for its help in preparing the manuscript for publication. Special thanks are due Olga Field for editing and checking the manuscript. However, all statements of facts or expressions of opinion are the sole responsibility of the author.

H. L. M.

New York,
May 1945

SOVIET FAR EASTERN POLICY

1931–1945

I. THE SETTING: THE SOVIET UNION IN 1931

FROM THE VANTAGE POINT of 1945 when the strength of the U.S.S.R. is one of the dominating facts in current events, it is not easy to recall how precarious was the whole new society at the time Japan invaded Manchuria fourteen years ago. The first Five-Year Plan was still in progress; socialization of industry had just been completed, following the abandonment of the New Economic Policy; collective farms were just being organized on a wide scale in the face of strong opposition; the machine-tractor stations had just been developed to give the collective farms the advantage of mechanization. Living was very difficult for all. Industry was young: there were virtually no automotive or chemical industries, to mention but two of the prerequisites of the modern power state. There were no Magnitogorsk or Kuznetsk iron and steel centers, no second tracks on the Trans-Siberian Railroad; the ground where Komsomolsk stands today was not even cleared. In short, the Soviets had only three years before regained the productive level of 1913, after the devastation of World War I and the Civil War which followed.

Internationally the Soviets were isolated in the Far East. The U.S.S.R. had what might be called normal relations with Japan alone of all the powers involved in the developing conflict, and Japan but six years before had withdrawn its troops from Siberia and the Soviet Far East. China had not resumed diplomatic relations with Moscow since the events of 1927 and 1929. When Chiang Kai-shek led the Kuomintang's split with the Chinese Communists, he also severed all relations with the Russians, and China was swept by a wave of anti-Soviet activities.[1] Although Moscow officially ignored this, as its diplomatic relations were with the old Peking government, it in turn cut off relations in 1929, as a result of the dispute and consequent armed conflict over the Chinese Eastern Railway (see below). In May 1930 an official delegation had been sent to Moscow by the Nanking and Mukden Chinese governments to negotiate a settlement, but the parleys had been interrupted and delayed so that by September 18, 1931, there still had been no exchange of diplomatic representatives between China and the Soviets. However, consulates had been reopened and the Khabarovsk Protocol, signed December 22, 1929,[2] provided a basis for the joint operation of the C.E.R.

Relations with Japan had been relatively good since the establishment of diplomatic and consular representation in 1925.[3] The change of government in Japan which had led to the final evacuation of Northern Sakhalin had given some assurance that the policy of aggression against the Russian Far East would be abandoned. Although the U.S.S.R. felt that Japan had played a part, along with the western powers, in delaying the establishment of diplomatic relations between the Soviet Union and the Peking government,[4] it nevertheless found the Japanese government unwilling to join the other powers in their protests to Russia and China over the Chinese Eastern Railway dispute in 1929.

[1] In 1927 there occurred the raid on the Soviet Embassy in Peking, the raid on its consulate in Shanghai, and the assassinations of Soviet consular officials after the Canton Commune.

[2] See Appendix, p. 182.

[3] See Appendix, p. 175.

[4] *Pravda* said that Japan occupied the same position with regard to Manchuria, and would willingly occupy the same position with regard to the Soviet Far East as France occupied with regard to the Ruhr. The Soviet press stated that the aims of Japan's hostile attitude toward the U.S.S.R. were twofold: to extend Japanese influence in Northern Manchuria and to prevent recognition of Russia by China before her recognition by Japan. Cf. *Russian Review*, published by the Russian Information Bureau, Washington, D.C., May 1, 1924, p. 339.

Japan, in that case, had remained neutral and refused to transport troops over the South Manchurian Railway. As a result, Molotov, then Chairman of the Council of Peoples Commissars, was able to report to the Congress of Soviets in March 1931 that following the establishment of diplomatic relations, no political conflicts had arisen with Japan and trade had expanded. Later that same year, just prior to Japan's invasion of Manchuria, further arrangements were completed for Japanese government-guaranteed credits to finance Soviet purchases of oil-well machinery, ships and port equipment, electrical apparatus, etc.[5]

The western powers were fully cut off from the Soviet Union in the Far East. The United States had never established diplomatic relations and had in fact indirectly opposed the U.S.S.R.'s policies in China as far as possible.[6] Although diplomatic relations with Great Britain had been restored in 1929 after the break in 1927,[7] an anti-Soviet campaign continued to rage in the British press. Moreover, the world depression was at its worst and cries of "Soviet dumping" were echoed in every industrial country. Molotov, in his report to the Congress of Soviets mentioned above, stressed that although Soviet trade was far below that of Tsarist Russia and the U.S.S.R. was the only country then increasing its imports, thus stimulating world trade, nevertheless these

[5] *Economic Review of the Soviet Union*, Published by the Amtorg Trading Corporation, New York, Sept. 1, 1931, p. 403.

[6] Cf. *Soviet-American Relations 1919–1933.* (In Russian) NKID, Moscow, 1934; and Frederick L. Schuman, *American Policy Toward Russia Since 1917.* International Publishers, New York, 1929, pp. 241–244.

[7] The Soviets held that the break in 1927 grew out of events in China: cf. Litvinov's note of May 28, 1927: " . . . It is evident to the whole world that the fundamental cause of the rupture is the defeat of the Conservative government's policy in China and an attempt to mask this defeat by a diversion directed against the Soviet Union, while the direct reason is the British Government's desire to divert public opinion from the failure of the absurd police raid on the Arcos and the Trade Delegation premises and to save the British Home Secretary from the scandalous position in which he found himself owing to this raid." *Soviet Union Review*, Published by the Soviet Union Information Bureau, Washington, D.C., July 1927, p. 114.

trade rivalries were adding to the already existing frictions between the Soviets and the major powers.

Of the international organizations aimed at keeping the peace, the Soviet Union was party only to the Kellogg Pact. It was not yet a member of the League of Nations. It had been excluded from the deliberations of the Washington Conference of 1921–1922 at which a structure of post-war international relationships in the Far East had been erected. Ironically, the absence of the U.S.S.R. from these arrangements was to be one of the pretexts used by Japan in later years for denouncing the Washington agreements.[8] Yet there was some evidence even at that time of a willingness on the part of the European powers to recognize that Moscow had a role to play in world affairs. The Soviet Union had been represented at disarmament conferences for a number of years. Soviet members had attended the sessions on a European Union in 1931, where their suggestion of an economic non-aggression pact was discussed; and the U.S.S.R. had participated in the International Wheat Conference. While these events had little direct bearing on the immediate Soviet position in the Far East, the fact that Moscow had made progress in Europe toward breaking through the international isolation of its earlier years and was dealing with other nations on something approaching a basis of equality was later to be of importance in the East.

Thus it was that the U.S.S.R., isolated and weak in the Far East, was faced in 1931 with the renewal of the northward drive of its historic enemy, Japan.

[8] Cf. *Problems of the Pacific, 1936*, Proceedings of the Sixth Conference of the Institute of Pacific Relations, University of Chicago Press, Chicago, 1937, p. 186.

II. THE MANCHURIAN CRISIS

THE FIRST Soviet press reports of the Japanese attack in Manchuria on September 18, 1931 set the tone that was to characterize Soviet attitude for many months to come. In addition to the military items, various reports took up a statement from Washington that the State Department did not believe the Mukden incident constituted a violation of the Kellogg Pact. One news item predicted that Chang Hsueh-liang would offer no resistance. A longer article, headed "Comedy in Geneva," described the meeting of the 65th session of the League of Nations Council which "happened to coincide" with the beginning of the Manchurian warfare. The Council's acceptance of Yoshizawa's statement that Japan was making an effort to settle the incident was derided as absurd, and stress was laid on the fact that the League had turned to Japan rather than to China to handle the situation.

Izvestia carried a feature article[1] reviewing the historical background of the incident and presenting the Soviet political analysis of its significance. It pointed out that the Japanese were dissatisfied with developments in China—specifically, Chinese railway construction which threatened to compete with Japanese lines; the rapprochement between Manchurian authorities and Nanking, and between Nanking and the western powers. It emphasized that "present events in Manchuria appear thus to be a new and extremely acute stage in the development of the permanent Japanese-Chinese conflict. It would be a mistake of course to consider these events exclusively in the framework of Japanese-Chinese

[1] N. Pakhomov, "Japanese Intervention in Manchuria," *Izvestia*, September 21, 1931. See Appendix, p. 211.

relations." The very fact that the Japanese had resorted to arms and actual occupation of the main centers was stressed as an indication of serious changes in the Far Eastern situation as a whole. The author remarked that the fact that Japan's aggression had not met with anything like as strong a reaction either from Geneva or Washington as China had expected created the impression that Japan's action was well prepared in the sense of getting the agreement of the other imperialist powers. But, he continued, even though Chinese hopes were disappointed, this fact by no means signified that the powers would not in their own interests oppose further Japanese penetration into Manchuria. The article predicted an increase in friction between the western powers and Japan, and termed the incident a very serious international event.

"This circumstance in itself is enough to make the Soviet public and the workers of the whole Soviet Union follow with close attention the further development of the events in the new Far Eastern zone of war danger, which carries with it the threat of new attempts at anti-Soviet provocations to which the imperialists can resort in order to conceal their aggressive policies. As for the working people of China, this new unheard of degradation imposed on their country doubtless will reveal to them the depths of the collapse and the degree of weakness to which the country has been brought by the Kuomintang, feudal-bourgeois reaction—the shameful agents of world imperialism."

This article, written only three days after the invasion of Manchuria began, is summarized at some length because its point of view persisted in the Russian comments published in succeeding months. All parties to the conflict were viewed with extreme suspicion. The Japanese were criticized for their aggressive designs; the Nanking government for its failure to resist; while the League and the western powers were suspected of collusion or even of trying to turn the

Japanese advance against the Soviet Union. That "only the masses of the people of Japan and China can avert the situation" was the conclusion running through Soviet comment. From the first week Moscow's fear of an anti-Soviet orientation of Japan's expansionist policy was heightened by items reported from the foreign press suggesting that Japan's action could be more easily condoned if she seized both North and South Manchuria rather than just the latter and thereby entrenched herself on the Soviet border.

SOVIET ENTANGLEMENT IN THE MANCHURIAN INCIDENT

By October 1931—less than a month after the outbreak of the Sino-Japanese War—the Soviets were already deeply involved in the conflict, both because their territory bordered on Manchuria and because of the Chinese Eastern Railway. The first protest was that of Moscow to Mukden on the massing of gunboats on the Sungari River on October 11; by October 28 the first note of what was to prove a lengthy Soviet-Japanese correspondence had been sent. On that day Ambassador Hirota called at *Narkomindel* (the Soviet Commissariat of Foreign Affairs). Expressing his satisfaction that since the beginning of the Manchurian incident there had been nothing to disturb Soviet-Japanese relations, he went on to report that there were rumors that Soviet instructors were serving in the army of General Ma Chen-shan and that General Ma had received material assistance from the Soviet Union. He also warned that for the Soviets to send troops into the Chinese Eastern Railway zone would aggravate the situation. Vice-Commissar of Foreign Affairs Karakhan replied the next day that the Soviet Government was amazed that the Japanese should pay attention to baseless rumors emanating from persons "in Japanese and Chinese circles who for some reason are interested in spreading provocative rumors in connection with the present situation in Manchuria." He added that "the government of the

U.S.S.R. in pursuing a policy of strict non-interference is not doing so because such a policy may be pleasing or displeasing to anyone. The Soviet Government pursues a policy of non-interference because it respects the international treaties which have been concluded with China. . . . "[2] On November 6 Voroshilov, then Commissar of Defense, denied rumors of a massing of Soviet troops and added: "The Soviet Government has not helped nor is it helping in any way either the Chinese or the Japanese in Manchuria . . . The Soviet Government believes that to render so-called assistance would be tantamount to direct intervention and consequently the partitioning of China and the suppression of Chinese independence. . . . "[3] He went on to suggest that all these rumors were Japanese in origin and were designed to use the bogey of the "red menace" in Manchuria to impress European and American public opinion. This conformed to the general Soviet view that America and the League of Nations powers were really accomplices of the Japanese in their anti-Chinese campaign. The Soviet press continued to be extremely pessimistic about the possibility of any effective action by the League.

Although Voroshilov had said that the Soviet Union desired continued amicable relations with Japan, the exchange of protests and denials did not abate. On November 14, 1931 Litvinov protested to Tokyo over statements by Japanese officials in Manchuria issued, according to Moscow, "with the aim of complicating the relations between Japan and the U.S.S.R." He also reminded Hirota of the Japanese pledge not to injure Soviet interests in Manchuria, which now were falling within the sphere of combat as Japanese troops prepared to cross the Chinese Eastern Railway near Tsitsihar.[4] The Japanese reply referred to Japan's neutrality in 1929 and

[2] *Soviet Union Review*, December 1931, pp. 235–236.
[3] *ibid.* p. 236.
[4] *ibid.* p. 237.

asked the same of the U.S.S.R.; it added that Soviet protests regarding false rumors should be addressed to the Chinese, who were spreading them "for the purpose of raising the morale of the Heilungkiang troops." The Japanese government requested further assurance that General Ma was not receiving Soviet aid; it declared that it had no intention of damaging the Chinese Eastern Railway and that in case of any armed clash near it, the responsibility would rest with the Chinese. In fact, Japan's note of November 19 declared specifically that, although the Japanese had been forced to cross the Chinese Eastern Railway, they had taken special precautions not to impair the line. They assured Moscow that as soon as the Chinese had restored order they would retreat south of Tsitsihar.[5]

Litvinov's reply to this note put clearly to Japan the Soviet position at that time. Having expressed his satisfaction with Japan's denial of the rumors, he went on to say:[6]

" . . . Insofar as in your statement, Mr. Ambassador, you draw a certain analogy between the present events in China and the Soviet-Chinese conflict in 1929, I am compelled to note the incorrectness of such an analogy. In spite of the gross violation by the Chinese authorities, entirely indubitable and apparent to everyone, of the treaty rights of the U.S.S.R., the Soviet government did not invade and had no intentions of invading Manchuria. Only after repeated attacks by the Chinese and Russian White Guard detachments on Soviet territory, did the Soviet troops cross the Manchurian border to repulse the attack, disarming the invaders and putting an end to further attacks. Furthermore, no question of the possibility of even temporary occupation of Chinese territory by Soviet troops, of the dismissal of existing authorities and the creation of new ones, ever arose. Nor was there at that time the remotest possibility of violating the

[5] *Soviet Union Review*, January 1932, p. 19.

[6] *Izvestia*, November 21, 1931, quoted in the *Soviet Union Review*, January 1932, pp. 19–20.

legal rights and interests of Japan. As soon as Soviet troops had carried out their restricted task, they were withdrawn to Soviet territory. . . ."

Litvinov then pointed out that the question of transporting troops over the Chinese Eastern Railway differed considerably from the case of the South Manchuria Railway, because Soviet renunciation of the Tsarist special regime for the Chinese Eastern Railway zone had meant that the line thenceforth was guarded by Chinese—not Soviet—troops and managed by a joint Chinese-Soviet board. Moreover, on November 12, the Soviet government had instructed "the Soviet part of the administration of the Chinese Eastern Railway to continue to maintain the principle of neutrality and not in any case to agree to transport the troops of either of the warring sides to the front by way of the Chinese Eastern Railway." Litvinov stated further that all these difficulties arose out of the Japanese northward advance: "I must, however, state that notwithstanding the first declaration made by you, Mr. Ambassador, on behalf of your Government with regard to instructions given for the utmost limitation of Japanese military operations in Manchuria that these operations since then have widened to a great extent and have gone far beyond the borders of the zone originally intended. This circumstance, increasing the possibility that the interests of the U.S.S.R. might be affected, cannot but give rise to serious alarm on the part of the Soviet Union."

It was therefore not surprising that Molotov's report from the Council of People's Commissars to the Central Executive Committee, which was made at the end of 1931, termed the Far Eastern conflict "the most important problem of our foreign policy." Molotov passed lightly over Soviet-Japanese relations, but stressed the League's failure either to stop hostilities by October 14 or to achieve any tangible results by sending the Commission of Inquiry. He concluded: "The League of Nations proved its complete lack of desire and ability to check to any degree the further development of military operations in Manchuria. This second decision of the League of Nations [to dispatch the Lytton Commission] makes mockery of the first [to halt hostilities] and virtually sanctions the military occupation and further development of military operations in Manchuria. All this compels us to strengthen our vigilance as regards happenings in the Far East. We must not forget that our border lies along the Manchurian line."[7]

Ten days after this speech was delivered, the necessity of guarding its own frontier led the Soviet Government to offer Japan a non-aggression pact. Yoshizawa, returning from his post as special delegate to the League in Geneva in order to assume the post of Foreign Minister, passed through Moscow, and on December 31, 1931 Litvinov first made the suggestion to him.[8] Almost a year elapsed before Japan replied, though in February 1932 Tass found it necessary to deny the first rumors emanating from other countries, that a secret agreement had been reached between Japan and the U.S.S.R. with regard to Manchuria.[9]

The Soviets began the year 1932 with inquiries to Japan on its intentions in northern Manchuria. In a note of February 24 they asked for information as to the character of the "newly organized Manchurian State," saying they found it difficult to determine how official were the demands of Japanese authorities in Manchuria, for instance, to use the Chinese Eastern Railway for Japanese troops, to reduce the rates, etc. Finally, the note returned to an old theme—the anti-Soviet activities of the Russian White Guards.[10]

[7] *Soviet Union Review*, February 1932, p. 27.

[8] Reported by Tass in *Izvestia*, January 17, 1933; the Tass report and the above mentioned replies are quoted in the *Soviet Union Review*, February 1933. See also, *Japan Yearbook, 1933*, The Foreign Affairs Association of Japan, Kenkyusha Press, Tokyo, 1933, p. 194.

[9] *Izvestia*, February 14, 1932, quoted in the *Soviet Union Review*, March 1932, p. 60.

[10] *Soviet Union Review*, April 1932, p. 93.

RUSSIAN WHITE-GUARD ACTIVITIES IN MANCHURIA

The importance with which the Soviets regarded the encouragement or even tolerance of White Guard activities had been long apparent in the Far East. Written into the Soviet treaties with China and Japan were the customary clauses regarding the prohibition by each signatory of activities of organizations directed against the other (Article VI of the Chinese Treaty and Article V of the Japanese). This type of clause had been invoked in the case of China on many occasions. The White Russians had been permitted by Chang Tso-lin to operate the Chinese Eastern Railway until the Mukden agreement in November 1924. In 1925 protests were made to Peking over the "First Russian Mixed Brigade"; White Russians were charged with complicity in the 1926 attack by Chang Tso-lin on the Chinese Eastern Railway; in the April 1927 raid on the Soviet Embassy in Peking; and in the 1929 Chinese Eastern Railway dispute. The question of White Guard activity carried over into Japan's regime in Manchuria, where the invaders encouraged and made extensive use of such activities[11] just as they had during the period of intervention in the Russian Far East.

The Japanese gave assurances that the Whites would be controlled and asked permission to transport a few troops over the eastern branch of the Chinese Eastern Railway to protect the lives and property of their people.[12] The Soviets granted this request, though remarking that in a strict sense it was contrary to both the 1925 agreement and the Portsmouth Treaty. Here, for the first time was introduced another recurring theme in Soviet notes. The background of the reference lay in the fact that during the negotiations for reestablishment of Soviet-Japanese diplomatic relations, Japan had demanded absolute assurance of the continuance

[11] Cf. *Contemporary Manchuria*, published by the Information and Publicity Department of the South Manchuria Railway Co., Dairen, Manchuria, September 1937.

[12] Cf. *Soviet Union Review*, April 1932, p. 94.

of its economic activities on Northern Sakhalin and its fishery rights in Soviet waters. The latter were guaranteed in the final settlement by the retention of the Portsmouth Treaty (1905), the only pre-war treaty perpetuated.[13]

For Japan, Portsmouth's chief significance lay in Article X, covering fishery rights. But since 1931 Moscow has made frequent references to other articles. In 1932 a note of February 27 pointed out that Article II had forbidden troop concentrations on the Soviet-Korean frontier. And on a number of occasions oblique references were made to Article III, prohibiting the maintenance of Japanese troops in Manchuria. Such remarks were subsequently made during negotiations on fishery rights, which rest basically on the Portsmouth Treaty.

Though the Soviets complied with the Japanese request to move troops over on the Chinese Eastern Railway, the tension between the two countries increased. An editorial in *Izvestia* on March 4, 1932, reiterated the Soviet government's sympathy for the Chinese people and its own complete neutrality, but, after enumerating recent developments, it concluded that "a careful analysis of these facts which we are now undertaking to clarify shows that the situation with which the Soviet Union is faced in the Far East requires that it strengthen its defenses, protect its border from outside attack, in particular through the strengthening of the military garrison on the Far Eastern borders of the U.S.S.R."[14]

THE LYTTON COMMISSION IN MANCHURIA

The arrival of the Lytton Commission in the Far East did not improve Soviet-Japanese relations. In April, 1932, the

[13] At the time of its extension China protested, but the Soviet Government replied that "the protest would have been timely if it had been made 20 years ago: while at present the rights conceded to the Japanese Government by the Tsarist Government remain valid by virtue of direct agreement between Japan and China." *Soviet Union Review*, April 1, 1925, p. 150. For text of Treaty see Appendix, p. 151.

[14] Quoted in *Soviet Union Review*, April 1932, p. 91.

Soviet press again charged the Japanese with inventing "red plots"—this time as window dressing for the benefit of the Lytton Commission. Nevertheless to sustain its neutral position, Moscow even requested the recall of a Chinese consul in Blagoveshchensk who was charged with abusing his official privileges by sending out appeals to the Manchurian population in code, over the signature of General Ma, who was supposedly in hiding in Heilungkiang.[15]

Despite the difficulties arising between Japan and the Soviet Union as a result of Japan's northward march and in spite of the fact that China again was negotiating for diplomatic relations with the Soviets (see below), Moscow persisted in deriding the Lytton Commission which had been dispatched by the League of Nations and refused to cooperate with it. On April 20, Secretary-General Drummond of the League had addressed a note to Moscow, stating:[16]

"I have been confidentially informed by Lord Lytton, President of the Commission which is now in the Far East for the purpose of making a report to the Council on the questions at issue between China and Japan, that the Commission feels that during its stay in Manchuria it might be of great help for it to be able to receive any information or evidence which officials of the Soviet Government in Manchuria might be authorized to furnish to it. Lord Lytton enquires whether a request to this end would meet with any objection on the part of the Soviet Government. I should be very grateful for any help or advice which you might give us in this matter."

Drummond's note was answered by Litvinov who refused the request on the ground that, although the U.S.S.R. would be ready to cooperate with any commission "which would really desire to put an end to the armed conflicts which are

[15] General Ma was later reported to have escaped from Manchuria through Soviet territory into Sinkiang.

[16] *League of Nations Secretariat Information Section, Communique No. 5658,* Geneva, May 5, 1932, pp. 1–2.

taking place in China," it could not help the Lytton Commission. Since it was not represented in the League of Nations, it could not "assume responsibility for the conclusions that the Commission of the League of Nations might reach."[17]

This attitude toward the League Commission apparently derived from two factors. On a later occasion Litvinov said that the reasons were "first, because we did not believe in the honesty and consistency of the governments participating in these actions and primarily because we did not seek, nor do we now seek, armed conflict with Japan."[18] This distrust of League activities dated back to its very foundation when the leading powers at Geneva had participated in the armed Intervention against the U.S.S.R., and it persisted in subsequent years when they had moved slowly in bringing the Soviets back into the family of nations. The Soviets were perhaps even more suspicious of Anglo-American activity in the Far East, where in the past they had always found themselves pursuing policies in conflict with the western powers as, for instance, in abolishing the old regime of special privileges in China. That England and America could not get together fully on opposing Japan's policies which were clearly contrary to their own best interests served merely to strengthen these suspicions. Writing later of this period, a Soviet scholar said:

"As regards the English government during this period, it looked favorably on the Manchurian adventure, hoping that Japan would be involved for a long time in Manchuria and would stop its activities in the rest of China (where there are large English investments) and in the South Seas (where English possessions are located). Inasmuch as England did not have important interests in Manchuria, English capital could look on with a certain satisfaction as Japan, by the seizure of Manchuria, knocked the feet out from under the

[17] *ibid.* p. 2.

[18] Maxim Litvinov, *Foreign Policy of the U.S.S.R.* (in Russian), Moscow, 1935, p. 72.

traditional American principles in China and created a base for an anti-Soviet war. There is no doubt but what in certain circles of the English conservatives the plan for an anti-Soviet war met with full approval."[19]

However, this deliberate aloofness did not extend into all phases of Soviet international relations. In the same year—1932—Litvinov had gone to the Disarmament Conference to plead for positive action to prevent the spread of war. He brought forward his proposals—first for total, then for partial disarmament—and finally he backed in the main the American proposal. At the same time he was forging a bastion of non-aggression pacts along the Soviet Union's western borders and succeeded in concluding such a pact with France.

The second deterrent to cooperation with the Lytton Commission—namely, unwillingness to take the risk of provoking retaliatory action from Japan—may have been even more compelling than distrust of the League. Japan's advance was meeting almost no opposition and there was little prospect that it would. China was still engaged in civil warfare. The Shanghai incident had shown even more clearly how much abuse the western powers were willing to take from Japan. The Soviets stood alone; it was clear that they could ill afford the risk of war.

The Special Far Eastern Army of the U.S.S.R. had been organized in 1929 and was retained after the Mukden incident revived the Far Eastern war danger, but it had little on which to base itself. The first Five-Year Plan, still in progress, aimed only to establish an industrial base in *western* Siberia (with the Kuznetsk-Magnitogorsk Combinat) for further economic development eastward to the Pacific. Aside from the lack of nearby industrial bases, an added factor was the critical agricultural situation of 1931 and 1932, which followed on drought and Kulak resistance to accelerated collectiviza-

[19] Motylev, *Origin and Development of The Pacific Ocean Nexus of Contradictions*, (in Russian), Sotsekgiz, Moscow, 1939, pp. 132–133.

tion. Moreover, internal political intrigue was continuing; Trotsky had just been exiled and Kamenev and Zinoviev were again expelled from the Communist Party for complicity in an anti-Party conspiracy. Neither economically nor politically was the situation favorable for taking on new risks on the distant Far Eastern frontier.

As a result the Soviets were ready to negotiate with both the Chinese and the Japanese. At the close of the year two trade arrangements were made with Japan—one to supply Soviet oil to Japan and the other to set up in Japan government-guaranteed credits for Soviet purchases. But more important was the settlement of a minor dispute over the Pacific fisheries—the first time that the question had arisen since the outbreak of Far Eastern warfare This issue, one of the recurring motifs of Soviet-Japanese relations, is reviewed more fully in a later chapter (p. 49ff).

The close of the year 1932 was marked by further friction when Manchukuo officials charged the Soviets with holding locomotives and rolling stock that rightly belonged to the Chinese Eastern Railway. While nothing more developed at that time, this question was to become the cause of acrid debate a year later. That it did not become so in 1932 may have been due partly to the fact that Japan sought a favor of the Russians—namely, evacuation via the U.S.S.R. of Japanese citizens from Manchuria Station (Manchouli) on the frontier, then held by the Chinese General Su Ping-wen. The Soviets complied and through negotiations with General Su effected the transfer in October.[20]

A few months later the Japanese succeeded in defeating General Su who fled with his army over the Soviet border. The Japanese then demanded that the Soviets deliver him to them—or at least intern him as a bandit operating against the true government of Manchukuo. The Soviets replied that it was none of Japan's business what they did with

[20] *Japan Weekly Chronicle*, November 3, 1932, pp. 594–595.

General Su, whom the Japanese government could hardly call a bandit when not many months before it had negotiated with him for the evacuation of its citizens. Moreover, the Japanese were brusquely told that they should put a stop to the activities of the White Guards before they complained of the Soviets harboring anti-Japanese elements. The final Japanese plea objected to the transfer of the General and his men to China where "they will not only conduct agitation harmful to Japan and Manchukuo, but they will be surrounded with sympathy by the Chinese and will probably become heroes, as was the case with General Ma."[21]

RELATIONS WITH CHINA

In the meantime Moscow and Nanking had been progressing toward a solution of their differences. Inasmuch as the attitude of the Chinese government had remained very anti-Soviet since 1927, its resumption of negotiations with Moscow was regarded abroad as a move of desperation. Professor Toynbee, for example, said that it resulted from China's "loss of faith in salvation through the League of Nations, and of the inexorable necessity of finding for China some 'very present help' in the sore trouble of Japanese aggression."[22]

The Khabarovsk Protocol had furnished a *modus vivendi* in Manchuria and a Chinese delegation representing both Nanking and Mukden had gone to Moscow in May 1930 to negotiate a final settlement. No parleys were held until October, however, apparently because Nanking refused to recognize the Khabarovsk Protocol which Mukden had accepted as the basis for regulating relations in Manchuria.[23]

[21] *Soviet Union Review*, January 1933, p. 6; see also *Japan Weekly Chronicle*, December 1, 8, and 15, 1932, pp. 814–815.

[22] A. J. Toynbee, *Survey of International Affairs, 1932*, Oxford University Press, London: Humphrey Milford, 1933, pp. 417–418.

[23] For exchange of notes in November 1930, see *China Year Book, 1931*, North China Daily News and Herald, Ltd., Shanghai, 1931, pp. 498–500.

In January 1931 Mo Teh-hui, the Nanking representative, returned to China for instructions and did not arrive back in Moscow until March. This time he brought instructions that seemed to imply both recognition of the Khabarovsk Protocol and a willingness to negotiate on all questions—not just on the Chinese Eastern Railway. The ground now appeared to be ready for conclusive discussions but negotiations dragged on intermittently for nearly two years more. Not until December 12, 1932, were diplomatic relations finally restored, and then the agreement merely affirmed the *status quo ante* 1929.[24] Evidently the other problems under discussion had not been solved. Nonetheless, the agreement did not fail to elicit hostile reactions from Japan. (In 1924 Japan had sought assurances that Soviet-Chinese relations would not injure its interests in Manchuria through the Chinese Eastern Railway agreement. The Soviets replied that the U.S.S.R. could not "take note of any reservations made by the Japanese Government in re the Chinese Eastern Railway.") No direct protest was made to Moscow but the Japanese press and various officials argued that the Soviets might have chosen a different time and place to negotiate with China (the agreement was arranged in Geneva during the discussions on the Lytton Report), that the "red menace" was serious and that it was pointless even to think of a non-aggression pact with the U.S.S.R. Japanese Foreign Minister Uchida said in the Diet:[25]

"There are those who fear whether the recent restoration of diplomatic relations between the Union of Soviet Socialist Republics and China might not add vigor to communist propaganda throughout the Orient. This is not an occasion for me to pass judgment upon this sort of opinion. However, should the red movement in the Yangtze Valley and South

[24] For text of notes, see Appendix, p. 216.

[25] *Contemporary Japan*, Published by the Foreign Affairs Association of Japan, Tokyo, March, 1933, Vol. 1, No. 4, pp. 766–767. See also *Japan Weekly Chronicle*, December 22, 1932, for articles on the "Red menace."

China, which have long suffered from the activities of communists and the depredations of Communist armies, gain in strength as a result of the Sino-Russian rapprochement, that would be a serious menace to peace in the Orient, against which Japan must certainly be on guard."

The Soviets remonstrated against this speech as an unfounded and provocative remark by a responsible official.

PUBLICATION OF THE LYTTON REPORT

The Lytton Report, published in October 1932, contained more Japanese allegations of this kind. In drawing up its conclusions the Commission had summarized the situation between Japan and Russia as follows:[26]

"The Russian Revolution of 1917, followed by the declarations of the Soviet government of July 25, 1919, and of October 27, 1920, regarding its policy towards the Chinese people and, later, by the Sino-Soviet agreements of May 31, 1924, and September 20, 1924, shattered the basis of Russo-Japanese understanding and cooperation in Manchuria. This fundamental reversal of policy radically changed the relations of the three powers in the Far East. Moreover, the Allied intervention (1918–1920), with its aftermath of friction between the Japanese and Soviet forces in Siberia (1920–1922), had accentuated the change in the relations between Japan and Russia. The attitude of the Soviet government gave a strong impetus to China's nationalistic aspirations. As the Soviet Government and the Third International had adopted a policy opposed to all imperialist powers which maintained relations with China on the basis of the existing treaties, it seemed probable that they would support China in the struggle for the recovery of sovereign rights. This development revived all the old anxieties and suspicions of Japan toward her Russian neighbor. This

[26] *Appeal by the Chinese Government, Report of the Commission of Enquiry* (The Lytton Report), League of Nations, Geneva, October 1, 1932, pp. 36–37.

country, with which she had once been at war, had, during the years which followed that war, become a friend and ally. Now this relationship was changed, and the possibility of a danger from across the North Manchurian border again became a matter of concern to Japan. The likelihood of an alliance between the Communist doctrines in the North and the anti-Japanese propaganda of the Kuomintang in the South made the desire to impose between the two a Manchuria which should be free from both increasingly felt in Japan. Japanese misgivings have been still further increased in the last few years by the predominant influence acquired by the U.S.S.R. in Outer Mongolia and the growth of Communism in China."

This analysis could mean but one thing to the Soviets—namely, that the Lytton Commission had accepted the Japanese "red menace" excuse at its face value, in spite of the fact that for six years Chiang Kai-shek's government had been doing its best to eradicate Chinese Communism and had refused even to entertain diplomatic relations with the Soviet Union.

Accordingly, in commenting on the report the Soviets recalled that the idea for the creation of the Commission was actually suggested by the Japanese—a delaying move in Soviet opinion. They pointed out that the Commission had leisurely progressed to the Far East via America; that even while making its investigation a series of incidents took place in Shanghai and another investigation was all that was undertaken. Furthermore, Manchukuo was organized and recognized by Japan when the Commission was still at work on its report.

The Soviet commentators recognized that the report was genuinely anti-Japanese in its conclusions, but—and this was the crux of the matter for the U.S.S.R.—it was not genuinely pro-Chinese. The recommendations—rejecting the *status quo ante*—proposed that while restoring formal

Chinese sovereignty in Manchuria, the regime should be in the nature of an international mandate in which Japan's special interest would be recognized but not permitted to dominate. In Moscow this plan seemed to mean merely substituting one form of imperialism for another in Manchuria. Equally ominous to the Soviets were the passages relating to foreign assistance in the political reconstruction of China proper.

The Soviets concluded[27] that while the western powers—at the insistence of the United States—were ready to condemn aggressive operations in Manchuria, to refuse them recognition and hope for eventual Japanese failure, they were totally unprepared to take any positive action to stop them. In fact, Moscow believed the western powers were not unwilling that Japan continue northward and become involved in a war with the U.S.S.R. After all, not only did the famous so-called "Tanaka Memorial" mention the inevitable Soviet-Japanese clash, but Matsuoka in his League speech on the Lytton report in December 1932[28] remarked that there were those who felt that Japan should attack the U.S.S.R. in order to blot out the menace of Communism in the East, a sentiment which was echoed in the statements of Japanese officials in Manchuria.

It cannot be over-emphasized in any survey of Soviet Far Eastern policy for this period that the Soviet fear of attack by a combination of powers was a constant factor. The year 1932 had witnessed a continuation of the almost world-wide campaign against Soviet trade and little had been done to lessen Moscow's feeling of isolation from the major world powers.

Thus, although the Lytton report had recognized the impor-

[27] Cf. *Izvestia,* October 13, 1932.

[28] Cf. *Japan's Case in the Sino-Japanese Dispute as Presented Before the Special Session of the Assembly of the League of Nations*, issued by the Japanese Delegation to the League of Nations, Geneva, 1933. Introduction.

tance of the U.S.S.R. in the Far East[29] and was regarded by the Soviets as a criticism of Japanese aggression, yet Moscow was unwilling to take part in any international operations in the Far East because of its mistrust of western policy. This attitude was brought out most clearly in Litvinov's note of March 7, 1933, declining to join the Committee of 19 set up by the League.[30]

He pointed out that not only was the U.S.S.R. not a League member, but thirteen of the twenty-two nations involved in the Advisory Committee did not have diplomatic relations with the Soviet Union. Thus, he declared, it is "permissible to doubt whether such states could really take into consideration the interests of the U.S.S.R." Consequently, he concluded, Moscow intended to follow a course of "strict neutrality," though it would naturally look with favor on action to secure a just and speedy termination of the conflict.

[29] "The Commission has not been able to obtain direct information as to the extent of the interests of the U.S.S.R in Manchuria, nor to ascertain the views of the government of the U.S.S.R. on the Manchurian question. But, even without sources of direct information, it cannot overlook the part played by Russia in Manchuria nor the important interests which the U.S.S.R. have in that region as owners of the Chinese Eastern Railway and of the territory beyond its north and northeast frontiers. It is clear that any solution of the problem of Manchuria which ignored the important interests of the U.S.S.R. would risk a future breach of the peace and would not be permanent." It further recommended in connection with the proposal of a Sino-Japanese Treaty of Conciliation and Arbitration, Non-Aggression and Mutual Assistance that "if the government of the U.S.S.R. desired to participate in the non-aggression and mutual assistance section of such a treaty, the appropriate clauses could be embodied in a separate tripartite agreement." *Lytton Report*, *op. cit.*, pp. 129–30, 138.

[30] For full text, see Appendix, p. 220.

III. THE SALE OF THE CHINESE EASTERN RAILWAY, 1933–1934

BY THE END of 1932 Soviet-Japanese relations showed no signs of improving, although Litvinov had been at pains to explain that the renewal of diplomatic relations with China was an entirely normal procedure—adding that "it is beyond doubt that the commencement of the present troubles in the Far East is in no small degree due to the fact that not all states situated on the shores of the Pacific Ocean have been maintaining diplomatic relations with one another."[1]

Litvinov asserted that the new Soviet-Chinese convention contained no secret agreement and was not directed against third countries. Nevertheless Japan took it as an occasion for a renewed press campaign against the Soviet Union and against any attempt the Soviets might make to gain recognition from the United States. Furthermore, in a note of December 13, 1932, the Japanese government had finally taken cognizance of the Soviet non-aggression pact first proposed a year earlier, and had pointed out that there were two views on the subject: "One opinion advocates the conclusion of a non-aggression pact which would guarantee the settlement of different questions of dispute which might arise between the two countries in the future. The other opposing view is that first of all the causes of possible disputes should be eliminated, and that only then might more general questions, such as that of a non-aggression pact, be considered."[2]

[1] December 12, 1932, Statement to Press, *Soviet Union Review*, January 1933, p. 3.

[2] *Soviet Union Review*, February 1933, p. 46. The publication of this correspondence regarding the proposal surprised Tokyo, according to the report in *Contemporary Japan*, (Vol. 1, No. 4, March, 1933, p. 712) which was substantially similar to that in the Soviet press.

The Japanese felt that the second view was the sounder of the two and concluded in the above note that "for the present moment the Japanese Government would prefer the exchange of opinion as to methods of averting difficulties which might arise as the result of contact between the troops of both sides." The note also proposed a Japanese-Soviet-Manchurian Commission for averting border incidents. The answer of Troyanovsky, then Soviet Ambassador in Tokyo, was that the Soviet government held to the first view and felt that a non-aggression pact should be signed even before all issues were cleared up as a form of reinforcing the Kellogg Pact, then the only international agreement to which both countries were party. However, he was ready to consider the Japanese proposal for a border commission to handle disputes locally as they might arise.

That the Soviets were not relying on agreements alone was made evident in the reports on the first Five-Year Plan and the proposals for the second. The first plan had been declared completed in four and a quarter years as of January 1, 1933, but in his report to the Central Committee of the Communist Party on January 10, 1933, Stalin pointed out that in fact they had fallen 6 per cent short of completing the schedules as originally laid down. "This is explained," he said, "by the fact that in view of the refusal of neighboring countries to sign non-aggression pacts with us, and the complications in the Far East, we were forced to shift a number of factories hastily to the production of modern implements of warfare, with the aim of strengthening our defenses."[3] The effect of the Far Eastern tension was also reflected in the plans adopted for the ensuing five-year period. Investment in the Far East, particularly in transportation, was sharply increased (the Trans-Siberian Railroad had yet to be double-tracked) and efforts were concentrated on adding to the economic and military strength of the area east of Lake Baikal.

[3] *Soviet Union Review*, February 1933, p. 33.

CHINESE EASTERN RAILWAY OFFERED FOR SALE

The need for such development was manifest when, in the spring of 1933, the question was raised of selling the Chinese Eastern Railway, hitherto the chief transport route for the Soviets in the East. As pointed out above, the Chinese Eastern Railway had long been a center of conflict between Tokyo and Moscow and on several occasions had been the subject of diplomatic exchanges. The temporary adjustments had, however, broken down almost completely by April 1933 and the operation of the line had come to a standstill. In a statement to Ota, Japanese Ambassador to Moscow, on April 16[4] Narkomindel listed all its complaints—a list so substantial as to suggest a remarkable tolerance on the part of the Soviets and to stress the extent to which they were willing to stand abuse at that time in order to avoid war. The statement opened with a reminder of the repeated Japanese assurances that Soviet rights in the Chinese Eastern Railway would not be infringed. It then enumerated the Manchurian-Japanese seizures of the transshipment stations at both the eastern and western terminals of the line, interrupting through traffic; the failure of the Manchurian authorities to pay for the transport of troops (the right of transport itself having been regarded as a major concession by Moscow); bandit attacks on the line; the arrest of Soviet employees by Manchurian officials with their Japanese advisers implicated; and the dispute over the ownership of rolling stock.[5]

The controversy continued in an exchange of notes between Mr. Kuznetsov, Assistant Chairman of the administration of the road, and Mr. Li Shao-keng, Chairman of the Board, a Manchukuoan appointee.[6] These notes grew increasingly acrimonious, with Mr. Li disputing the Soviet ownership of

[4] *Izvestia*, April 18, 1933.

[5] For details, cf. memorandum of April 15, 1933, quoted in the *Soviet Union Review*, June 1933, p. 130.

[6] Cf. *Japan Weekly Chronicle*, June 8, 1933, pp. 780–781, also *Contemporary Japan* Vol. II, No. 2, September, 1933, pp. 366–374.

the line and the validity of the Peking and Mukden agreements. Mr. Kuznetsov denied categorically any such interpretation and listed the wrecks, the arrests and the losses incurred by the line and its employees since the Manchurian authorities began their campaign against it about a year earlier. The matter became so serious that on May 2 Litvinov suggested the sale of the line "as one of the most radical means"[7] of settling the conflicts which were complicating the relations of the Soviets both with Japan and Manchuria.

Before considering the negotiations for the sale, which dragged on for nearly two years and were interrupted frequently by new outbursts of violence, it may be useful to review briefly the history of the line down to that time. Following the Sino-Japanese war in 1894 China had turned to Russia for aid through the Li-Lobanov agreement of 1896. In return Russia was granted the right to build the Chinese Eastern Railway and two years later the concession was extended to include a South Manchurian line terminating in the Liaotung Peninsula, on which Port Arthur and Dairen were leased to Russia. As part of the settlement of the Russo-Japanese War in 1905 the Treaty of Portsmouth gave the South Manchuria Railway as well as the Liaotung Peninsula leases to Japan, leaving Russia in a dominant position only in North Manchuria. This new arrangement was ratified by China in the Peking Protocol of 1905.

Following the Revolution in Russia, the Chinese Eastern Railway and other Russian railways in the east were placed under the jurisdiction of an international railway commission headed by John F. Stevens, an American. And the Chinese Eastern Railway remained something of an international charge until 1924 at the time of the establishment of diplomatic relations between China and the Soviet Union. In fact the Washington Conference adopted two resolutions

[7] *Soviet Union Review*, June 1933, p. 134, quoted from *Izvestia*, May 12, 1933.

regarding the line; one for its better management and the other holding the Chinese government responsible for the obligations of the line to foreign creditors.

In the meantime the new Soviet Government had stated its position in the declarations of July 25, 1919 and October 27, 1920,[8] renouncing all special rights and privileges enjoyed by Tsarist Russia along with the other powers (Boxer Indemnity, extraterritoriality and land concessions along the C.E.R. administered by Russian officials and guarded by Russian troops). These principles were embodied in the Treaty of 1924 with China. Article IX dealt specifically with the Railroad, which was declared "a purely commercial enterprise."[9] A detailed agreement was signed in the same year

[8] Victor A. Yakhontoff, *Russia and the Soviet Union in the Far East*, Coward-McCann, Inc., New York, 1931, pp. 381–383.

[9] Text of Article IX is as follows:

"The governments of the two Contracting Parties agree to settle at the aforementioned Conference the question of the Chinese Eastern Railway in conformity with the principles as hereinafter provided:

"1. The governments of the two Contracting Parties declare that the Chinese Eastern Railway is a purely commercial enterprise.

"The governments of the two Contracting Parties mutually declare that with the exception of matters pertaining to the business operations which are under the direct control of the Chinese Eastern Railway, all other matters affecting the rights of the National and the Local Governments of the Republic of China—such as judicial matters, matters relating to civil administration, military administration, police, municipal government, taxation and landed property (with the exception of lands required by the said Railway)—shall be administered by the Chinese Authorities.

"2. The Government of the Union of Soviet Socialist Republics agrees to the redemption by the Government of the Republic of China, with Chinese capital, of the Chinese Eastern Railway, as well as all appurtenant properties and the transfer to China of all shares and bonds of the said Railway.

"3. The governments of the two Contracting Parties shall settle at the Conference as provided in Article II of the present Agreement the amount and conditions governing the redemption as well as the procedure for the transfer of the Chinese Eastern Railway.

"4. The government of the Union of Soviet Socialist Republics agrees to be responsible for the entire claims of the shareholders, bond holders and reditors of the Chinese Eastern Railway incurred prior to the Revolution of March 9, 1917.

"5. The governments of the two Contracting Parties mutually agree that the future of the Chinese Eastern Railway shall be determined by the Union of Soviet Socialist Republics and the Republic of China, to the exclusion of any

providing for the management of the line. However, since the Peking government was not in actual control of the line it was necessary to conclude another agreement with Chang Tso-lin, the *de facto* ruler of Manchuria at that time. The chief difference in that agreement lay in the provision for the reversion of the line to China in 1956 instead of 1976. Upon the acceptance of this agreement by the Peking government, the line was turned over to joint Soviet-Chinese management.

The first major dispute over its operation came in 1926 when a controversy arose with Chang Tso-lin over the question of payments to the line for the transport of troops. Raids and arrests followed, but the difficulty was finally settled. In 1929, however, trouble flared up again and this time the Manchurian authorities received the backing of the Chinese National government. Diplomatic relations were broken by the Soviets, and rail connections were interrupted. By September protests and counter-protests were passing rapidly through the German Embassy between Nanking, Mukden and Moscow. Border conflicts resulted in which Russian White Guard units participated, and on November 16, 1929 Soviet forces entered Manchuria. Ten days later Chang Hsueh-liang agreed to negotiate; on December 3 a preliminary agreement was signed at Nikolaevsk-Ussurisk and on December 22 the Khabarovsk Protocol was signed for both Mukden and Nanking. The *status quo ante* on the railroad was thus

---

third party or parties.

"6. The governments of the two Contracting Parties agree to draw up an arrangement for the provisional management of the Chinese Eastern Railway pending the settlement of the questions as provided under Sec. 3 of the present article.

"7. Until the various questions relating to the Chinese Eastern Railway are settled at the Conference as provided in Article II of the present Agreement the rights of the two governments arising out of the Contract of August 27 (September 8), 1896, for the Construction and Operation of the Chinese Eastern Railway, which do not conflict with the present Agreement and the Agreement for the Provisional Management of the said Railway and which do not prejudice China's rights of sovereignty, shall be maintained."

restored, both sides agreed to release their prisoners, consulates were reopened (without however, the resumption of diplomatic relations) and by January 22, 1930, traffic again was moving over the line.

The progress of subsequent negotiations between Nanking and Moscow has already been reviewed, but it should be mentioned that Chinese purchase of Soviet rights had been among the possible adjustments discussed regarding the Chinese Eastern Railway. It was therefore not surprising that Litvinov should make the same suggestion to the new masters of Manchuria when the railroad again threatened to involve the U.S.S.R. in hostilities.

The Chinese government promptly protested the proposed sale as a violation of paragraph 5 of Article IX of the 1924 Agreement which read: "The governments of the two Contracting Powers mutually agree that the future of the Chinese Eastern Railway shall be determined by the Union of Soviet Socialist Republics and the Republic of China to the exclusion of any third party or parties."

Litvinov's statement to the press on May 12, 1933 gives a full exposition of the Soviet view of the sale.[10] He attached considerable importance to "the fact that the Nanking government and its subordinate authorities have ceased to be the actual partners of the U.S.S.R. on the C.E.R. for more than a year and a half," and accordingly were not able to carry out their obligations in regard to the line. It was for this reason that the U.S.S.R. felt free to dispose of this "purely commercial enterprise" in order to eliminate a source of conflict. Other Soviet comment on the Chinese protest was less polite, pointing out that should the U.S.S.R. turn over its rights in the railway to local authorities, China would lose nothing because "if and when Manchuria is again conquered by the latter (though there is little hope of that as long as the reactionary Kuomintang is in power), then China will get back

[10] For full text, see Appendix, p. 222.

the Chinese Eastern Railway along with everything else."[11] The Soviets were particularly incensed that the Nanking government, which in their eyes had systematically yielded to the Japanese and had even sabotaged efforts at resistance in Shanghai and North China, should suddenly, by filing such a protest, try to make it appear to the world that it was the U.S.S.R. which was violating Chinese sovereignty and injuring its national interests by selling the Chinese Eastern Railway to the local authorities in Manchuria. Soviet comment subsequently emphasized the fact that less than a month later Nanking signed the Tangku truce which aroused antagonism in China itself.[12]

It was not only the total collapse of Chinese resistance that made the Soviets regard as imperative an adjustment of their differences with Japan; the situation in Europe also impelled them toward a settlement. Hitler had come to power with his avowedly anti-Soviet program and friction was already developing. Relations with Great Britain were also severely strained because of the Metro-Vickers trial and the practical cessation of trade through the imposition of mutual embargoes. Thus, although Soviet relations in Europe and elsewhere were destined to improve before the close of the year, the negotiations for the sale of the Chinese Eastern Railway were undertaken at a time when the Soviets were peculiarly isolated.

On May 29, 1933, Ambassador Ota was reported to have said that although the economic significance of the Chinese Eastern Railway had been decreased by the construction of other lines, it was important to settle the disputes centering

[11] Terentev, *The Seat of War in The Far East*, (in Russian), Partizdat, Moscow, 1934, fn. p. 191.

[12] Toynbee reports that following the fall of Jehol and other Japanese victories the "Nanking government—in whose counsels the Commander-in-Chief still manifestly held the casting vote—took the line of least resistance and compromised with Japan . . . it became clear that those in power in Nanking had decided to accommodate themselves to the facts of the situation and might even prove responsive to suggestions for Sino-Japanese cooperation in China's internal affairs." *Survey of International Affairs*, 1933, *op. cit.*, p. 483.

about it because it had become a source of friction between Japan, Manchukuo and the Soviet Union.[13] Three days before, in continuing the exchange of protests regarding abuses, he had disclaimed responsibility for the actions of Manchurian officials or of their Japanese advisers who, he said, were acting under instructions from the Manchukuo government. He reported that the matter had been taken up with the Manchukuo government which had expressed its readiness to buy the line, to which the Japanese had no objection. Consequently he was offering the services of Japan as the intermediary in the negotiations.

The first conference was held in Tokyo on June 26. The Soviet delegation's first proposal was based on an estimated total cost of the line of 411,691,976 gold rubles and an average net income of 20 million gold rubles per year from 1924 to 1930 (11,000,000 gold rubles in 1932 despite the disturbances).[14] It placed the price at 250,000,000 gold rubles (the equivalent of about 625,000,000 yen)—half to be paid in goods over two years, one-quarter in cash at the time of the sale and one-quarter in 4 per cent bonds payable in three years. Manchukuo's counter-offer was at 50,000,000 yen and the Soviets lowered their figure to 200,000,000 gold rubles, but at this point negotiations deadlocked and recriminations began again. In September the Soviets protested a series of arrests and made charges of a carefully planned campaign inspired by Tokyo, designed to lead to seizure of the line.[15] Receiving no satisfactory reply, on October 9

[13] *Japan Weekly Chronicle*, June 15, 1933, p. 825. For further Japanese comment on the negotiations, see *Japan Weekly Chronicle*, June 8, pp. 780–781, July 6, pp. 17–18, and July 13, 1933, pp. 43–46.

[14] *Soviet Union Review*, November 1933, p. 241.

[15] *Japan Weekly Chronicle*, July 13, 1933, p. 45 reported an interview between Mr. Ohashi, a Manchukuo delegate in the C.E.R. negotiations, and Mr. Togo of the Japanese Foreign Office, in which the former said, among other things, that "in case the negotiations break off owing to Soviet Russia's refusal to accept the Manchukuo terms, Manchukuo is ready to take over the railway by actual force by dint of her right of joint control under the Soviet-Mukden Agreement of 1924." The Foreign Office was reported to endorse this plan and "if necessary, to render friendly help to Manchoukuo. . . . "

Moscow carried out its threat to publish documents purporting to prove Japanese responsibility for the campaign against the Chinese Eastern Railway. Following this revelation, the Chinese Eastern Railway vanished from the headlines for a short period.

ESTABLISHMENT OF DIPLOMATIC RELATIONS WITH THE UNITED STATES

Meanwhile the Soviet position in other parts of the world had been improving markedly. The first indication came in the form of an invitation from the United States to attend the World Economic Conference in London in June, 1933. Although this conference turned out to be the scene of the first of a number of serious incidents between the Soviet Union and Germany,[16] it also gave Litvinov the chance to complete the line of non-aggression pacts along his western frontier, reinforced with a general pact defining aggression. Relations were also patched up with Britain in July.

The most important step, however, was the establishment of diplomatic relations with the United States. Ever since the Russian Revolution the United States had remained adamant in its refusal to recognize the new regime, and in the early years[17] had declined even to attend conferences where Soviet delegations were present. Nevertheless, trade between the two countries had expanded substantially in the years of the first Five-Year Plan, reaching a peak in 1930 and 1931 when the value of American exports to the Soviet Union exceeded one hundred million dollars. The volume of trade then fell off rapidly until in 1933 sales to the U.S.S.R. totaled only nine million dollars. The decline increased the pressure for

[16] The German delegation presented a memorandum asking for land for those without "lebensraum" and pointing to Russia with the statement that "war, revolution and international ruin found their point of departure in Russia, in the great regions of the East. That destructive process still continues. The moment has come to stop it." *Soviet Union Review*, August 1933, p. 172.

[17] For a full account, see Frederick L. Schuman, *American Policy Toward Russia Since 1917*, International Publishers, New York, 1928.

the establishment of diplomatic relations, and on October 10, 1933 President Roosevelt invited President Kalinin to send a representative to Washington in an effort "to end the present abnormal relations" between the peoples of the two countries. On November 16, 1933 through an exchange of notes between Roosevelt and Litvinov, diplomatic relations were formally established with the hope that "our nations henceforth may cooperate for their mutual benefit and for the preservation of the peace of the world."[18]

Although nothing was said which had direct bearing on the situation in the Far East, some observers read such a reference into Kalinin's reply to Roosevelt's invitation, when he observed that the absence of relations between the two countries had complicated "the process of consolidating world peace" and encouraged "the forces tending to disturb that peace."[19] The American press confined itself largely to the commercial aspects of the agreement, but in the American Foundation report on Soviet-American relations, one of the points in the list of arguments favoring recognition read:[20] "If the United States genuinely desires to check imperialism in the Far East, it must cooperate with Russia. It can do so adequately only if there are normal diplomatic relations between the two countries."

The foreign press was unanimous in its view that the Far Eastern situation was a major consideration in the American decision. It recognized the American dilemma with regard to its desire to play a strong hand in the Sino-Japanese conflict, as evidenced by Roosevelt's continuation of the Stimson doctrine. But the only country on the spot and vitally concerned was the U.S.S.R. with which the United States

[18] For the full text of the exchange of notes, see *Establishment of Diplomatic Relations with the Union of Soviet Socialist Republics*, U.S. Government Printing Office, Washington, D.C., 1933.

[19] Cf. *The United States in World Affairs*, Council on Foreign Relations, Harper and Brothers, New York, 1934, p. 243.

[20] *The United States and the Soviet Union*, The American Foundation, New York, 1933, p. 7.

had no diplomatic relations. In historical perspective it also appears that Far Eastern affairs so often had played a prominent role in the relations between the two countries that they could not fail to be an important element in the decision. A final indication of the significance of the Far East in American-Soviet discussions was the fact that the Soviets waived all claims arising out of America's Siberian Intervention as a result of Litvinov's "examination of certain documents of the years 1918 to 1921 relating to the attitude of the American government toward the expedition into Siberia, the operations there of foreign military forces and the inviolability of the territory of the U.S.S.R."

Whether or not the Chinese situation chiefly motivated Roosevelt's move, recognition by the United States came as a major triumph for the Soviet Union, marking the end of an era—the end of diplomatic isolation. Litvinov commented that in the establishment of relations one should "see not only one more recognition of us by a great power, but the fall of the last position, the last fort in that attack upon us by the capitalist world, which after the October Revolution, took the form of non-recognition and boycott."[21] This fact was to be signalized by Soviet admission to the League of Nations the following year.

Recognition by the United States did not, however, mean improved Soviet relations with Japan. In his report to the Central Executive Committee of the U.S.S.R. in December 1933, Litvinov summarized the growing difficulties encountered with Japan along with the steps taken to meet them:[22]

"From the time of the signing of the Peking Agreement until the end of 1931 the best good-neighbor relations existed between us and Japan. There were no conflicts, no serious misunderstandings, and whatever misunderstandings arose were settled by peaceful diplomatic negotiations. There were no threats from one side or

[21] Maxim Litvinov, *op. cit.*, p. 62.
[22] *ibid.*, pp. 71–73.

the other. We were so trusting in our relations with Japan—for she had at that time given us no reason for distrust—that we had left our Far Eastern frontier almost without protection. This situation began to change after Japan began its military operations in Manchuria. Along with the rest of the world, we could not but see in those operations a violation by Japan of many obligations, which she had voluntarily taken upon herself in the form of international treaties. The Japanese Government, as you remember, at that time gave explanations for those operations which explained nothing and convinced no one. She also gave us official assurances that her troops would not go further than a definite line in Manchuria proper and that in any case our interests, specifically interests in the C.E.R., would not suffer. These assurances were repeatedly given us, as the Japanese troops advanced, until the completed occupation of the whole of Manchuria and the formation of so-called 'Manchukuo' were effected. These actions were, as you know, characterized by all the outside world, including the League of Nations to which Japan herself belonged, as a violation of such agreements as the Washington Nine-Power Treaty, the Covenant of the League of Nations and the Kellogg Pact. The occupation of Manchuria was, however, also a violation of the Portsmouth Treaty, confirmed by the Peking Agreement under which Japan did not have the right to maintain troops in Manchuria above a certain minimum. We declined to take part in the international actions undertaken and planned at that time, first, because we did not believe in the honesty and consistency of the governments participating in these actions and primarily because we did not seek, nor do we now seek, armed conflict with Japan. We asked from Japan only one thing: the observance of our commercial interests in the C.E.R., and we had no other interests in Manchuria. Contrary to all the solemn promises and assurances the Japanese representatives in Manchuria soon, however, began a direct attack on these interests. . . . The calmer and more patiently we behaved, the more provocative became the Japanese authorities in Manchuria. The impression created was that they were consciously provoking us to action more forceful than protests. Not wishing to give in to this provocation, we made the proposal on May 2 of this year that Japan buy the C.E.R. from us. . . .

"It was not, however, only a question of the C.E.R. Along with infringing our rights on the railroad, political figures in Japan, including official representatives of the Japanese Government began to discuss openly and even in the press the question of war against the Soviet Union for the purpose of seizing the Primore and the whole Far Eastern Krai. The matter did not stop at discussion and in Manchuria near our border a large number of Japanese troops were concentrated, war materials were brought, railroads and highways were built, etc. In this way the danger not only of the seizure of our railroad by Japanese arms, but a direct threat to our frontier was created. Under these circumstances there was nothing left for our Government to do but to begin to fortify our frontier, transferring the necessary forces for that purpose and taking other military measures."

In December 1933 special measures were taken to encourage migration to the Soviet Far East from other parts of the U.S.S.R. Collective farmers were exempted from agricultural taxes; wages for workers were raised 10 to 30 per cent; for the Red Army 20 to 30 per cent; and prices to be paid by the Government for fish products were increased 20 per cent.[22]

The advent of Hirota, former Ambassador to Moscow, to the Japanese Foreign Office brought a short relaxation of tension and also a suggestion (in November 1933) that paragraph 3 of Article II of the Portsmouth Treaty, demilitarizing the Korean-Siberian border, be extended to cover the whole Soviet-Manchurian border. The Soviets turned down this proposal for obvious strategic reasons which were explicitly stated when Japan renewed the offer at the end of 1934.

Negotiations for the sale of the C.E.R. had been resumed in January 1934 and were carried on intermittently until August. By this time the Soviets had lowered their price to 160,000,000 yen, two-thirds of which might be paid in goods. Hirota rejected the offer, clinging to his own figure of 120,000,000 yen plus the retirement pensions to be paid to Soviet employees by Manchukuo. His answer, in fact, practically took the form of an ultimatum. Shortly afterwards the Manchukuo delegation left for home though the Japanese had indicated that further negotiations should be handled directly by Manchukuo.

[22] *Economic Review of the Soviet Union*, January 1934, p. 23.

The final breakdown of the railway negotiations was only one symptom of a developing international situation which Moscow regarded as extremely ominous. Even though Japan had withdrawn from the League in March 1933 and had set up its puppet administration in Manchukuo, there had been indications early in 1934 of an effort to reach some kind of compromise with the western powers and with China. By April, however, the Amau statement, arrogating to Japan the right to veto all financial and commercial operations of foreign powers in China, had further alienated Britain and the United States from Japan. This estrangement was accentuated again when Japan denounced the Washington Naval treaty at the end of the year.

The year 1934 also witnessed the first steps toward close collaboration between Japan and Germany, a development of particular concern to Moscow. Both had left the League in connection with their programs of treaty revision; both were outspokenly anti-Soviet in official statements of policy. The first outright demonstration of the new German-Japanese affinity came with the visit of a Japanese naval squadron to Germany during the summer of 1934, followed up by the negotiation of trade agreements and by the dispatch of Japanese military and naval experts to Germany. As a token of the new-found friendship the German press began to admit the Japanese into the select circle of "superior races" which were destined to rule over inferior peoples of lesser blood.

For Moscow this rapprochement was considered the more alarming because Poland was being drawn into the German-Japanese combination against the U.S.S.R., with evidences too of Japanese attempts to involve Iran and Afghanistan. Soviet writings of this period could find no basis for a German-Japanese alliance or even an entente other than an anti-Soviet war.[23] The foreign press also recognized the serious threat

[23] Cf. I. Lemin, "German-Japanese Relations," and A. N., "The Preparation of Japan for a Big War," *Tikhii Okean*, No. 1, 1935.

of a Japanese-Soviet war and more than once during 1934 warned of its imminence. Consequently Moscow exerted every possible effort to remove any excuse for provocation by Japan—even at a sacrifice. In regard to the Chinese Eastern Railway, however, no settlement proved feasible until after Soviet admission to the League of Nations had strengthened the country's international position.

SOVIET ADMISSION TO THE LEAGUE OF NATIONS

Far Eastern considerations were among the determinants of American recognition of the U.S.S.R. and this action in its turn gave impetus to the subsequent admission of the Soviet Union to the League. But it was Hitler's rise to power in Europe which finally impelled France to take the lead in bringing Litvinov to Geneva. The question had first been raised at the spring meeting of the League. On September 15, 1934 an invitation was dispatched to Moscow and the same day the Soviets replied in the affirmative, accepting "the international obligations and decisions binding upon its members in conformity with Article I of the Covenant."[24] The final vote was taken on September 18; 39 countries voted in favor; 7 abstained and 3 voted against. The U.S.S.R. was given a permanent place on the League Council. A warm-hearted welcome from China was thus expressed by Mr. Quo:[25]

"If China is the foundation of Asia, as she is, Russia is the uniting arch of Europe and Asia. China warmly welcomes the prospect of her immediate entrance into the comity of the League of Nations. Russia's collaborative labors in the Disarmament Conference are a happy augury of her influence now that she is about to enter the League membership. She

[24] *Economic Review of the Soviet Union*, October 1934, p. 192. The only exception noted was that disputes arising before Soviet entry should not come under the provisions for arbitration or judicial settlement provided in Articles 12 and 13.

[25] W. W. Willoughby, *The Sino-Japanese Controversy and the League of Nations*, Johns Hopkins University Press, Baltimore, 1935, p. 516.

has contributed the most clear and acute definition of the aggressor. China is Russia's neighbor over the longest stretch of continuous boundary anywhere in Asia or Europe. We have a common interest in the preservation of peace in the Far East and the Pacific, and we are glad that from now on our joint efforts for peace can be coordinated within the framework of the League."

This turning point in Soviet relations with the major countries of western Europe indicated a trend which had been foreshadowed by the efforts to establish an Eastern Locarno including the Soviets and which reached its peak in the negotiation of the Franco-Soviet mutual assistance pact in 1935. For the Soviets it meant that the British and French were ceasing to regard the U.S.S.R. as their most serious adversary and were trying to organize against the outbreak of war. Since this change was highly significant, it is of interest to quote at length from Litvinov's maiden speech at the League Assembly, made on September 18, 1934:[26]

" . . . At the time when the League of Nations was being formed to proclaim the organization of peace, the people of our country had as yet not been enabled to enjoy the blessings of peace. They still had to defend their internal peace with arms, and to contend for long their right to internal self-determination and their external independence. Even after the most extreme forms of intervention in the affairs of our state were over, the hostility of the outer world continued to be manifested in the most varying degrees and forms.

"All this makes it quite obvious that the relations between the Soviet state and the League of Nations could not be other than those existing between itself and the states belonging to the League. Not only this, but the people in the Soviet Union naturally feared that these nations united in the League might give collective expression to their hostility towards the Soviet Union and combine their anti-Soviet activities. . . . To this I must frankly add that the Soviet Government could not have agreed with all the decisions of the League at that time and that, had we taken part in drawing

[26] *The Soviet Union in the Struggle for Peace*, Co-Operative Publishing Society of Foreign Workers in the U.S.S.R., Moscow, 1936, pp. 100–108.

up the Covenant of the League, we would have contested certain of its articles. . . . All this, however, has not been important enough to prevent the Soviet Union from entering the League, especially since any new member of an organization can be morally responsible only for decisions made with its participation and agreement.

"In order to make our position quite clear, I should like further to state that the idea in itself of an association of nations contains nothing theoretically inacceptable for the Soviet state and its ideology. . . . The Soviet state has, however, never excluded the possibility of some form or other of association of states having different political and social systems, so long as there is no mutual hostility and if it is for the attainment of common aims. For such an association it considers that the essential conditions would be, first, the extension to every state belonging to such an association of the liberty to preserve what I might call its state personality and the social-economic system chosen by it—in other words reciprocal non-interference in the domestic affairs of the states therein associated; and secondly, the existence of common aims."

After enumerating instances of Soviet participation in international conferences, such as the disarmament conference, he went on: "It needed, however, one great dominating common aim to prove incontestably to all nations, including those of the Soviet Union, the desirability—nay the necessity—for closer cooperation between the Soviet Union and the League of Nations, and even for the entry of the Soviet Union into the League. The discovery of such a common aim has been greatly facilitated by the events of the last two or three years."

Litvinov's speech closed with references to the war-making nations of Asia and Europe who aim at the "refashioning of the map of Europe and Asia by the sword," and he urged something more than "paper obstacles." Molotov expressed the same views more concisely in his report to the Congress of Soviets, January 28, 1935:[27] "Recent events have served to emphasize the change that has occurred in the position of the

[27] *ibid.*, p. 40.

League of Nations. The more bellicose and aggressive elements have begun to withdraw from the League of Nations. . . . Inasmuch as the League of Nations may now play a certain favorable part in maintaining peace, the Soviet Union could not but admit the expediency of collaborating with the League of Nations in this matter, although we are not prone to over-estimate the importance of such organizations."

RAILWAY NEGOTIATIONS RESUMED

Meanwhile negotiations with Japan over the Chinese Eastern Railway had been resumed despite the arrest of more Soviet employees and charges from Manchukuo that the Soviets were trying to wreck the line. A Tass report of October 31, 1934 described the subsequent exchanges as follows: On September 6, Hirota offered 130,000,000 yen for the line; on September 12 Yurenev replied that the Soviets did not think petty bargaining was appropriate after 15 months of negotiations, that although the Soviets had offered to sell for 160,000,000 yen on July 30, a figure "apparently lower than the real value of the line," they would split the difference and accept 145,000,000. Hirota countered with 140,000,000 and on September 19 this figure was accepted by Moscow, exclusive of the pensions to former employees. It was agreed that two-thirds of the price should be paid in trade, one-sixth in cash at the time of sale and one-sixth over a period of three years. Next came the question of a guarantee of the time payments inasmuch as delivery of the road and its management was to take place immediately. Three months of negotiations followed. The Japanese charged that it was an insult both to Manchukuo and to Japan for the Soviets to show such lack of faith as to demand guarantees from Japan. Moreover, the two parties could not agree on a method of settling of disputes that might subsequently arise in carrying out the contract. The Soviets claimed to be endeavoring to close the matter in such a way as to prevent all future possibilities of conflict on the subject and charged that "a number of the Japanese proposals are of such a nature that were they to be utilized as a basis for the agreement, they would present opportunities for fresh attempts being made to use the C.E.R. question as a source of conflict between the two nations even after the railroad had been sold."[28] In November and December further "disorders" occurred on the line, but on December 12 the Japanese finally agreed to guarantee the sale price.

None of the verbal warfare then being waged over alleged Soviet activities in Mongolia apparently was intended by either side as a means of holding up the C.E.R. negotiations. Hirota even found himself in the position of having to answer complaints in the Diet that the money from the C.E.R. sale might be used for more communistic activity in Manchuria and China. During February more and more of the Soviet employees of the C.E.R. who had been arrested during the previous summer were released by the Manchurian authorities.[29] The Japanese press reported that agreement would soon be reached and details were discussed concerning a loan to be made by a group of Japanese banks to Manchukuo to cover the cost. On March 12, 1935 the three documents effecting the sale were initialled and the formal signing took place on the 23rd.[30]

The arrangement comprised three separate agreements: the agreement between the U.S.S.R. and Manchukuo on details of transfer of ownership; the tri-partite protocol regarding the arrangements for payment in kind; the final protocol dealing with details such as the schools and cooperatives formerly run for the Soviet employees of the line. And

[28] Tass, November 21, 1934. Quoted in *Economic Review of the Soviet Union*, December 1934, p. 270.

[29] Cf. *Izvestia*, February 15, 17, 27 and March 29, 1935.

[30] Text of the agreements is published in English in *Information Bulletins Nos. 66–150*, Publications of the Department of Foreign Affairs, Manchukuo Government, Hsinking, Manchukuo, May 1936, pp. 35–55.

in addition there was an exchange of notes between Japan and the U.S.S.R. in which the former guaranteed the payments. The price was fixed at 140,000,000 yen plus about 30,000,000 yen in pensions to Soviet employees. One-sixth of the purchase price was paid in cash at the signing, one-sixth in cash payments to be paid over three years, and two-thirds in goods, with deliveries to be made by Japan and Manchukuo over a period of three years. Within three weeks most of the Soviet employees had returned to the Soviet Union and on April 5 a trade commission was set up to handle the deliveries of goods.

The conclusion of these long and stormy negotiations was marked by a number of friendly exchanges between the two countries. In an interview to the press Litvinov even went so far as to say that the Japanese demilitarization proposals might be discussed.[31] "As regards the question of so-called demilitarization, I must state in truth that this word does not exactly describe the state of affairs in the Far East. Too often in history has demilitarization followed the conclusion of military operations. But there has been no war between the U.S.S.R. and Japan, and I hope there will not be. Although in the present instance it is a question of voluntary mutual demilitarization, I nevertheless consider that such a statement of the question ought to be avoided. It would be perfectly normal, however, if, as the tension aroused in the Far East by the events of the past four years relaxes, the interested sides would make a study and enter into a calm discussion of the question of the mutual withdrawal for a definite distance of a certain section of the armed forces of both sides, including aviation, taking into consideration of course the geographical position of each side."

As usual, Litvinov ended with a reiteration of the argument for a non-aggression pact.

Prior to this statement, the Chinese Government had filed

[31] *Izvestia*, March 15, 1935.

a protest against the sale of the C.E.R. along the same lines as that entered in 1933, but following the Litvinov interview it went further and sent a memorandum on the subject to the British, American, Japanese, French, Italian, Portuguese, Belgian and Netherlands governments.[31] Referring again to the provisions of the 1924 Sino-Soviet treaty, the note read:

"While Russia might have deemed fit to surrender her own interests in the Chinese Eastern Railway to a third party—be it real or fictitious—China can never recognize any party as a successor to any of the rights and interests in the railway.

"No railway can be held or operated by any persons or organizations in the territory of China without her explicit consent. Russia's present action constitutes without the shadow of a doubt, a direct violation of China's contractual as well as sovereign rights.

"The painful fact that the Chinese Government has been prevented by circumstances—for which it is not responsible—from exercising its rights in connection with the administration of the Chinese Eastern Railway, does not in the least affect the validity of the provisions of the agreement of 1924, nor the status of the railway. . . . "

Izvestia answered this protest indirectly in an editorial on March 24th which asserted:[32] "Every thinking Chinese patriot knows that the U.S.S.R. would have been deeply happy if it had been possible to turn over the railroad to the representatives of the great Chinese people, friendship with whom is especially valued by the people of the U.S.S.R. But the Chinese people are not master of the situation in Manchuria and they would gain nothing if the C.E.R. became the object of a war which might have destroyed this Far Eastern railroad."

After twenty months of negotiations the sale of the railroad was finally completed. The reasons for the mutual interest

[31] *China Year Book, 1935*, North China Daily News & Herald, Ltd., Shanghai, p. 139.

[32] See Appendix, p. 225.

in closing this deal lay to a considerable extent outside of the Far East. Japan, it is true, was beginning to make cautious southward moves along the coast of China and was registering real progress in bringing the Chinese National government, still deeply engrossed in its anti-Communist warfare, into "cooperation with its program in China." But in Europe far more momentous events were distracting the world. The Abyssinian War was brewing and Japan found itself involved as the chief foreign adviser to Ethiopia. Even more serious was Nazi activity. On March 16 1935, four days after the C.E.R. contract was initialed, Hitler denounced the military clauses of the Versailles treaty and introduced universal military service. The immediate result of this action was the arrival of Eden and Laval in Moscow. After the many months of bandying the question of an Eastern Locarno from conference to conference, the project of a Franco-Soviet pact was announced on the eve of the Stresa conference and on May 2 it was signed. To the Soviets the European situation remained a powderkeg; both Germany and Poland were conducting a rabid anti-Soviet press campaign; Britain and France were at odds over the proper tactics to meet the situation; and the Soviets were worried that a gap would be left in the security arrangements, leaving the road open for an attack on their borders.[33]

[33] Cf. Soviet comment on the London project for a western European regional pact, "Without The Soviet Government it is impossible to protect peace in Europe," *Izvestia*, February 21, 1935 and later on the Stresa conference.

IV. *FRONTIER AND FISHERIES DISPUTES, 1935–1936*

IN THE THREE-MONTH INTERVAL while the last details of the sale of the Chinese Eastern Railway were being worked out, a number of other issues developed between the Soviet Union and Japan. The parliaments of the two countries were meeting simultaneously, so that a kind of indirect verbal exchange at long distance took place. At the end of January Foreign Minister Hirota reported that he hoped the C.E.R. deal would soon be closed and that the Soviets would then consider demilitarization of the border. But, he added, because of the "sovietization of Sinkiang" and the activities of the Chinese Red Army the Japanese government would have to continue on the alert.[1] Soviet editorial comment was to the effect that talk of demilitarization was useless in the face of what was going on and that the references to the sovietization of Sinkiang were only cover for those "who consider China a pie waiting to be cut up and who are looking for an excuse to select the best piece."[2]

Molotov reinforced this comment a few days later in a speech to the Seventh Congress of Soviets, wherein he stated specifically that the U.S.S.R. considered Sinkiang an integral part of China. Hirota continued his side of the argument in answer to questions in Parliament, declaring that no non-aggression pact could be concluded until all issues were settled, but at the same time advocating extension of the Portsmouth demilitarization provisions to the whole border. In his closing remarks to the All-Union Congress, Molotov retorted

[1] *Contemporary Japan*, Vol. III, No. 4, March, 1935, pp. 704–705.
[2] *Izvestia*, January 24, 1935.

that while the Soviets were fully observing the demilitarization clauses of the 1905 treaty regarding the Sakhalin and Korean frontiers as well as the limitation on railway guards in Manchuria, Japan on the other hand was flagrantly violating the latter. The Japanese press then took up the cudgels and stated that since the Soviets had given up their rights to railroad guards in their 1924 treaties with China, they had no right to worry about Japan's guards. *Izvestia* replied that Japan's obligations under the Portsmouth Treaty were not changed by the Soviet-Chinese Treaty. And so the battle of words continued. Yurenev even protested against a speech made by Saito, then Japanese Ambassador to the United States, at the Chicago Council on Foreign Relations in which he justified Japan's actions in China as a defense against Soviet machinations within that country.

The real significance of all this seemed to lie in the fact that Japan was moving westward deeper into Inner Mongolia and was beginning to use "Pan-Islamic" slogans for intrigue among the Mohammedan population in western China. In January occurred the first of the serious border incidents on the Mongol-Manchurian border near Lake Khalkha, and a commission was set up to deal with it. At the same time Japan persistently stressed Soviet penetration, but its charges that the Soviets were building a railroad from China to Ulan Bator were denied by Moscow.[3] Japan's campaign against Soviet influence in Sinkiang even aroused anxiety in China; so that at the end of January, Sheng Shih-tsai, governor of the province,[4] wired Nanking reaffirming his loyalty and explaining that some foreign technical advisers were in the province,

[3] *Izvestia*, February 23, 1935.

[4] Sheng Shih-tsai's regime in Sinkiang was established in Dec. 1933 after a period of civil war. For accounts of this very confused period, cf. Owen Lattimore, *Inner Asian Frontiers of China*, American Geographical Society, New York, 1940, pp. 199ff. and *Mongol Journeys*, Doubleday, Doran and Co., Inc., New York, 1941; also, Edgar Snow, *Battle for Asia*, Random House, New York, 1941.

but none in governmental positions. He also reported that the Soviets had offered commercial credits to be repaid in kind. Ho Ying-chin replied for the Nanking government, assuring Sheng that he did not need to be worried over the effects of the Japanese-inspired rumors.[5]

JAPANESE FISHERIES IN SOVIET WATERS

Fishing off the Russian coast, especially off Kamchatka, had been in the hands of the Japanese since 1869. By 1924 these fishing grounds—primarily salmon and some crab—were yielding the Japanese about 12 million poods or 432 million lbs., of fish products annually. Not until that year did the Soviet government enter the business, taking over the leases on most of the fishery districts on the Kamchatka and Bolshaya Rivers. By 1927 it also had begun to enter the field of fish-canning on both Kamchatka and Sakhalin.

Japanese fishing in Russian territorial waters and the establishment of bases for processing the fish on Russian soil had gone on without any official arrangements up to the time of the Russo-Japanese war. Although the 1875 Treaty, exchanging Sakhalin for the Kurile Islands, gave Japan most-favored-nation treatment in regard to the fisheries, some friction had arisen subsequently over the treaty's operation. At Portsmouth the Japanese therefore insisted that their fishing rights be written into the treaty. Accordingly, Article XI reads: "Russia engages to arrange with Japan for granting to Japanese subjects rights of fishery along the coasts of the Russian possessions in the Japan, Okhotsk and Behring Seas."

The detailed arrangements for the procedure under which such rights were to be implemented and controlled were made in the fishery convention of 1907. This arrangement expired in 1919 and from that time until 1923 the Japanese had taken the matter into their own hands. In 1923, when Soviet control had been extended over the entire mainland, the

[5] A Reuters dispatch from Shanghai, quoted by *Izvestia*, January 30, 1935.

question of fisheries was one of the first to be handled. A mixed Russo-Japanese commission was set up to establish the indebtedness of the Japanese fishing enterprises for their rents, etc. during the war years, with a figure of 6,265,000 gold rubles finally agreed upon.

In the meantime, the Soviet government had taken independent action and by a decree of May 8, 1923, annulled all treaties, concessions, contracts and other agreements relating to the fisheries and seal-hunting grounds of the Far East, which were concluded before the date on which the Far Eastern Republic was fused with R.S.F.S.R.[6] The decree also provided that the fishing grounds—except for those in areas closed for strategic reasons and in rivers where natives and settlers lived—would be leased at auction to Russian citizens or foreigners. It made the foreign leases subject to all Soviet regulations as to conservation, sanitary provisions, and so on.

Under this law, public auctions, held on April 15, 1924, in Vladivostok gave the Japanese 219 sea fisheries and the Russians 72. Since the rent had been increased by 15 per cent, the Japanese paid 1,152,000 gold rubles as compared with 1,120,000 rubles for the 255 lots which they had held the year before. The Russians had also introduced new regulations limiting the catch and the methods of treating the catch. They had, moreover, given 13 of the best lots formerly held by the Japanese, to the Soviet state fisheries.

Following the establishment of diplomatic relations, which carried with it the extension of the provisions of the Portsmouth Treaty, it was agreed that the 1907 Convention would be revised and that until then the Soviet arrangements made in 1924 would remain in force. The new convention, concluded on January 23, 1928, provided that the Japanese could obtain fishery grounds at auction in all but 37 gulfs and bays, that Soviet state fisheries could not participate

[6] Cf. *Russian Review*, November 1923.

in the auctions and that their catch should be limited to 2,000,000 poods.[7] At that time there were three such state organizations—the Far Eastern State Fisheries, the Okaro (Okhotsk-Kamchatka joint stock company) and the Far Eastern Marine Products Company formed in 1923 and 1924.

The first difficulty[8] arising over the agreement concerned the rate of payment, which was supposed to be made in gold rubles (102.5 sen). The Japanese were charged with dealing on the "Black Bourse" to obtain rubles and in December 1930 the Vladivostok Branch of the Bank of Chosen was closed as a result of participating in this speculation. In 1931 there was widespread agitation on the matter in Japan, and an attempt was made on the life of the Soviet trade representative in Tokyo. In April a temporary settlement was reached, fixing 32.5 sen per ruble as the rate for "obligations now due, with the understanding that negotiations would be continued to settle upon the final rate."[9]

At the auctions in February 1932 thirty Japanese firms took part, acquiring 101 fishing grounds for 654,020 rubles as against 25 lots obtained by Soviet citizens and cooperatives. But of the total Salmon lots (some leases ran for more than one year and Soviet State fisheries holdings were not included in those auctioned), the Soviets had increased their holdings to 42 per cent, as against 12 per cent in 1924. While Japanese fisheries held more lots than eight years earlier—371 as against 299—the Soviets apparently were getting the bulk of the new lots being opened up. In crab fishing, where the Soviet share had always been larger, the same trend was evident. Thus, while Japanese production remained relatively stable—35 million yen in 1926 and 32 million in 1932—Soviet competition was increasing.

[7] one pood = 36 lbs.

[8] For a detailed account of the fisheries difficulties cf. Kathleen Barnes, "Fisheries, Mainstay of Soviet-Japanese Friction." *Far Eastern Survey*, March 27, 1940, also H. E. Gregory and K. Barnes, *North Pacific Fisheries*, American Council, Institute of Pacific Relations, New York 1939.

[9] *Soviet Union Review*, June 1931, p. 131.

Because of this situation further revisions in the 1928 agreement were sought by both sides. The Hirota-Karakhan Agreement reached on August 13, 1932, raised to 5,000,000 poods the former 2,000,000-pood limit on the catch of the Soviet state fisheries. The original limitation had supposedly represented approximately 20 per cent of the total catch, while the new figure approximated 37 per cent. In return it was agreed that the Japanese-held lots (with the exception of 60) should not be put up for auction again until the expiration of the convention in 1936. This arrangement meant that the annual auction would henceforth cover only new fishing grounds, those held by the Soviet citizens plus the 60 excluded from the Japanese agreement, leaving about 280 in Japanese hands without auction. This settlement kept the fisheries off the agenda of Soviet-Japanese negotiations until 1934.

In February 1934 the Soviets announced a new exchange rate for the payment on fishery leases—namely 75 sen per ruble instead of the 32.5 sen per ruble agreed on in 1931. The Japanese declared this change illegal and refused to take part in the auctions which therefore had to be postponed. By May the question was settled; the rate remained at 32.5 sen and it was agreed that the Japanese might pay by purchasing debentures of the Kamchatka Company.[10] By this device, the price in rubles nominally remained at the higher figure, but the actual yen price was lowered.

In March 1935 the Japanese government had passed a law bringing fishing operations in the North Pacific under its direct purview. The net result of this action was to consolidate the fishing business in the hands of one or two big firms who were then able to exert pressure more than ever through the Foreign Office. The spring auctions went off uneventfully, but the basic Convention of 1928 was due to

[10] B. Sokolov, "Fisheries Question in the Concession-Waters of the U.S.S.R.," *Tikhii Okean*, No. 2, 1936, p. 92.

lapse on May 27, 1936. Unless one of the parties requested its revision twelve months in advance, it would automatically be prolonged for another twelve years. In April 1935 the Japanese notified Moscow that they did not consider basic revision was necessary but that they would like various changes and wanted negotiations to start at once. The Soviets were agreeable to this arrangement and suggested a temporary three-year prolongation of the August 1932 supplementary agreement, which had given the Japanese the right to use most of the fishing lots without putting them up for auction.

In the negotiations that followed immediately, the Japanese sought to discover before May 27, 1935 the Soviet position on all other questions which they had raised. The Japanese were reported to desire abolition of the fishing grounds auction system, payments of ground rents in yen instead of rubles, maintenance of open-sea fisheries, adjustment in the number of Japanese and Russian grounds, reduction or elimination of Soviet state-operated fishing grounds and continuation of the Hirota-Karakhan Agreement.[11] The Soviet government was willing to try to settle the question of payments in the short time remaining. But on all other points it was prepared to negotiate only after the question of the extension of the existing 1928 Convention was settled affirmatively. The Japanese found this attitude unsatisfactory and on May 25 notified the Commissariat of Foreign Affairs that they wanted a basic revision of the whole arrangement, to which request the Soviet Government agreed.[12] Nothing of importance was reported regarding the negotiations until the end of 1935, when the Japanese press stated that they had broken down because the Soviets were trying to push the Japanese out of their fishery grounds. As proof they cited the increased proportion of lots held by the Soviets. *Izvestia*

[11] *Japan Weekly Chronicle*, April 11, 1935, p. 484.
[12] *ibid.*, June 6, 1935, p. 739.

countered by denying that the negotiations had broken down, but reported that they were delayed because the Japanese were trying to obtain rights that they had never held under the 1928 Convention. It pointed further to the increase in the absolute number of lots held by Japanese firms as refutation of the Japanese charges that they were being ousted from the North Pacific fisheries.[13]

BORDER COMMISSIONS DISCUSSED

During the summer months of 1935 the Japanese had slowly edged their way farther south of the Great Wall and were attempting with some degree of success to obtain the Chinese Government's acquiescence in the establishment of other autonomous administrations in North China. At the same time Japanese activities in Inner Mongolia and Northern Manchuria had resulted in border incidents with both Soviet troops and those of Outer Mongolia. Early in July, Ambassador Yurenev, who had succeeded Troyanovsky in Tokyo, protested the series of frontier violations that had taken place since May along the whole border from Grodekovo and Bezymianny Height (later scene of the Changkufeng conflict) to the inland waterways leading to Khabarovsk and to Blagoveshchensk. On these occasions no actual fighting had occurred and Yurenev signified his willingness to accept the Japanese proposal of June 26 to set up a border commission to handle the incidents. His plan called for a commission composed of Soviet delegates on the one hand and Japanese-Manchukuo delegates on the other.

Nothing was accomplished on this score, however, and in October new incidents occurred, this time accompanied by fighting. In answer to Yurenev's protest and a renewed request for the organization of a commission, Hirota replied that the Soviets were at fault; that the incidents arose because the border lacked clear definition; that a commission should

[13] *Izvestia*, December 12, 1935.

be set up to define the line between Lake Khanka and the Tumen River, and finally that these incidents really were a matter for negotiation between the U.S.S.R. and Manchukuo.[14] Yurenev denied all of these points. He insisted that the border was clearly defined by treaties binding on Manchukuo and that no such boundary difficulties had arisen before the Japanese invasion of Manchuria. He pointed out that he had never received an answer to his suggestion for a mixed commission to investigate the incidents and added that to consider these matters as no affair of Japan's was foolish since obviously any complication between Moscow and Changchun (Hsinking) would inevitably affect Soviet-Japanese relations.

Still no results were reported; in December 1935 Yurenev again protested this time against the appearance of ships flying the Japanese flag on the Amur and Ussuri Rivers, in violation of both Article I of the Aigun Treaty of 1858 and Article I of the agreement reached in 1934 with Manchukuo confining shipping on the Amur to Manchurian and Soviet ships.[15] The treaties on which the border arrangements were based were as follows:

(1) The Treaty of Nerchinsk of 1689, defining the border east from the Aigun River; (2) the Treaty of Kiakhta of 1727, marking the border further west near Lake Baikal; (3) the Treaty of Aigun of 1858, ceding Russia the left bank of the Amur River from the Aigun to the Ussuri Rivers; (4) the Treaty of Tientsin of 1858, providing for a detailed survey of the Amur boundary; (5) the Treaty of Peking of 1860, granting to Russia the Maritime Province formerly jointly owned by China and Russia; this treaty delimited the border along the Ussuri River to Lake Khanka and thence south to where it crosses the Tumen River. (6) The survey for the last two of these treaties was made in 1861, and by 1886 many

[14] *Japan Weekly Chronicle*, October 24, 1935 and October 31, 1935.
[15] Cf. *Economic Review of the Soviet Union*, October 1934.

of the wooden boundary posts had disintegrated. To remark the line a new commission was convened in 1886 out of which grew the Hunchung Treaty of June 26, 1886.[16]

All of these frontier definitions were carried over in the 1924 agreement regarding the resumption of relations between China and the Soviet Union, Article VII of which reads: "The governments of the two Contracting Parties agree to redemarcate their national boundaries at the Conference as provided in Article II of the present Agreement, and pending such redemarcation, to maintain the present boundaries."

This redemarcation never took place, however, and although most of the frontier was bounded by rivers, sections of land frontier and river islands remained which were to provide the pretext for innumerable border conflicts in the ensuing years and concerning which no border commission could be agreed upon. Nonetheless the Soviets stood ready to sign a non-aggression pact with Japan; and on December 30, 1935, in fact the Soviet press denied Shigemitsu's report that the idea had been dropped by both sides.

MONGOL-MANCHUKUO BORDER NEGOTIATIONS

In 1935 and early 1936 the Mongolian-Manchurian border was the scene of the most significant developments. In June 1935 delegates from Mongol People's Republic and Manchukuo convened in Manchouli to effect a settlement of the incident of the previous January. The Mongol government tried to limit discussions to this one point, but the Manchukuo delegates sought to take up all questions.[17] On June 23 the situation was further complicated by seizure of a Japanese and White Russian surveying party by Mongol frontier guards who after some difficulty turned the captives over to

[16] Cf. Cyrus H. Peake, "Changkufeng and Russo-Japanese Border Disputes," *Amerasia*, October 1938, pp. 386–7.

[17] *Japan Weekly Chronicle*, June 20, 1935, p. 799; also, July 4, 1935, pp. 18–21 and July 28, 1935.

the Manchurian frontier post. In Manchouli the Manchukuo delegates demanded that the Mongol government assume responsibility for the incident and that Manchukuo be permitted to maintain permanent representatives on Mongol territory with the right of freedom of movement. They asserted that if this demand were refused they would insist on the withdrawal of Mongol troops from the Tamsyk-Sume sector of the border. The request was supported by a similar statement from the representative of the Kwantung Army, who added the demand that the Kwantung Army be permitted to maintain representatives in Outer Mongolia and to build telegraph lines there. In reply the Mongol government gave notice of its willingness to return the equipment to the seized surveyors and to set up a mixed commission to determine on whose territory the incident had taken place. On July 14 the Kwantung Army repeated its demands in the form of an ultimatum and asked for the withdrawal of Mongol troops from the entire border.

Three days later the Manchukuo delegates, having received the Mongol rejection of their plan to have representatives stationed on Mongol territory, proposed instead an exchange of representatives to be stationed along the frontier. The Mongols accepted this plan solely for the purpose of dealing with border disputes. In reply the Manchurian delegates proposed that they should station their representatives in Bain-Tumen, Tamsyk-Sume and Ulan Bator, while the Mongols should send representatives to Hailar, Manchouli and Changchun. The Mongols thereupon pointed out that the original arrangement called for the exchange of only one representative each and that they were to remain at the border in order to be near at hand in case of incident. They indicated their readiness to work out the details of an agreement on this basis, and recalled their delegation to Ulan Bator for instructions, proposing that negotiations should be resumed in September.

In October Manchukuo repeated in ultimatum form its demand for three commissions, including one in Ulan Bator. The Mongols again rejected it and suggested *two commissions*—one at Manchouli to handle disputes over the northern sector of the frontier as far as the Kerulon River; the other at Tamsyk-Sume for the southern sector. On November 25, 1935, the negotiations broke down completely as a result of an impasse over the establishment of diplomatic relations between the two sides. By December new border incidents were reported near Lake Buir Nor and on December 22 the Mongol government filed a strong protest in Changchun.

SOVIET-MONGOL RELATIONS

By this time the matter was clearly becoming part and parcel of Soviet-Japanese relations. The Soviet press had treated the question with gravity and on December 9 *Pravda* warned that "The Tokyo government is well informed as to what a dangerous adventure it would be for it to try to carry out any of the threats" against the Mongol Republic made by Manchukuo in the official communique at the time the negotiations were broken off.

Soviet concern for the defense of Outer Mongolia dates from the time of the Revolution when the histories of the two countries overlapped. In 1919 the Revolutionary Party of Mongolia was set up in Kiakhta on the Siberian border. In 1921 Baron Ungern von Sternberg, driven from Siberia, seized and sacked Urga, only to be defeated finally by combined Mongol and Soviet troops. Growing out of this cooperation, a treaty of friendship annulling past Russian privileges in Outer Mongolia was signed on November 5, 1921. From that time until May 1, 1925, Soviet troops remained in Mongol territory. When eventually they were withdrawn, a note expressing the gratitude of the Mongol government was sent to Moscow.[18]

[18] *Tikhii Okean*, No. 3, 1936, p. 74.

"The Mongol working people and its government consider that henceforth the people of the Soviet Union and of our Republic are bound by an unseverable community of fate, interests and the great ideas of real rule by the people, and that in the future the lives of both Republics will pass in true friendship and in mutual support in difficult moments, and, particularly, the people and Government of our Republic firmly trust in the aid of the U.S.S.R. and the Red Army, if contrary to expectations, conditions develop similar to those of 1921 . . . "

Since that time the two governments have exchanged diplomatic representatives and have had very close economic relations, but the U.S.S.R. throughout has recognized the sovereignty of China over the area. This was specifically stated in Article V of the 1924 treaty with China: "The government of the U.S.S.R. recognizes that Outer Mongolia is an integral part of the Republic of China and respects China's sovereignty therein."

The 1924 treaty also guaranteed the withdrawal of Soviet troops.

As with other eastern countries bordering on it, the Soviet Union has followed a policy of economic assistance toward Outer Mongolia. Its trade with Mongolia has been carried on through the *Sovmontuvtorg*, which engages in the exchange of Soviet textiles, sugar, flour and industrial metal manufactures for Mongolian wool, hides and livestock. The Soviet Union has offered favorable trade terms and low credits for the construction of manufacturing plants such as the Industrial Combinat, the Khatylsk wool-washing plant, etc. Certain enterprises such as the Mongoltrans, Avtokontor, Mongolsherst, Mongsovbuner and the Industrial Combinat originally were jointly operated but subsequently became entirely Mongol owned. Soviet technical and financial aid nevertheless has continued.[19]

[19] For sources on the Mongol People's Republic, See: *Planovoe Khoziaistvo*,

The internal development of the Mongol People's Republic has passed through a number of phases and undergone a number of crises. From 1930 to 1932 a program of complete socialization and collectivization was attempted, including a state trade monopoly and a campaign against the Lama monasteries. This program failed utterly and even provoked uprisings. In 1932 a change was effected which recognized that the country lacked "the prerequisites for going directly over into socialist construction." The present economy is called "anti-imperialist and anti-feudal" and is based on privately-owned, nomadic livestock-raising—in marked contrast to conditions in the Central Asian and Buriat Mongol territories within the U.S.S.R. where a socialist economy has been established.[20]

When the 1935 Mongol-Manchurian frontier crisis came to a head, Gendun, President of the Council of Ministers of the Mongol People's Republic, went to Moscow. In an interview in January 1936 he declared that Japan was aiming to set up a second Manchukuo in Outer Mongolia as a base for further attack on China and the U.S.S.R. and expressed his confidence that the Soviet Union would support the Mongols if they were attacked.[21] On January 25, 1936, according to Soviet reports the Mongol government requested a mutual assistance pact with the U.S.S.R.[22]

The increased strain in Soviet-Japanese relations at the close of 1935 must be viewed in conjunction with world developments at the time. Soviet relations with the United States had somewhat deteriorated, in spite of the conclusion

---

No. 6, 1936; *Tikhii Okean*, No. 1, 1935; No. 3, 1936; also S. Viktorov and N. Khalkhin, *The Mongolian People's Republic* (in Russian), Moscow, 1936; Owen Lattimore, *Inner Asian Frontiers of China*, *op. cit.*; *Problems of the Pacific*, 1936, *op. cit.*, pp. 133–141 and Kathleen Barnes, "Outer Mongolia on the World Stage," *Far Eastern Survey*, August 30, 1939.

[20] *Tikhii Okean*, No. 3, 1936, p. 91.

[21] *Izvestia*, January 3, 1936.

[22] Y. Ryzhik, "Economic and Cultural Construction in the Mongol People's Republic," (in Russian) *Planovoe Khoziaistvo*, No. 6, 1936, p. 190.

of a trade agreement on July 14, 1935.[23] In January debt negotiations had broken down as a result of failure to reach agreement on the financial terms of loans to be advanced by the United States.[24] In August 1935 both the United States and Great Britain protested against speeches made at the Seventh Congress of the Communist International in Moscow. Moscow rejected the protests, holding that its anti-propaganda agreements applied only to its officials and calling attention to activities of White Guard Russians in America.[25] Just prior to this in June, the Soviet government had made objection to an article by Admiral Sterling (United States Navy, retired) calling for a crusade against Bolshevism.[26]

In Europe the Ethiopian war was the chief topic of debate at the League of Nations. The Soviet Union had urged full sanctions against Italy and was participating in the partial arrangements agreed on. In reply to an Italian protest, the Soviet government had described its stand as being in full support of collective security.[27] But the Hoare-Laval proposals, following the Anglo-German naval agreement, served to heighten Soviet anxiety. Further causes for alarm were the unceasing anti-Soviet campaign in Germany (as evidenced in Hitler's interview with the United Press in November) and the rumors that Laval had concluded the Franco-Soviet pact only to prevent a Soviet-German understanding and actually was ready to undertake negotiations with Germany.[28] These

[23] The Soviets agreed to purchase up to $30,000,000 in American goods in return for obtaining the benefits granted under the trade agreements program. This pact was renewed in 1936. In subsequent years—1937–1940—the Soviet guarantee was raised to $40,000,000 and the United States granted most-favored-nation treatment. Cf. *U.S. Department of State Bulletins.*

[22] Cf. Secretary Hull's statement in Press Release, U.S. Department of State, January 31, 1935, and Litvinov's statement, *Economic Review of the Soviet Union*, April, 1935, p. 87.

[25] Cf. *New York Times*, August 28, 1935, and the Roy Howard-Stalin interview in *The Soviet Union in the Struggle for Peace*, *op. cit.*, pp. 33–36.

[26] Cf. *Izvestia*, June 21, 1935.

[27] Cf. *Izvestia*, November 24, 1935.

[28] *Frankfurter Zeitung*, November 28, 1935, as reported in *Izvestia*, November 29, 1935. Cf. also A. Toynbee, *Survey of International Affairs*, 1935, Oxford University Press, London: Humphrey Milford, 1936, Vol. II., p. 83 and p. 89.

reports coincided with the first stories of a German-Japanese military agreement. *Izvestia* reported from London on December 30, 1935, that a secret military alliance between the two countries was being negotiated, directed against the U.S.S.R. and England, and to be made public under the guise of an "anti-comintern pact" in order to "disarm" England.

The only hopeful elements seen by Moscow in the international situation were the reports of growing anti-Japanese sentiment in China as signalized by the Canton movement and the ousting of Wang Ching-wei from the Chinese National Government. At the same time renewed British activity in China through the Leith-Ross Mission was regarded as an attempt to counteract to some degree previous Japanese successes with the Chinese government and to facilitate a Japanese-British agreement with respect to control over China on a basis somewhat more favorable to British interests.[29]

That the Soviets saw a close relation between European and Far Eastern developments was indicated by various items in the Moscow press charging that Germany had requested Japan to stir up border incidents with the U.S.S.R. in order to prevent the ratification of the Franco-Soviet mutual assistance pact. The Soviet press freely predicted more incidents, which indeed did follow in rapid succession all during the spring of 1936 both on the border between Manchuria and Mongolia and on the Siberian frontier. As a result the border-commission plan was put forward once more. After an incident in which Japanese and Manchukuo troops pursued deserting Manchurian forces across the border, the Far Eastern army of the U.S.S.R. issued a communique suggesting an "impartial" commission to investigate. The Japanese reply referred to the Carolina case in American history and charged that Soviet propaganda among the

[29] Cf. A. Kantorovich, "The Powers in the Far East," (in Russian) *Izvestia*, December 5, 1935.

deserters had been the cause of the whole incident. When the matter was aired diplomatically early in February, Moscow suggested a commission to include a neutral third power. The Japanese rejected this plan, arguing that the main problem was to "demarcate" the border, since its "unclearness" was the cause for the disputes. The Soviet reply to Ambassador Ota (February 21) dropped the "third party" proposal, but insisted on equal representation for the U.S.S.R., as against the combined Japanese-Manchukuo delegation. Moscow also suggested that in view of the number of incidents on the Mongolian border it might be well to set up a commission there as well. However, on the point of "demarcating" the frontier the Soviets remained adamant: there could be no question of "demarcation," only "redemarcation" of the *existing* frontier could be discussed. In a long editorial[30] *Izvestia* charged, first, that although the idea of a border commission had originated with the Japanese in December 1933, the Kwantung Army did not really want to settle the border clashes, because only a continuing "crisis" could enable them to secure enormous budgetary appropriations; second, that in attempting to use the "redemarcation" provisions of the Mukden and Peking treaties of 1924 (Art. III and Art. VII respectively) as ground for their demands, the Japanese were clearly misreading the text.

Concurrently trouble was again brewing on the Mongolian frontier as the Japanese moved in closer to Kalgan. On March 1 Stalin told Roy Howard that:[31] "If Japan should venture to attack the Mongolian People's Republic and encroach upon its independence, we will have to help the Mongolian People's Republic. Stomoniakov, Litvinov's assistant, recently informed the Japanese Ambassador in Moscow of this and pointed to the immutable friendly relations which the U.S.S.R. has been maintaining with the

[30] *Izvestia*, February 20, 1936.
[31] *The Soviet Union in the Struggle for Peace*, *op. cit.*, p. 30.

Mongolian People's Republic since 1921. We will help the Mongolian People's Republic just as we helped it in 1921."

This statement was followed by opening of negotiations between Outer Mongolia and Manchukuo. Though both countries had agreed in principle on a border commission, still to be determined were the exact terms of reference for its work. Increasingly the Soviet government insisted that the success of these negotiations formed an integral part of a Soviet-Japanese commission agreement. On March 16 Ambassador Ota proposed to redemarcate the line between Lake Khanka and the Tumen River where the U.S.S.R., Manchuria and Korea converge; contingent upon this, Japan would further be willing to establish a permanent commission to handle all incidents that might arise in that vicinity. Vice-Commissar of Foreign Affairs Stomoniakov replied that acceptance of the Japanese plan must depend on a broader settlement including the Mongolia-Manchukuo border and a subsequent extension of the commission principle to the entire frontier.

Such exchanges did not affect the frequency of clashes, which included both border incidents and the seizure of Soviet ships by Japanese authorities. Finally on March 31 Ota and Stomoniakov conferred again: Ota said that Japan could not understand what basis the two countries could use to interfere in the Manchukuo-Mongol negotiations. Stomoniakov in reply pointed out that so far as the Soviet Union was concerned a mutual-assistance agreement with the Mongol People's Republic had existed since 1921 and that a new protocol had been signed in Ulan Bator on March 12 (on March 28, *Izvestia* had already reported approval of the pact by the Small Hural of the Mongol Republic).

The text of this new pact was made public on April 8.[32] It referred to a gentlemen's agreement of November 27, 1934 and pledged consultation and cooperation in case of danger of

[32] See Appendix, p. 185.

attack. The Chinese Government immediately filed a protest, on the basis of Article V of the 1924 Agreement, which reads: "Insofar as Outer Mongolia is an integral part of the Chinese Republic, no foreign state may conclude with it any treaties or agreements."[33]

Litvinov rejected this protest on the grounds that the pact did not "violate to the slightest degree the sovereignty of China" nor did it contain "any territorial pretensions whatsoever on the part of the U.S.S.R. in relation to China or the Mongol People's Republic."[34] He reaffirmed Soviet recognition of Chinese sovereignty over Outer Mongolia and referred to the agreement made in 1924 with the provincial authorities of Manchuria as an analogous case. In closing he said that he hoped the Chinese government would become convinced that the agreement "corresponds to the interests of both the Mongolian and Chinese peoples." The Chinese government, however rejected the reply because it did not consider the 1924 Mukden agreement a precedent for dealing directly with Chinese provincial authorities instead of the National Government. According to the Chinese, the 1924 arrangement was "originally an illegal act on the part of the Soviet Government, an act contrary to international practice" which "was only rectified subsequently by the Chinese government" when it ratified it in March 1925.[35]

The Soviet press charged editorially that the Chinese government had been forced to make this protest by the Japanese, who insisted that the absence of a protest would be taken to mean the existence of a secret Soviet-Chinese pact. The Soviet reply was, however, found unsatisfactory by the Chinese government which lodged two more similar protests on April 11 and June 4, 1936.[36]

The spring of 1936 was an immensely complicated period

[33] *Moscow Daily News*, April 9, 1936.
[34] *ibid.*
[35] *China Yearbook*, 1936, p. 23.
[36] *Chinese Yearbook*, 1937, p. 308.

in Soviet-Japanese relations and there was every evidence of a conflict of purposes within Japan itself. Following the February coup in Tokyo however, Ambassador Ota had reported to Litvinov that the change was purely internal and that the new government was, as before, seeking an improvement of relations, especially in regard to the new fisheries convention. A similar note was struck by an *Izvestia* article[37] marking the anniversary of the sale of the Chinese Eastern Railway. Pointing out, first, that everything had, to date, run smoothly in repatriating former Soviet employees as well as in placing orders for the goods to be taken in payment, it added: "Experience shows that where the provocative hands of adventurist warmongers are absent, where the deciding voice belongs to representatives of the sensible business groups of Japan who understand the real interests of their country, there good business relations can be established without any particular trouble." In April Ambassador Ota reiterated at a dinner his belief that if economic questions could be settled, all other problems would resolve themselves.[38]

In reality, however, little progress was being made on the new fisheries convention. After nearly a year's interval—June 28, 1935 to March 13, 1936—negotiations had been resumed with a Japanese counter offer to the Soviet plan of June 1935. A Tass dispatch published on April 27,[39] outlined the Soviet counterproposal: extension for five years of the leases of the majority of the lots without auction, as provided in the agreement of August 13, 1932; the renewal of the ten-year leases on cannery concessions and lots attached thereto, which for the most part were to expire in 1938; the retention of provisions for payment in debentures, with a gold clause to offset currency fluctuation. Moscow refused to consider, as contrary to Soviet law, the Japanese proposal of a twelve-year extension of leases without auction; nor would it agree

[37] *Izvestia*, March 24, 1936.
[38] *ibid.*, April 26, 1936.
[39] *ibid.*, April 27, 1936.

to Japanese participation in decisions regarding the opening of new lots or the regulation of fishery practices in the rivers and bays. Although the editorial accompanying the Tass dispatch expressed the hope that agreement could be reached before the old convention lapsed in May, it was obvious that neither side had moved more than a few inches from its original position. The tone of the *Izvestia* comment reflected annoyance at Japanese charges that the Soviets were trying to squeeze out the Japanese fisheries. It cited figures on the catch in Japanese lots:

1911–1916	3,529,000	centners
1917–1922	4,689,000	"
1923–1928	5,231,000	"
1929–1934	6,800,000	"

It also showed a similar rise in the number of Japanese canneries and their output:

In 1911—			
2	canneries produced	3,300	cases of canned goods
In 1916—			
10	" "	222,400	" " " "
In 1934—			
35	" "	1,397,500	" " " "

The editorial concluded that the Japanese were in fact annoyed more by the increase in Soviet fishery operations than by any decline in their own.

No progress was made toward resolving the deadlock, but on May 25 the old convention was extended to the end of 1936 as it became increasingly apparent that Soviet-Japanese relations as a whole were seriously deteriorating. A sharper note had already been sounded by Arita, the new Japanese foreign minister, in his speech of May 6[40] when he charged that "the wanton resort to arms on a dogmatic assumption

[40] *Contemporary Japan*, June 1936, p. 154.

that a trespass has been committed on their territories where there exists no clear border demarcation can serve no useful purpose and only injure the friendly relations between the nations concerned." He claimed that the basic reason for the bad relations was inadequate understanding by Soviet officials of Japan's position in East Asia and their unfounded fear and suspicion which led them to retain "excessive" armed forces in the Far East. He stressed that Japan, because of its concern for the peace of East Asia, could "not remain indifferent to that fact." War Minister Terauchi as reported in *Izvestia*[41] virtually admitted that the Japanese army opposed a non-aggression pact. In an editorial reply, *Izvestia*[42] emphasized that the offer of such a pact still held and it inveighed against the war-making factions in Japan who were seeking both enlarged military appropriations and more extensive control over the economy and government of the country.

In addition to border incidents, other points of friction developed. The Japanese charge of Soviet complicity in the Ling Seng conspiracy in Inner Mongolia was promptly refuted by Tass;[43] as was a rumor of a new railroad from Verkhneudinsk to Kalgan. *Izvestia*[44] pointed out the absurdity of such a project since much of the railroad would have to pass through territory likely to become an "independent-Kuo" tomorrow. In Japan itself arrests of Japanese employed by the Soviet Embassy were made while the Soviets for their part took measures against Japanese inspection boats in the fisheries regions—actions which Tokyo regarded as reprisals against the special regulations introduced for Soviet vessels in Japanese ports.

The press war raged fiercely. On June 18, 1936, *Izvestia*

[41] *Izvestia*, May 15, 1936. See also *Japan Weekly Chronicle*, May 21, 1936, p. 640.

[42] *Izvestia*, May 15, 1936.

[43] *Izvestia*, April 23, 1936.

[44] *Izvestia*, May 29, 1936.

published an editorial accusing the Hirota government of being a front for the most aggressive army elements who had engineered the February coup. The editorial is interesting because it gave the fullest Soviet reply to the idea often hinted at by the Japanese press and in speeches that a demilitarized zone would provide a solution to the border difficulties. Rejecting the proposal of a 50 km. demilitarized zone such as provided in Article IX of the Portsmouth Treaty, *Izvestia* argued: (1) If the Japanese do not like us as neighbors, they should not have entered Manchuria. (2) When they refer to the Portsmouth Treaty, they should remember that it recognized Chinese sovereignty over Manchuria and they (the Japanese) have violated it. Moreover, Article 9 referred specifically to Sakhalin and the Straits of La Perouse and Tartary—which Japan now plans to fortify. (3) It is stupid to consider your adversary to be more foolish than he is—particularly since he never was foolish. The U.S.S.R. has built a defense line behind which runs a railway which at some places is less than 50 km. from the border. How then can the Japanese dream that we would give up our fortifications! Obviously the demilitarization proposal is just a ruse—a blind to mislead the Japanese public into support for further adventurist policies.

Reviewing the fruitless efforts to get border commissions, *Izvestia* then commented on the fact that Japan had refused a non-aggression pact on the ground that not only were the Soviets trying to Sovietize the world, beginning with China, but that they also wanted a warm-water port. In reply to this charge, *Izvestia* merely stated that the Soviet Union did not regard the signing of a pact as a "token of love" but as a basis for improving relations especially with countries with which conflicts prevailed.

To complete the picture of Soviet-Japanese friction, the Chinese Eastern Railway came back into the news. In April Manchukuo suspended its pension payment to former employees and Arita told Ambassador Yurenev that this was to offset outstanding debts of the former C.E.R. management. The Soviets contended that such claims were supposed to be presented in court and that as yet no accounting had been submitted. After a series of protests in Tokyo, Manchukuo agreed to renew the pensions but threatened to suspend the principal payments on the sale price of the railroad if the Soviets did not settle the counterclaims.

The charged atmosphere between Japan and the U.S.S.R. continued throughout the summer as a result of numerous incidents in several areas: border incidents in July near Manchouli; detention of Japanese vessels in Soviet waters for illegal fishing off Kamchatka; a Soviet protest against the intrusion of Japanese destroyers within the 12-mile sea frontier zone; interference with railway connections at Pogranichnaya; and the removal of frontier markers near Turi Rog.

Yet all these difficulties were overshadowed by more alarming developments in Europe. The first of these occurred with German remilitarization of the Rhineland on the excuse that the Franco-Soviet mutual assistance pact about to be ratified by France violated the Locarno Treaty and was directed against German security. In a speech to the League of Nations on March 17, 1936, Litvinov went on record for collective action, claiming that the U.S.S.R. was interested "not less but more than others in the non-violation of peace both today and for a decade to come, and not only in one sector of Europe, but throughout the whole of Europe and the whole world."[45] He declared his government ready to take part in any such collective action.

Four months later at the Sixteenth Plenary Session of the League, meeting for final action on the Ethiopian war, Litvinov again made a strong plea for collective action,

[45] M. Litvinov, *Against Aggression*, International Publishers, New York, 1939, p. 33.

claiming that even in its feeble attempt at sanctions against Italy, the League had "made a huge step forward in comparison with the past."[46] While clinging to the old Soviet contention that complete disarmament was the only guarantee against war, he saw in Article XVI of the Covenant a powerful weapon. "In an ideal League," he said, "military sanctions, too, should be obligatory for all. But if we are as yet unable to rise to such heights of international solidarity, we should make it our concern to have all continents and, for a start, at least all Europe covered with a system of regional pacts, on the strength of which groups of states would undertake to protect particular sectors from aggression."[47]

The first reaction to the German move had helped to bring the other powers closer to reconciliation. Despite wide divergency of objectives, the U.S.S.R. and Great Britain were able to agree on revision of the Straits Convention at Montreux; at the end of July the basis was laid for an Anglo-Soviet naval agreement (excluding limitations on the Soviet Far Eastern navy in the absence of a Soviet-Japanese agreement). Britain then granted the Soviet Union a five-year credit of £10,000,000 at five per cent to finance Anglo-Soviet trade. It is interesting to note that on his return to Tokyo Ambassador Ota was quoted as attributing this newfound Anglo-Soviet friendship to fear of the German-Japanese rapprochement.[48]

The reconciliation, however, was brief, for the Spanish war soon intervened, with all the ensuing friction over "nonintervention," an obligation from which the Soviets finally released themselves at the end of the year. Antagonism

[46] *ibid.*, p. 43.

[47] *ibid.*, p. 44. In August Litvinov submitted the Soviet proposals for strengthening the League Covenant, including the waiving of unanimity necessary for the application of sanctions and advocating regional mutual assistance pacts. Cf. Maxim Litvinov, *Foreign Policy of the U.S.S.R.*, *op. cit.*, p. 420.

[48] At the beginning of 1937, the Japanese press reported also a secret Anglo-Soviet accord on spheres of influence in China. Cf. *Japan Weekly Chronicle*, January 14, 1937, p. 46.

between the U.S.S.R. on the one hand and Germany and Italy on the other was growing acute, while in the Far East the partnership of Japan in what was to become known as the Axis was a matter of open speculation.

Although on his return to Tokyo Ambassador Ota, with the backing of certain segments of the Japanese press, had recommended the conclusion of a non-aggression pact with the Soviets, his successor in Moscow, Shigemitsu, concurred with other Japanese spokesmen in considering such a pact "premature." However, some progress was made toward clearing up specific points of dispute. In October negotiations reopened at Manchouli between the Mongol Republic and Manchukuo concerning the two border commissions for their common frontier. And on October 3, Tass announced that all basic questions on the fisheries had been agreed upon and the text of a new convention was being edited.[49] On the same day an agreement was signed between the Soviet Commissariat of Heavy Industry and the Japanese oil concessionaires on Sakhalin.

THE SAKHALIN OIL AND COAL CONCESSIONS

The Sakhalin oil and coal concessions furnished the single point of contact between the Soviet Union and Japan where a minimum of irritation had occurred in the years since September 1931. Sakhalin Island, originally a joint Russian-Japanese possession, had been transferred to Russian ownership in 1875 in exchange for the grant of sovereignty to Japan over the Kurile Islands. By the Treaty of Portsmouth, Japan had regained the southern half of the Island, below the 50° parallel. During the intervention in Siberia Japan had also held Northern Sakhalin, the last Russian territory to be evacuated in 1925. Indeed, it was the question of economic concessions in Sakhalin that had held up Soviet-Japanese negotiations in 1924.[50]

[49] *Izvestia*, October 3, 1936.

[50] It will be recalled that an oil concession on Sakhalin had been granted to

Oil had been discovered on the eastern shore of the island in 1890 and the Japanese became actively interested in its exploitation during the First World War. They began drilling in 1918 after their occupation of the island and in 1920 had started production in the Okha area. There were also known to be considerable coal reserves on the island. With the establishment of Soviet-Japanese relations in January 1925, Article III of Protocol A (attached to the Peking Convention) provided for complete Japanese evacuation of the island by May 1925 and Protocol B outlined the basic principles governing the coal and oil concessions to be granted to Japanese citizens on Sakhalin.[51] In December of that year three such concession agreements were signed, each to run for 45 years.

Oil concessions were granted to prospect and exploit deposits at Okha, Nutovo, Piltun, Ekhabi, Chaivo, Niyvo, Ugleikuty and Katangli. On each the field was to be checkerboarded (15–40 *dessatins* in area), with every other square going to the Japanese, including those on which wells already were operating. It was estimated that about 5,940 acres of petroliferous land were thereby handed over to the concessionaires without even including the 433 sq. mile area on which they were granted a ten-year right to prospect.[52] In 1927 an area of 281,221 acres was added to the prospecting zone on the eastern shore.[53] Half of any new deposits discovered were in turn to go to the concessionaire. These

---

the Sinclair Exploration Company in May, 1921 by the Far Eastern Republic and had been confirmed by the Soviet Government in 1923. The contract, giving monopoly rights, was conditioned on operations beginning before January 1924, which implied that Sinclair would have to force Japanese evacuation. This fact indeed may have been the original objective of granting the concession. Cf. Louis Fischer, *Oil Imperialism*, International Publishers, New York, 1926, Chapter VII, "The United States, Japan and Russia;" also *Foreign Relations of The United States, 1925*, U.S. Government Printing Office, Washington, D.C., Vol. II, p. 697.

[51] For text, cf. Yakhontoff, *op. cit.*, pp. 404–10.

[52] *Russian Review*, January 15, 1926, p. 22.

[53] *Economic Review of the Soviet Union*, March 15, 1927.

prospecting privileges were extended for five years by the 1936 agreement. Payment for the contract was fixed at a pro-rata share of production amounting to 5 per cent on an annual output of 30,000 m. tons and rising to 15 per cent on 620,000 m. tons. A sliding scale of 15–45 per cent was set for payment on gusher production and a scale of 10–35 per cent on gasoline from well-gases. In addition there was a rental of 4 per cent of the value attached to the use of existing equipment. The original coal concessions located at Vladimirovka, the Machi River and the Agnovsk district were thought to account for 15 per cent of the proven coal reserves on the Soviet half of the island. The payments ranged from 5 to 8 per cent of production depending on output (5 per cent on 100,000 m. tons, increasing by 0.25 per cent on every additional 50,000, to a maximum of 8 per cent).

The concessionaires were allowed to export their products and import supplies duty-free and to build auxiliary buildings at will. But in most other matters they were subject to Soviet law. While they were permitted to employ foreign labor to the extent of 50 per cent in skilled categories and 25 per cent in unskilled (the percentages were to be raised every three years in favor of Soviet citizens), they were strictly obligated to obey all provisions of the Soviet labor code, including the social insurance provision. Permission had to be obtained to construct refineries, pipelines, by-product plants and utilities. And, finally, all disputes were to be settled by the Supreme Court of the Soviet Union. A five-year extension of exploration rights in 1936 was combined with added responsibility for the provision by the concessionaires of housing facilities on a par with those required of the Soviet enterprises there. Further provisions were also made for supplying workers to the Japanese enterprises.

THE GERMAN-JAPANESE ANTI-COMINTERN PACT

Agreement was reached by the Japanese firms and the Soviet Commissariat of Heavy Industry on October 10, 1936 (rather than through the foreign offices) and in the nick of time. The ill-fated fisheries convention negotiated simultaneously and already initialled was scheduled to be signed in November, but on November 21 *Izvestia* appeared with an editorial announcing that "the two most aggressive powers in the world—Germany and Japan, have formed a bloc"; that the object of the "conspiracy against peace" was not merely Soviet territory, but the British Empire and the United States as well, not to mention Europe as a whole; and that the answer to its threat was "organization of collective security and real protection for peace."[54] Three days later the "anti-Comintern" pact was made public.[55] Litvinov officially stated the Soviet position to the Supreme Soviet as follows:[56]

"As for the Japanese-German Agreement which has been published, I would recommend you not to seek for any meaning in it, since it really has no meaning for the simple reason that it is only a cover for another agreement which was simultaneously discussed and initialled, probably also signed, and which was not published and is not intended for publication.

"I declare with all sense of the responsibility of my words that it was precisely to the working out of this secret document, in which the word Communism is not even mentioned to which were devoted the fifteen months of negotiations between the Japanese military attache and the German super-diplomat.

" . . . All the three states, well known for their aggressiveness and their attempts against the territories of others, are fighting against the principles of collective security and the indivisibility of peace. This in itself lends a sinister character to those agreements and indicates their menace to universal peace, security and the interest of many countries. . . .

"Nor will the reputation for sincerity of the Japanese government be enhanced: this government assured us of its desire for the establishment of peaceful relations with the Soviet Union and urged us for the sake of this to meet it in the settlement of several questions

[54] For Soviet comment, see also A. Kantorovich, "Conspiracy of The Aggressors," *Izvestia*, December 4, 1936.

[55] For text, Cf. *Contemporary Japan*, December, 1936, pp. 514–517.

[56] Maxim Litvinov, *Against Aggression*, *op. cit.*, pp. 76–78.

in dispute in which it was interested. Now, however, it has concluded a secret aggressive agreement with Germany. The Japanese government also assured us that it was still considering the non-aggression pact we proposed to it and that such a pact might be concluded after the settlement of all questions in dispute; now however, it has made the conclusion of such pacts dependent upon Germany's consent, lessening thereby the independence of its own foreign policy.

"The anti-democratic, aggressive Fascist countries have had their say. They have stated that they do not want to participate in general international cooperation for the organization of peace, for guaranteeing security to all nations. They issue one challenge after another to peace loving and, in the first place, to the democratic nations. It now rests with those nations to speak."

The immediate Soviet reaction was a refusal to sign the new fisheries convention. Both Arita and Shigemitsu failed signally to explain the agreement to the satisfaction of Moscow, and during conversations on the 8th, 9th and 14th of December, Litvinov made clear to Shigemitsu the Soviet position. In regard to border commissions, he insisted that the frontiers of the 1924 Soviet-Chinese treaty must be recognized and that Japan could not be a "third" party to the negotiations but must constitute the second party jointly with Manchukuo. On the fisheries he pointed out that it was Japan that had denounced the 1928 convention and that the question now did not relate to any change of Japanese rights under the Peking or Portsmouth treaties, but simply to the conditions for carrying on the enterprises—a subject which had always remained within the exclusive competence of the Soviet Government. As a stop-gap, however, a one-year extension of the old fisheries convention was signed on December 28.

Needless to say, press comment became acrimonious and Matsuoka, then head of the South Manchuria Railway, took a leaf from Hitler's book by announcing that he would like to plant the Japanese flag on the Urals.

THE SIAN INCIDENT

In China, however, an event was taking place destined to change the whole pattern of Far Eastern relations. The kidnaping of Chiang Kai-shek by Chang Hsueh-liang's troops at Sian in December 1936 had brought an immediate charge from Tokyo that Chang was trying to set up an independent government with Soviet support.[57] The Soviet press quickly retorted that, intentionally or not, the kidnaping was pro-Japanese in effect. The extreme anxiety with which the Soviet press followed developments in Sian was based on the same analysis that they had made of the Canton-Nanking conflict earlier in the year. At that time Soviet comment had pointed out that while the Canton faction was cloaking its actions with anti-Japanese slogans, its real motives were more dubious and that China's only hope lay in Chiang Kai-shek's assumption of leadership of the popular sentiment for national liberation by restoring internal peace. "The key to successful Chinese resistance is its unity."[58]

In regard to the Sian incident, the Soviet press pointed out that it coincided with a crisis in Japanese-Chinese relations resulting from the unsuccessful attempt of "Manchukuo-Mongol troops" to invade Suiyuan, and also from British financial assistance to China. Internecine warfare in China at that moment could only play into Japanese hands and open the way for their further penetration into the northwest provinces. Moscow further emphasized that insofar as the Nanking government was following a policy of resisting Japan, a united front for struggle against Japan made no sense as a front against Nanking but only as a front with Nanking. At first the Soviets even detected the hand of Wang Ching-wei in the Sian move and they referred back to the statements of the Chinese Communists made in the sum-

[57] Cf. *Japan Weekly Chronicle*, December 24, 1936, p. 814.

[58] A. Kantorovich, "Smoke Screen or Provocation," *Izvestia*, June 10, 1936.

mer of 1936 on the subject of the united front with Nanking against Japan.[59]

As events unfolded in Sian, however, the Soviet press showed less alarm over Chang Hsueh-liang's actions and more concern over the efforts of certain groups in the Kuomintang to dispatch an immediate punitive expedition—even at the risk of endangering the lives of the Generalissimo and his party. The enthusiastic seconding of this proposal by the Japanese gave the lie, in Soviet eyes, to the patriotism of those Chinese who sponsored such action. It was therefore with great relief and satisfaction at the growing Chinese desire to settle internal difficulties for the sake of unity against Japan that the Soviets hailed the peaceful solution of the Sian crisis. From it they thought three lessons could be drawn:[60] First, that despite the disruptive work of Japanese agents, real progress was being made toward national unity; second, that the success of Nanking as the central organizing force in China was due to its moving, however hesitantly, in the direction of meeting the public demand for a firmer policy against Japan; third, that a rising against Nanking, which objectively was to Japan's advantage, was possible only to the extent that Nanking continued to compromise with Japan.

In retrospect, Soviet Far Eastern commentators[61] regarded the Sian coup as an understandable, though misguided, expression of exasperation on the part of former Manchurian troops when confronted both with Nanking's orders for them to fight the Chinese Communists and the tendency of Nanking to accept Axis diplomatic recognition of Manchukuo. In the final solution of the incident, combining as it did reestablishment of Chiang Kai-shek's authority and recognition of

[59] See reference, Edgar Snow, *Red Star Over China*, Random House, New York, 1938, p. 413ff.

[60] "After the Liberation of Chiang Kai-shek," *Izvestia*, December 27, 1936. See Appendix, p. 234.

[61] Cf. G. Voitinsky, "The People's Front Movement in China and Japanese Imperialism," (in Russian) *Tikhii Okean*, No. 1, 1937.

the validity of the general demands of the northern troops, Moscow foresaw a powerful reinforcement of the anti-Japanese national front. Voitinsky's prophecy that "the Japanese military is taking every possible step in order, by provocation and direct military force to forestall, and where possible to crush the people's front in China"[62] soon was to materialize in the second Japanese invasion of China.

[62] *ibid.*, p. 22.

V. FROM THE SINO-JAPANESE WAR TO THE EUROPEAN WAR, 1937–1939

IN THE MONTHS between the Sian incident and Japan's second invasion of China in July 1937, Soviet relations with Japan grew increasingly strained with neither side attempting to cloak animosity in politeness. The tone was set in January 1937 by the second of the great Moscow trials, involving Radek, Pyatakov and others. Although the purge had been going on since the assassination of Kirov in December 1934 and the first major trial (that of Kamenev and Zinoviev) was held in the middle of 1936, the international aspects of the charges were not particularly emphasized until the 1937 trial. At this time the indictment included the accusation that the Trotskyite Parallel Center had carried on negotiations with agents of foreign governments and was prepared to cede the Ukraine to Germany and the Maritime Province and the Amur region to Japan.[1] The testimony cited meetings with Hess in Germany and officials of the German and Japanese embassies in Moscow. With the Japanese the principal contact was a "Mr. H" who, according to subsequent press reports, was an attaché and left the country in April after the trials.

These were not the only sensational revelations; the Soviet press continued throughout the year to carry stories of espionage and espionage methods, used primarily by the Japanese to obtain military information and to sabotage Soviet industry and transport. On the other hand the Hayashi government in Japan continued to blame tension

[1] Reports of the Court Proceedings in the case of the *Anti-Soviet Trotskyite Center*, Commissariat of Justice, Moscow, 1937, p. 9 and elsewhere.

in the Far East on Soviet policy—both in building up its armaments and in its "Comintern" activities.[2]

During the spring a series of minor incidents flared up. The border at Pogranichnaia was closed by the Soviets in January because of maltreatment of Soviet train crews at the transfer junction; Tokyo protested the search of its ships in Vladivostok and charged that the Soviets were contemplating stoppage of shipping between Vladivostok and Japan. In April and May minor border incidents occurred and a Japanese official was arrested in Alexandrovsk on charges of espionage. But these pinpricks were without serious result. Shipments of goods in payment for the Chinese Eastern Railway were reported to be progressing satisfactorily, with 65 million yen worth of tea, cement, textiles, chemicals and paints already received by the Soviets and special orders for ships, electrical machinery, etc., placed with Japanese firms.[3]

On the eve of Japan's renewed attack on China, however, a passage-at-arms took place between the Japanese and Soviets which was subsequently known as the Amur Island incident. In point of fact the incident had only slight military significance and differed but little from the incidents checkering Japanese-Soviet relations for five years past; yet the wide publicity which it received both in Japan and abroad served as a fitting prelude to Lukuochiao.

The course of the incident was as follows. South of Blagoveshchensk the Amur broadens and branches into two channels on either side of a group of small islands. In the spring of 1937 the Soviets blocked the channel on the north side of the islands, leaving only the south channel open to navigation, in order to prevent ships from observing the fortifications along their shore. Beginning on May 31 a number of minor clashes occurred when Japanese-Manchurian patrol boats tried to enter the northern channel or to

[2] Cf. *Japan Weekly Chronicle*, March 4, 1937, p. 257 and March 11, 1937, p. 290.
[3] *Izvestia*, May 24, 1937.

land on the islands. By June the Soviets had established a regular frontier post on the islands which gave rise to negotiations over their ownership, on the basis of differences in the interpretation of certain treaties. The Japanese held that the boundary lay along the bed of the river and that at that point in the river the bed was north of the islands, which therefore must belong to Manchukuo. Moscow claimed that the line was established by the treaty of 1860 with China and that while the islands were not mentioned specifically in it, the map attached, accepted by both sides in 1861, clearly indicated that the boundary lay south of the islands. A change in the river course did not, they claimed, change the frontier. As circumstantial evidence the Japanese pointed to Manchurian placer miners working on the islands. The Soviets countered with reference to Russian farmers on the islands and also to the Russian names of the islands which even the Japanese had used previously (Bolshoi—large; Sennukha—hayfield; Iziubrennii—Manchurian deer; Vinogradi—grape). They also brought up the allotment of land to a cossack farmer in successive land surveys.

Obviously the matter demanded negotiation and on June 29 discussions began between Litvinov and Shigemitsu. The former suggested the simultaneous withdrawal of troops by both sides; the latter agreed to submit the plan to his government for approval. The very next day a Japanese cutter sank a Soviet patrol boat. Diplomatic conversations followed with renewed suggestions of troop withdrawals and the establishment of a border commission. When on July 2 Shigemitsu reported that the Japanese cutters had already left, it was announced that the Soviet Commissar of Defense had issued instructions for the withdrawal of the Soviet cutters and armed patrol from the islands.

The dispute appeared well on its way toward a peaceful settlement but on July 6 Japanese troops landed on Bolshoi Island, stating that no agreement for permanent withdrawal had been reached. Moreover, other minor incidents broke out along the frontier and Litvinov filed a protest. By now, however, the Japanese had struck at Lukuochiao and events in China overshadowed the recurring border incidents. Yet the political significance of the island controversy was not inconsiderable. The Soviets claimed that the Japanese were trying to seize the islands and to engage in espionage along the whole river border. The line taken by the Japanese press was very different.[4] It took up the theme of General Homma, who had just returned from the U.S.S.R., to the effect that the purge trials had caused confusion in the Soviet Union and that the Red Army in the Far East had been measurably weakened (Tukhachevsky and seven other high army officers had been executed early in June). The Amur incident was variously interpreted as a Soviet attempt to distract foreign attention from its internal troubles or as an effort by the internal enemies of the Soviet Government to involve it in war as a prelude to an uprising. Once the Japanese had returned to the islands in force, their press taunted the Soviets with being so anxious to liquidate the incident that they had voluntarily evacuated without an agreement of any kind.

In retrospect the importance of the clash seems to lie chiefly in its propaganda value, for the foreign press readily took up the Japanese theory of Soviet demoralization. Still it is not entirely clear why so much was made of this particular incident. Ambassador Davies, in Moscow at the time, regarded it as sufficiently dangerous to call upon Litvinov and Shigemitsu and urge that the incident be localized.[5] Ambassador Davies also reported in *Mission to Moscow* that later in 1938 he had been told by a Japanese official that the incidents were designed to test Soviet defenses.[6]

[4] e.g. *Japanese Weekly Chronicle*, July 1, 1937, p. 17; July 8, 1937, pp. 43–44; July 15, 1937, pp. 95–96.

[5] Joseph E. Davies, *Mission to Moscow*, Simon and Schuster, New York, 1941, pp. 164–166.

[6] "Later in 1938 in Europe a high Japanese official told me that the Japanese

THE OUTBREAK OF THE SINO-JAPANESE WAR

The Japanese attack on North China on July 7, 1937 was immediately interpreted by Moscow as a serious danger heralding a renewed threat of large-scale conflict similar to that endangering Europe as a result of the Spanish war. On July 22 *Izvestia* carried a front-page analysis of the situation, comparing it to the events of 1931 and pointing out that once more the Japanese were trying to create the impression that it was just a local incident, whereas in fact it was "the beginning of the second stage of the conquest of China long and thoroughly prepared by the Japanese Imperialists." Expressing concern over the apparent British reaction, *Izvestia* continued:[7]

"There is no doubt whatever that Japan succeeded in carrying out her plans in Manchuria only as a result of the passivity of the western powers . . . Certain English politicians, having misjudged the correlation of forces in the Far East, evidently presupposed that Japanese aggression in Manchuria would unfold in an entirely different direction than toward North and Central China. . . .

"Against the background of 1931–32, it is especially lamentable and alarming that in her attitude to the present conflict, England is again adopting the position of 1931 . . . Conservative politicians obviously are influenced by threats of bluff and blackmail irrespective of whether they are fabricated in the Far East or in Central Europe."

The article went on to forecast Japanese operations far beyond North China and then summarized the essential differences between 1931 and 1937: the increased strength of the Soviet Union; the real rise in an anti-Japanese movement

---

government had deliberately projected these tests of Soviet resistance and military strength; and that the Japanese were surprised and impressed with the mechanized strength and effectiveness of the Red Army in the East." *ibid.*, p. 166.

[7] For full text, see Appendix, p. 240.

in China; internal weaknesses of Japan. Accordingly, *Izvestia* concluded that the policies of the western powers might again prove decisive, not only for the future of China, but for the whole world situation. This analysis was elaborated in subsequent articles in the periodical press,[8] and cause for pessimism was found in Britain's policy of vacillation—British negotiations with Japan during May being regarded by Moscow as an attempt to reach a settlement at the expense of China.

Grounds for optimism, on the other hand, were found in the growing unity of China which at last was making China a positive force in international policy rather than merely "a helpless toy in the hands of the imperialists." Moscow also entertained some hope of a collective system in the East. Earlier in the year *Izvestia* had strongly endorsed the idea of a regional security pact for the Pacific as suggested by the Australian government in May 1937 at the British Empire Conference:[9]

" . . . Here as in Europe, the preservation of peace demands its collective organization as the only possible way to stop the aggressor and ensure the security of peaceful countries. The Australian project for a regional pact is therefore a step in the right direction and deserves the support of all.

"The conclusion of a regional pact, in accordance with the Australian project, would serve the interests of all countries of the Pacific, each of which is threatened separately at present . . .

" . . . For the success of this policy, however, first of all it is necessary that the powers should not refuse in advance to participate in a real struggle for peace in the Pacific, that they should not prefer to seek agreement with the aggressor and

[8] G. Voitinsky, "Japanese Aggression in China," and I. Lemin, "The International Position of Japan at the New Stage of its Aggression in China," (both in Russian) *Tikhii Okean*, No. 3–4, 1937.

[9] For full text, see Appendix, p. 237.

should not retreat before his impudent demands." There was, further, the feeling that England, America and France could not but react in a positive fashion to the now obvious threat to their Far Eastern position implicit in Japan's new forward moves.

The Chinese government gave immediate recognition to the increased importance of Soviet aid by including the U.S.S.R. as well as the signatories of the Nine Power Treaty among the nations to which it dispatched its note of protest on the Japanese treaty violation (July 16). Less than three weeks later American warships made a courtesy call at Vladivostok, the first since the Revolution. This visit, coming after the trans-Polar flights of Soviet airmen to the United States, was hailed as a token of good will and mutual support. And the unflagging determination to resist expressed by Chinese leaders was in welcome contrast to the policy previously pursued by Chiang Kai-shek.[10] Not until the Brussels Conference did the Soviet press again show resentment over the policies of the other major powers.

In the meantime the U.S.S.R. had itself been drawn into the conflict, as was Great Britain by the shooting of the British Ambassador and later on the United States by the sinking of the *Panay*. On August 1 the Tientsin consulate of the U.S.S.R. was raided by White Russians with the alleged connivance of the Japanese. Although an apology was received, the Shanghai consulate was attacked a few weeks later on charges that the Chinese were sending out signals from it. Ambassador Shigemitsu's statement to foreign correspondents in Moscow regarding the Tientsin raid and his denial of a forthcoming attack on the Shanghai consulate, which followed almost immediately, were both the subject of a bitterly sarcastic attack by *Pravda*.[11]

[10] Ya. Maksimov, "Three Speeches of Chiang Kai-shek" (in Russian), *Izvestia*, July 29, 1937.

[11] Cf. *Moscow Daily News*, August 20, 1937. For the Japanese version, see *Japan Weekly Chronicle*, August 12, 1937, p. 221.

The first major change in the Soviet position came with the Soviet-Chinese non-aggression pact,[12] signed on August 21 and published on August 30. Soviet comment recalled that such a pact had been projected in 1933, and while at that time "certain aspects of the internal and foreign policy of China were an obstacle to the conclusion" of the pact, recent events had awakened the interest of the Chinese government. The Chinese spoke of the treaty as "a beginning of collective security for the Pacific countries through mutual assurances of non-aggression."[13] The Japanese, needless to say, regarded it as a "conspiracy" between the anti-Japanese Chinese Government and the Communists, and Hirota declared that Japan, as the bulwark against the penetration of Communism into East Asia could not afford to remain indifferent to it.[14]

THE LEAGUE OF NATIONS AND THE BRUSSELS CONFERENCE

Two weeks after the announcement of the treaty, China appealed to the League of Nations (under Articles 10, 11 and 17 of the Covenant) for action against Japan's aggression. What action the League would take was regarded in Moscow as a test of the strength of the collective security principle. From the Soviet point of view the success of the Nyon conference for "piracy" control in the Mediterranean (in connection with the Spanish Civil War) had set a hopeful precedent for the forthcoming meeting, in contrast to the unbroken failures of the Spanish "non-intervention" committee. *Pravda's* editorial[15] on the opening of the League meeting repeated the time-worn phrases regarding the failures of the League in the Abyssinian, Spanish and Chinese situations because of which "the blood of whole peoples" had been spilt. It held that to stop the aggressor and restore the authority of

[12] See Appendix, p. 187.
[13] *Chinese Year Book 1938–39*, The Commercial Press, Ltd., China, 1939, p. 615.
[14] *Japan Weekly Chronicle*, September 9, 1937, p. 359.
[15] *Pravda*, September 22, 1937.

the League required "collective repulse of the fascists by all the governments interested in peace, the collective defense of indivisible peace . . . Only in this way is it possible to check and even extinguish the flames of world war now being lighted by Germany, Italy and Japan."

In his opening speech, Litvinov spoke in the same vein[16] and advanced with eloquence a plea for action by the League. The action finally taken—for the first time naming Japan as an aggressor and condemning its bombing of defenseless cities in China—he regarded as an encouraging sign.[17] But reference of the whole question to the signatories of the Nine-Power Treaty again raised fears that the real object was to pass the buck and arrange some form of meeting which the aggressors themselves could attend. The outcome Moscow regarded as the final test of the League: "It could become either the center of the organization of collective repulse to the aggressor, or a discussion club having no significance of any kind."[18]

The U.S.S.R. was invited to attend the Brussels meeting of the Nine-Power Treaty signatories and accepted. The Soviet estimate of the international forces operating at that time throws considerable light on their subsequent attitude and on Litvinov's departure before the meetings were over. According to Ambassador Davies, Litvinov was "exceedingly pessimistic" about the whole procedure and this same view found reflection in the Soviet press.[19] As regards the United

[16] "Thus we have had four aggressions in the course of five years. We see how aggression, when it meets with no check, passes from one continent to another, assuming larger and larger dimensions every time. Yet I am firmly convinced that a resolute policy pursued by the League of Nations in one case of aggression would rid us of all the other cases. Then—and only then—would all States become convinced that aggression does not pay, that aggression should not be undertaken . . . " *League of Nations, Verbatim Record of the Eighteenth Ordinary Session of the Assembly*, Eighth Plenary Meeting, September 21, 1937, p. 8.

[17] Cf. "Sino-Japanese Conflict," *League of Nations Official Journal, Special Supplement No. 177*, Geneva, 1937.

[18] *Izvestia*, September 27, 1937.

[19] Joseph E. Davies, *op. cit.*, p. 241ff.

States, the Soviets thought that Washington was probably fully aware of the need for some kind of joint action in the Pacific. Moscow was impressed with Roosevelt's famous Chicago speech calling for a quarantine against aggressors, although it gave note at the same time to the fact that the United States remained the principal purveyor of war supplies to Japan. Its own relations with the United States had somewhat improved: the new trade pact of 1937 for the first time had granted the Soviets most-favored-nation treatment in return for an increase in the purchase guarantee to $40,000,000, and Litvinov's reply to Secretary Hull's declaration of July 16, calling for peaceful settlement of international disputes, had been well received.[20] British policy, however, was viewed with extreme suspicion. Not only had the Anglo-Italian exchange of notes regarding the Mediterranean in August met with disfavor but Moscow generally assumed that British policy aimed not so much to oppose the aggressive powers but rather to split their alignment by reaching agreements with each separately. In the Far East particularly, Moscow felt that England was still prepared to attempt to strike a bargain with Japan.

As for the Axis, the Soviets considered that the possibilities for cooperation with Germany and Italy gave Japan one major advantage over its position in 1931. Specifically, the inclusion of Italy at Brussels meant that at least one power present could maneuver in Japan's behalf. As *Pravda* put it:[21] "The composition of the Brussels conference, even in the case of Japan's absence, makes it impossible in advance for the conference to reach any positive decisions. The basis for activity under these circumstances can result only

[20] For Hull's Statement, cf. *Press Releases*, The Department of State, Vol. 17, No. 407, July 17, 1937, pp. 41–42. For Litvinov's reply, *ibid.*, Vol. 17, No. 411, August 14, 1937, p. 105. Litvinov urged counteraction against the aggressors, both through activization of the League of Nations and through regional pacts of mutual assistance and other accords.

[21] *Pravda*, October 28, 1937.

in empty chatter, under cover of which the Japanese militarists will continue their criminal war against the Chinese people."

In his opening speech to the conference Litvinov warned against the dangers that beset such a gathering, from the point of view both of postponing action and of attempting to conduct negotiations with the aggressor:[22] "In the process of negotiations connected with consistent concessions to the aggressor it is possible to overstep the line on which persons, undoubtedly inspired by the best intentions slip, without noticing it themselves, into the viewpoint of the aggressor, commence to speak in his language, actually justifying and encouraging his actions."

The Brussels discussions turned out to be as equivocal as the Soviets had feared; Litvinov returned to Moscow before the conference had closed with the adoption of a resolution even weaker than that of the League.

At the same time two other developments were causing anxiety in Moscow. The first was the formal signing, in the midst of the Brussels conference, of the Italo-Japanese agreement completing the Axis Triangle. For some months it had been apparent that this step would be taken and the Soviet press had already carried a number of articles on the subject.[23] Stress had been laid on the fact that the signing of such a pact constituted a threat to the other powers and meant a stepping up of war-like moves in all quarters of the globe. *Izvestia* also warned Japan that the new agreement would not improve Soviet-Japanese relations and recalled that the German-Japanese pact had cost Japan the new fisheries convention. With Italy a formal protest was filed to the effect that the agreement ran contrary to Article IV of the Soviet-Italian non-aggression pact restraining either signatory from joining any international grouping directed against the other.

[22] *Moscow Daily News*, November 4, 1937. See Appendix, p. 246.

[23] e.g., *Izvestia*, August 4, 1937, and November 2, 1937; *Pravda*, September 15, 1937 and October 17, 1937.

In Lord Halifax's trip to Berlin lay the second source of worry to the Soviets. *Pravda*[24] commented that while the motives and results of the trip were not quite clear, it might mean granting Hitler a free hand in Austria and Czechoslovakia; it was "already apparent that the present policy of the English rulers is contrary to the interests of peace."

Having viewed with some optimism the prospects of international action to aid China after July 1937, largely because of a belief that the United States would exert real pressure in that direction—by the close of the Brussels conference the Soviets were clearly disabused of any such illusions. Litvinov's speech to his electors in November 1937, was bitterly sarcastic:[25]

" . . . Take another example—the Far East. Japan is flooding China with her troops . . . in short, is doing everything that used to be called 'war.' She declares authoritatively, loudly and repeatedly, that she intends to continue her offensive until she carries out her aims and China opens negotiations with her, with the object of capitulating, of course. At the same time, she warns us that she will not brook anybody's mediation. China applies to the League of Nations for protection, referring to the corresponding points in the League Covenant. The League forms a committee, the committee appoints a sub-committee, and the latter elects an editorial committee. A paper is drafted and addressed to Japan: 'We do not approve of your offensive. Probably it is based on a misunderstanding. Please come to confirm this, and, lest you feel lonely among us, we are inviting your kindred spirit and friend, Germany.' From Japan comes confirmation that there is no misunderstanding at all, that she is on the warpath quite deliberately and agrees to discuss matters only with China and only on terms of the latter's surrender. Disarmed by this reply, the League decides to refer the question to the Powers most concerned in Far Eastern affairs, signatories to the so-called Washington Treaty, which is violated by Japan for the second time (it was violated the first time by the occupation of Manchuria). And so the Brussels Conference is called, and the Soviet Union is also invited, although

[24] *Pravda*, November 27, 1937.
[25] Maxim Litvinov, *Against Aggression*, *op. cit.*, p. 105ff.

she is not a signatory to the Washington Treaty. What does the Conference do? Its activity was very neatly hit off in a cartoon which I saw in a foreign newspaper. This shows the honorable delegates of eighteen states, not without great effort and strain, dragging a letter to the post-box for Japan. In this letter, as you know, they again demand Japan's confirmation whether she is deliberately committing her aggression in China and request her to stop and accept mediation. Confirmation is not long in coming. Japan, even with an inflection of resentment, replies that there is no need to bother her; she has repeatedly stated that she is attacking China quite deliberately and for quite definite aims. She does not need anybody's mediation; she is ready to negotiate only with China—about capitulation, of course—and the only thing the Conference can do is to make China agree to this capitulation. This reply disarmed the Brussels Conference, just as the first reply disarmed the League of Nations, and the Conference was closed.

"I see it is quite a puzzle to you how experienced *bourgeois* diplomats could fail to understand the meaning of the aggressor's tactics. You think they are only pretending to disbelieve the aggressor's statements, and, under cover of negotiations for confirmations and explanations, they are groping for a deal with the aggressor. You can think so if you like, but my position does not allow me to express such doubts, and I must leave them to your responsibility. I can speak only about the official position of other states."

From then on, outside of the regular appeals at Geneva, Soviet Far Eastern relations were conducted almost exclusively on a bilateral basis. Litvinov's efforts to secure collective action were of necessity centered in Europe, the scene of greatest need. His various appeals (February 1, 1938 to the League Committee of 28; of March 17, 1938 to the press of the world following the occupation of Austria; September 21, 1938, on the very eve of Munich) all fell on deaf ears and there was no basis for negotiations in the Far East. The pattern remained set in terms of Soviet-Chinese and Soviet-Japanese relationships.

FRICTION WITH JAPAN

During the second half of 1937 every one of the usual sources of dispute between the U.S.S.R. and Japan had been up for debate, and a few new ones had been added. In August Moscow reported that Manchukuo had again suspended pension payments to the former employees of the Chinese Eastern Railway. The Sakhalin concessions were twice the subject of dispute—in August and September.[26] The first new question to arise concerned the building of a pipeline for which the Japanese concessionaire was supposed to obtain permission from Soviet authorities but which he proposed to build in any case since the permission was so slow in coming. Soviet comment carried veiled threats that such a violation of the contract might be taken as grounds for its cancellation. The second issue concerned the labor force of both the oil and coal concessions. The Soviet government charged that after applying for several thousand workers, the concessionaires had then delayed in employing them and shortly thereafter began dismissing them in large numbers. The Japanese claimed that obstacles put in the way of the operation of the concessions were forcing them to close down. But the Soviets pointed out that "reducing output means a decrease in the income of the Soviet government from these concessions," an action which could not be tolerated.

As for the border situation, no improvement had been made. In fact, the Manchukuo-Mongol negotiations for a commission had again broken down in June 1937, while in September a Japanese gunboat was detained in Soviet waters.

The fisheries question came up only briefly at the end of the year when the 1928 agreement was again extended to cover 1938. But the Soviet press charged that the Japanese were withholding news of the extension in order to whip up anti-Soviet sentiment at home. The tension between the two countries was also reflected in a number of statements by General Araki—one in October saying that it would probably be necessary to attack Russia in order to wipe out the Com-

[26] Cf. *Izvestia*, August 6, 1937 and *Moscow Daily News*, September 26, 1937; also *Japan Weekly Chronicle*, September 30, 1937, p. 454.

munist influence in China, and a subsequent interview to the same general effect which the Soviets protested. The closing of Soviet consulates in Manchuria together with Moscow's withdrawal of recognition from the Japanese consulates in Odessa and Novosibirsk occurred in September—months before the Soviets requested the closing of consulates of other foreign powers.

Developments in China had also served to accentuate Soviet-Japanese friction. In addition to the raids on Soviet consulates mentioned above and Japan's objection to the Soviet-Chinese non-aggression treaty, exchanges had gone back and forth over the bombing of Nanking. On September 25 the Chinese government sent the Soviet government a note drawing attention to Japanese bombings of civilians and asking the Soviet government (as it did the other powers) to cooperate in putting a stop to the "total war." The Soviet diplomatic mission in China had already received warning from the Japanese military authorities of their intention to bomb Nanking. The Soviets protested and stated that they would hold Japan responsible for any damages to their citizens or embassy. On September 26 a further protest was sent to Tokyo by Litvinov.

SOVIET TRADE WITH CHINA

From the Japanese side complaints began to be heard against Soviet military supplies sent to the Chinese government. Soviet trade with China proper, never large, had in the past been shipped primarily by sea to the big coastal ports of China. With the loss of these cities to the Japanese, increased attention had been directed to the routes across the common land frontiers, although the bulk of Soviet trade with Free China during the first years after 1937 still passed over the Burma Road or through various coastal points.

Soviet trade statistics show 17 land border points,[27] (many

[27] Overland border points between the Soviet Union and China and the

of purely local significance) which handle Soviet trade with Sinkiang, western Mongolia and Tanna Tuva. Other roads have in the past been well-developed trade routes within a few hundred miles of the border. These are capable of extension along old caravan routes into China Proper. Of the routes for which considerable tonnage is recorded, probably only four represent trade with China proper, namely those through Khorgos, Bakhti, Zaisan and Iliisk.[28]

From the North a well-worn trade route runs south from the Trans-Siberian Railroad, east of Lake Baikal, to the Mongol border at Kiakhta (which is probably as far as the

---

Mongol People's Republic are as follows:

Murgabsk	From Tadzhikistan to Kashgar
Irkeshtam	From south Kirgizia to Kashgar
Pokrovsk	From central Kirgizia to Kashgar
Khorgos	(Near Dzharkent) from Alma Ata to Kuldja
Bakhti	From Sergiopol on the Turk-Sib Railway to Chuguchak
Zaisan	From Semipalatinsk to northern Sinkiang
Iliisk	(On the Turk-Sib Railway and the River Ili) from just north of Alma Ata to Kuldja by River
Kosh-Agach	From Barnaul into the Mongol People's Republic from the extreme west, to Ulan Kom
Semiozersk	Into Tanna Tuva from the northwest
Bolsheporozh	Into Tanna Tuva from the northeast
Mondinsk	From Irkutsk west into the Mongol People's Republic at Lake Kossogol
Kiakhta	South from Ulan Ude into Ulan Bator (Urga)
Solovevsk	South from Chita into the Eastern end of the Mongol People's Republic
Otporovsk	Western terminus of the Chinese Eastern Railway
Blagoveshchensk	Central Manchurian border (on the Amur River)
Turii Rog	At Lake Khanka (near junction of Manchuria-Korea-Siberia)
Grodekovo	The eastern terminus of the Chinese Eastern Railway

Source: *Statistika Vneshnei Torgovli SSSR*, Moscow, No. 12, December, 1937, p. 51.

[28] Kosh Agach is situated on the Chuisk Tract, the historic route through the Altai Mountains into western Mongolia. While it has been developed into a motor road across the frontier, it peters out at the eastern end. Mondinsk and Solovevsk are border points on roads into local regions of Outer Mongolia and are not linked to through trade routes.

railroad runs) to Ulan Bator, capital of the Mongol People's Republic. The southward extension into China passes through Ude to Kalgan. But since the Japanese occupied the Kalgan area well before 1937, it is doubtful whether much trade has come into Free China through Outer Mongolia, although there are alternative, less-traveled roads westward to Ninghsia. The principal land route remains that through Sinkiang.[29] From the Soviet side a number of routes run into Northern Sinkiang, all connecting with the Turk-Sib Railroad. The shortest and best is from Sergiopol to Chuguchak, some 100 miles from the railroad. Others follow the course of the Ili river from Alma Ata to Kuldja. According to reports the roads are well-developed and carry considerable truck traffic as far as Hami. Out of Sinkiang there are also alternative routes—one northeastward toward Ninghsia and the other—the main road, along the old Imperial Highway to the rail terminal near Sianfu. The volume of trade on this route is said to have been gradually increased but its potentialities are limited by the difficulty of maintaining a sufficient gasoline supply for the 2,500-mile stretch east from Hami to the railroad.

Early in 1938 Japanese protests against Soviet aid to China were called groundless by Litvinov, both because "the sale of arms, including airplanes, to China is entirely in accord with standard procedure of international law . . . especially in view of the fact that arms are provided to China, just as, incidentally, to Japan, by many countries,"[30] and because the Japanese denied the existence of a war in China. In point of fact, there was no trade agreement between China and the U.S.S.R. at that time; not until October 1938 was the first of a series of credit and barter agreements signed.

[29] For a fuller discussion, cf. Owen Lattimore, "Chinese Turkistan-Siberian Supply Road," *Pacific Affairs*, December, 1940, p. 593ff.; also Martin Norins, *Gateway to Asia: Sinkiang*, John Day, New York, 1944.

[30] *Izvestia*, April 5, 1938. For Japanese protests, see *Japan Weekly Chronicle*, April 14, 1938, p. 453; April 21, 1938, p. 483; May 12, 1938, p. 580.

(Ambassador Davies has reported an earlier credit of 100,000,-000 Chinese dollars in August 1937, presumably at the time the non-aggression pact was signed.[31])

A number of protests were exchanged between the Soviet and Japanese governments during the first months of 1938. The first concerned the holding of a Soviet mailplane which had lost its way and landed in Manchukuo in December 1937. Despite energetic diplomatic activity on the part of Soviet officials, no progress had been made in obtaining the release of its crew or cargo. At the January meeting of the Supreme Soviet Andrei Zhdanov, one of the most important figures in the Communist Party and the government, took occasion to criticize the Commissariat of Foreign Affairs on the grounds that it "should be more resolute in its attitude towards the arrogant, hooligan and provocative conduct of the agents of Japan and that puppet state called Manchoukuo."[32] A few days later Moscow took retaliatory action against Japan by suspending parcel post connections with Manchuria. In February and March the Japanese seized and held two Soviet ships which had called at Japanese ports, evidently with the object of forcing the Soviets to exchange the Japanese they had arrested as spies for the Russian passengers and crews. Thereupon the Soviets detained eight Japanese previously scheduled for deportation. Finally, Manchukuo refused to honor the obligations for the final payment on the Chinese Eastern Railway in March 1938 on the ground that the Soviet government still owed considerable debts in connection with the line. In answer, the Soviets seized more Japanese fishing smacks, demanded the closing of the Japanese consulate at Okha on Sakhalin and refused to grant certain requests by the Sakhalin concessionaires. On April 4 Soviet Ambassador Slavutski asked Hirota for a general settlement of all

[31] Joseph E. Davies, *op. cit.*, p. 248.

[32] *First Session of the First Supreme Soviet of the U.S.S.R., Moscow, Jan. 12–19, 1938.* Co-operative Publishing Society of Foreign Workers in the U.S.S.R. Moscow, 1938, p. 100. See also p. 115 for Molotov's acceptance of the criticism.

these points. The Japanese replied that several questions, such as that regarding the mailplane, should be addressed to Manchukuo, that the Soviets must indicate more precisely what concessions they were prepared to make in regard to the Sakhalin affair, and that they must agree to sign the new long-term fisheries convention immediately and consent to the retention of Japanese consulates in Khabarovsk, Blagoveshchensk and elsewhere.

At the end of April[33] Moscow reportedly rejected the Japanese demands, both because direct negotiations with Manchukuo had already proved unsuccessful and because it held that the Japanese government "could not consider itself free from responsibility for the injuries to Soviet interests caused by Manchukuo." The Soviets renewed their offer to settle the small points of friction "which do not bear on the general policy of both governments and are the cause of inconvenience to one side without any advantage to the other." Such minor incidents along with retaliations continued through the year, breaking out into the serious clash at Changkufeng in July and only reaching partial settlement in the fisheries negotiations that went on until the next April.

THE CHANGKUFENG INCIDENT

The so-called "Changkufeng" incident (or as the Soviet term it, the fighting at Lake Hasan) first came to public attention in July 1938 when the Japanese Ambassador asked for the withdrawal of Soviet troops from frontier positions occupied by them on July 11 on the heights west of Lake Hasan (near the junction of the borders of Manchuria, Korea and the Soviet Maritime Province). On July 15 the Soviet government rejected the demand and asserted Soviet ownership of the hills on the basis of the maps attached to the Hunchung treaty of 1886.[34]

[33] *Izvestia*, April 28, 1938.

[34] For Soviet version of this conflict, see *Izvestia*, especially July 22, August 1, 2, 3, 5, 8, 1938. Throughout the conflict the Soviet press was filled with accounts of mass meetings held at factories and farms, calling for defense of the Motherland and defeat of the Japanese invaders.

On July 20 Shigemitsu repeated his demand, basing his claim on other documents and on the assertion of some Manchurians that they were accustomed to go to the hills for religious ceremonies. He concluded according to Soviet report, by saying that if the Red Army refused to comply, Japan would be compelled to resort to force. He also protested the shooting of a Japanese gendarme. Litvinov rejected all the Ambassador's assertions. He inquired as to when the Japanese had begun to regard treaties as invalid unless published (Shigemitsu had stated that Japan would not recognize the Hunchung map since it has not been made public). He stated that the Red Army did not intend to move its troops on its own territory at the behest of foreign governments; that the gendarme was killed on Soviet territory where he had no business to be; and finally, that even though the Japanese may have found intimidation effective as a diplomatic weapon elsewhere, Shigemitsu need not expect to score any successes in Moscow by using such threats. Litvinov also protested the distribution of provocative leaflets in the Soviet Embassy in Tokyo.

On July 31 fighting began in earnest when artillery was brought into action. Four days later Shigemitsu visited Litvinov to report that the Japanese government would prefer to settle the incident by peaceful means and suggested the return to the situation prior to July 11. He further suggested that since agreement had been reached in principle on setting up border commissions, the matter should be turned over to such a commission to determine the exact location of the frontier on the basis of various documents. Litvinov replied that it was up to the Japanese government to demonstrate its peaceful intentions by halting the attack. He insisted on recognition of the validity of the Hunchung agreement as a prerequisite for negotiations and reiterated the old point that as far as the Soviets were concerned the agreement on border commissions related solely to "redemarcating" the border, i.e. putting up new markers or making new surveys on the basis of *existing* treaties defining the frontier which had been signed in the past by China and Russia. He was ready to negotiate only after a return to the status prior to July 29 when Japanese troops began their attacks.

In the meantime the fighting had continued fiercely with substantial losses on both sides. At an interview on August 7 Litvinov pointed out that this could hardly be termed a border incident since border guards were not usually equipped with heavy artillery. Shigemitsu renewed his proposal for negotiation through a border commission, with a halt to military operations as they then stood with subsequent withdrawal on both sides. However, Litvinov held out for complete withdrawal of Japanese troops before negotiations. Japan agreed that the Hunchung agreement should serve as one of the documents with which the commission should work, but Litvinov insisted it be the *only* document, since no more recent agreement existed between Russia and China. He counterproposed that as soon as the Japanese retired to the positions held prior to July 29, a two-party commission consisting of two representatives of the U.S.S.R. and one each from Manchukuo and Japan should proceed to mark the border as established in the Hunchung treaty. Litvinov closed the interview by reporting another incident with casualties near Grodekovo. He said that henceforth the Soviet government did not intend to leave unpunished any sporadic attacks on its border guards or even temporary occupation of Soviet territory by Japanese troops. He declared that it was determined in the future to use the strongest measures in such cases, including the use of artillery and aviation. "Let the Japanese government force the Kwantung and Korean armies to respect the existing frontier. It is time to put an end to the endless 'incidents' and clashes on the frontier."[35] On the same day *Pravda's* editorial charged

[35] *Pravda*, August 8, 1938.

that the Japanese military—the Kwantung Army—was trying to "drag Japan into war with the U.S.S.R."

On August 10, Litvinov proposed an armistice on the following terms: (1) Fighting should stop at noon on August 11; (2) Both sides should retain their positions as of midnight August 10; (3) The border should be "redemarcated" by a mixed commission of two Soviet representatives; two Japan-Manchurian representatives and one mediator chosen by both sides from a third country; (4) The work of the commission should be based on treaties and maps signed by Russia and China.

Shigemitsu accepted points 1 and 2; on point 3 he rejected the mediator, a move which Litvinov accepted; on point 4 he wished to add other material, which according to *Pravda* the Soviets had never seen and now rejected.

A truce was finally arranged on this basis and although the local commissions did not succeed in settling questions of the frontier, active hostilities did cease. Moscow estimated its dead and wounded at 263 and 611 respectively and gave considerably higher figures for Japanese losses.

NEGOTIATIONS ON FISHERIES

The termination of this incident did not serve to improve relations between the two countries. Both Voroshilov and Molotov in their November 7 speeches made scathing attacks on Japan over the Lake Hasan battle, Molotov even went so far as to say that "the whole question of the events in the district of Lake Hasan was actually decided not in Tokyo, but in another place, somewhere in Europe and most probably in Berlin. The Japanese military probably wanted to support their Fascist friends in Germany. . . ."[36] Moreover, from the spring and summer a whole list of unresolved disputes remained, many of which were aired in the negotiations for renewal of the fisheries agreement. As these negotia-

[36] *Pravda*, November 9, 1938.

tions were spread out over more than four months, the points at issue will be summarized here.[37] The first group concerned the relation between the fisheries agreement and other outstanding issues. It will be recalled that Manchukuo had refused to make the last payment on the Chinese Eastern Railway in March—because of counterclaims against the Soviet government. The Japanese insisted that before they would consider this matter, the U.S.S.R. must sign immediately the eight-year convention negotiated in 1936 (see above). Litvinov asserted that the Soviet government could not consider a long-term agreement until Japan "has fulfilled at least its obligations" regarding the Chinese Eastern Railway payments. He offered, however, to sign a one-year extension of the old agreement with certain changes: lots held by Japanese would be left to them until their leases expired; lots whose leases had expired would be put up again for auction except about 40 "which for reasons of the conservation of fisheries or for strategic reasons" would be withdrawn; and contracts on canneries would be extended for a year. After the usual exchange of comments on the Portsmouth Treaty—Ambassador Togo charging Soviet violation of fisheries obligations and Litvinov pointing out Japanese infractions in maintaining troops in Manchuria and fortifying LaPerouse Straits—the argument was reduced to two main issues; the auctions and the so-called "stabilization" of the lots.

The original 1928 convention had provided for the disposal of all lots by auction except those held by the Soviet State Fisheries Trusts, but the 1932 supplementary agreement had allowed the renewal of Japanese leases without auction. Ambassador Togo held that to return to auctions would infringe Japanese rights or at least render such rights valueless. Litvinov reiterated that the only rights the Japanese

[37] For the Soviet version, see Tass dispatches of December 8, 10, 15, and 24, 1938 and January 28, and April 3, 1939.

retained after the expiration of the one-year extension at the end of 1938 were the very general fishing privileges provided in the Portsmouth Treaty. All arrangements were subject to negotiation and ultimately remained at the discretion of the Soviet government which had in no way relinquished sovereignty over the fisheries. The same applied to the second question, "stabilization." Togo insisted that if any lots were taken from the Japanese for strategic or other reasons, they would have to be replaced by other equally good ones selected by the Japanese; that the number of lots must be "stable." He added that any change in this principle would be a blow to "historic feelings of the Japanese people" and might lead to dire consequences. Litvinov replied that the number had never been "stable"—once the Japanese had held as few as 100 lots in contrast to their present total of more than 300. Moreover, he denied any such tradition as mentioned by Togo and again stressed the absence of any legal obligations on such matters.

The negotiations stretched out over so long a period that the Soviets held their own auctions in March 1939 without the Japanese, and when final agreement was reached on April 2, under pressure of the approaching opening of the new season, the auctions had to be repeated. In the renewal agreement both sides appeared to have been relatively satisfied with the compromise. The Soviets established in principle their rights to alter the terms of the basic arrangements and the Japanese obtained in practice fairly liberal terms. The 1928 convention was extended to December 31, 1939, with the exception of Article 8, Protocol A.[38] Although 37 lots were withdrawn, three new ones were granted the Japanese, and in addition Soviet fishing organizations relinquished 10 which they had obtained at the March auctions. The new leases extended over three years under the old terms

[38] This clause provided that lots once opened for exploitation could not be closed but had to continue to be offered for lease.

while cannery leases were extended for a year. The Soviets also retained the 5,000,000-pood catch limit on State fisheries as stipulated in the 1932 agreement and gave assurances that *Dalryba* (Far Eastern Fisheries Administration) would not raise the valuation on fisheries lots more than 10 per cent. In the absence of any settlement of the Chinese Eastern Railway debt, there was no mention of the question of negotiations for a long-term convention.

THE DEVELOPING INTERNATIONAL CRISIS

The 100th meeting of the Council of the League of Nations in January 1938[39] dealt with the question of implementing the October 1937 resolution on aid to China. Wellington Koo asked for full sanctions against Japan under Article 16; but in discussions among Eden, Delbos, Koo, and Litvinov, the French and British took the stand that sanctions would prove ineffective in the Far East. In the Soviet press the suspicion was voiced that the powers would again invoke the old excuse that Geneva could not take action because of the absence of the United States. (Litvinov mentioned the same suspicion to Ambassador Davies before Brussels.[40]) Litvinov proposed financial aid to China while Koo went further and requested arms plus a ban on the sale of oil to Japan. But a further obstacle was Poland's opposition to anti-Japanese action. Consequently Poland was regarded by Moscow as an Axis agent assigned to sabotage the work of the League from within. The final resolution merely reiterated the October position and urged those powers specially interested in the Far East to let no opportunity go by for taking more effective measures to stop the war.

At the same time, speaking before the Committee of 28 which had been set up to deal with the revision of the League

[39] *League of Nations, One-hundredth Session of the Council, Minutes, 2nd Meeting,* January 27, 1938; also *Official Journal,* Special supplement, No. 169, February, 1938, pp. 120–121.

[40] Davies, *op. cit.*, p. 247.

Covenant, Litvinov took the position that the League could well act as an obstacle to war and that its covenant should be strengthened and Article 16 reinforced. "There are no states," he said, "or such a bloc of states which could stand up to the combined forces of the members of the League, even in its present composition. . . . Collective security means Article 16, and we should preserve it and, when it proves possible, strengthen it."[41]

The Nazi occupation of Austria in March had impelled Litvinov to address an urgent appeal for action to the world (March 17, 1938) through a statement to the press: "Tomorrow might be too late, but today there is time yet, if all states, particularly great states, take up a firm, unambiguous stand on the problem of the collective salvation of peace."[42] But Soviet ambassadors failed to receive any reactions to this statement from the governments to which they were accredited.

At the 101st Council meeting in May,[43] Litvinov again found himself battling England and France on a move to approve the recognition of Abyssinia following the Anglo-Italian agreement; on the question of "non-intervention" as a policy of blockade against the Spanish government; and on the resolution exempting Switzerland from participating in actions under Article 16. Again Litvinov hurled charges of internal wrecking to weaken the League. *Pravda*[44] discussing Britain's agreement with Italy and also with Japan (on the Chinese customs revenues), concluded that "up to 1931 English imperialism supported the League of Nations. The present course of English foreign policy, openly pursued by Chamberlain, consists of protecting the interests of England principally outside of the League. The reason is quite simple: the fascist aggressors have left the League and the

[41] *Moscow Daily News*, February 2, 1938.

[42] Litvinov, *Against Aggression*, *op. cit.*, p. 116.

[43] *League of Nations, One-hundred and First Session of the Council, Minutes, 2nd meeting*, May 10, 1938.

[44] P. Poliakov, "Policy of the 'Bag of Gold,'" *Pravda*, May 12, 1938.

English bourgeoisie are trying to reach agreement with each of these aggressors separately. The basis of these negotiations is concessions to the aggressors at the expense of other states which are members of the League."

The backlog of disagreement between Moscow and London on fundamental international policy, which eventually was to make cooperation impossible in the final crisis of 1939, was growing more marked at each meeting of the League. The Soviet position was carefully summed up in a very long and serious speech analyzing the whole range of international relations since Versailles, delivered by Litvinov on June 23, 1938, during the election campaign for the Supreme Soviet of the R.S.F.S.R.[45] In September his analysis was given full corroboration by the Munich agreement.

This is not the place to elaborate on the course of events leading up to Soviet exclusion from the settlement concerning Czechoslovakia, to which Moscow was bound by a mutual-assistance pact. But for its bearing on subsequent events, it should be recalled that the League of Nations was in session during this period and that the usual appeal from China was being heard.[46] *Izvestia* commented: "In the course of these three weeks of intense crisis when the really basic question of

[45] *Moscow News*, July 5, 1938.

[46] When another League resolution on China was adopted, Litvinov said: "I wish to assure the representative of China of our sympathy and our understanding of his disappointment with the report presented to us. I agree with him that this report does not correspond with what China had a right to expect from the League of Nations. It is impossible to restrain the aggressors with such reports or to stop aggression. The fact that we have had to limit ourselves to such reports is even more regrettable at the present moment when so much is being done outside the League to encourage aggression and to assure the success of the aggressors. My government would have been willing to go further than this report and to undertake participation in such coordination of collective measures, which would have permitted the League of Nations to fulfill all of its obligations to China.

"Individual measures can do little to stop aggression, if these measures are not undertaken by other members of the League. My government would have been most ready to participate in such coordination of collective measures, but inasmuch as the other governments do not find this possible for themselves, it is necessary for me to vote for this report." (*Pravda*, October 2, 1938.)

war and peace was being settled, the League of Nations in fact did not exist."[47]

Furthermore, the Soviets considered the Franco-Soviet Pact dead—abrogated by the one-sided action of France.[48]

At the successive meetings of the Council of the League of Nations, the question of aid to China was regularly placed on the agenda by Wellington Koo. The 104th Session in January 1939 heard his plea for economic and financial assistance. When a resolution was put forward of which Jordan of New Zealand said "it would be difficult to find a weaker resolution than the present one and yet one which contains some tangible proposals,"[49] Souritz, the Soviet representative, remarked on the more and more apparent tendency to draw a distinction between "League of Nations theories" and so-called realistic policy. He pointed out that the League had in fact grown out of the realities of a frightful war. He reaffirmed the readiness of the U.S.S.R. to carry out any League decision on measures to defend the collective security of nations—"that security which has been so much derided but which must be made a reality if we are indeed one day to win peace for all in honor and in justice."[50]

Although the Soviets continued to attend the Geneva meetings and to urge collective action, officially they expressed their distrust of the motives of the other major European powers. Early in March they formally withdrew from the Non-Intervention Committee. At the Eighteenth Party Congress Stalin made a report on foreign relations which served as the formulation of Soviet policy for that period.

[47] *Izvestia*, September 30, 1938.

[48] Cf. *Le Journal de Moscou*, October 4, 1938, an editorial reading in part: "In effect, France has with its own hands and without having consulted the U.S.S.R., annulled the Soviet-Czech pact which was a corollary to the Franco-Soviet Pact and one of the important elements of a regional eastern pact. . . . The loss of its allies and isolation, this is the price which France will have to pay for capitulation before the aggressor."

[49] *League of Nations, Official Journal*, No. 2, February 1939, p. 100.

[50] *ibid.*, p. 101.

Because of the importance the Soviets attached to that speech and because of the light it threw on the subsequent course of Soviet diplomacy, it is not out of place to summarize it here.[51]

In analyzing the five-year period since the last Party Congress, Stalin discussed the economic depression in the capitalist countries, pointing out that the aggressive nations whose economies had been converted to a war basis were not yet suffering from the economic depression that had set in at the close of 1937 in the other major imperialist countries. They were, however, using up their resources and reserves and eventually would fall into an even deeper crisis. Stalin then went on to recount the political consequences of the economic difficulties such as the territorial claims of the Axis, and he concluded that "a new redivision of the world by means of war becomes imminent." Next he discussed the evolution of the crisis and elaborated on the paradox of the lack of resistance by England, France and the United States to the infringement of their own interests, which he attributed to their rejection of collective security in favor of a policy of "non-intervention" or "neutrality."

"The policy of non-intervention reveals an eagerness, a desire, not to hinder the aggressors in their nefarious work: not to hinder Japan, say, from embroiling herself in a war with China, or, better still, with the Soviet Union; not to hinder Germany, say, from enmeshing herself in European affairs, from embroiling herself in a war with the Soviet Union; to allow all the belligerents to sink deeply into the mire of war, to encourage them surreptitiously in this; to allow them to weaken and exhaust one another; and then, when they become weak enough, to appear on the scene with fresh strength, to appear, of course, 'in the interests of peace,' and to dictate conditions to the enfeebled belligerents."

After elaborating on what he considered to be attempts to

[51] For full text, see *The Land of Socialism Today and Tomorrow*, Foreign Languages Publishing House, Moscow, 1939, p. 8ff.

stir up war between Germany and the Soviet Union, he concluded "that the big and dangerous political game started by the supporters of the policy of non-intervention may end in a fiasco for them." In the light of this situation, Stalin outlined the fundamental course to be pursued by Soviet foreign policy: "(1) To continue the policy of peace and of strengthening business relations with all countries; (2) To be cautious and not allow our country to be drawn into conflicts by warmongers who are accustomed to have others pull the chestnuts out of the fire for them; (3) To strengthen the might of our Red Army and Red Navy to the utmost; (4) To strengthen the international bonds of friendship with the working people of all countries, who are interested in peace and friendship among nations."

This statement did not by itself mark any sharp break with previous formulations: indeed it was followed up by Litvinov's proposal for a conference of France, Great Britain, Poland, Rumania, Turkey and the U.S.S.R. to discuss the situation resulting from Germany's complete absorption of Czechoslovakia. Britain rejected the idea as "premature" but suggested conversations between England and the U.S.S.R. The negotiations that followed (in which France participated) stretched out through the summer. Although they specifically excluded any question of similar cooperative action in the Far East,[52] it will be necessary to discuss them briefly because of the increasingly close connection between events in the Far East and in Europe. In his first speech as Foreign Commissar, delivered on May 31 to the Third Session of the Supreme Soviet, Molotov outlined the fundamental requirements for Soviet participation in a defensive alliance,[53] and

[52] The Soviet press on two occasions denied that Far Eastern considerations were holding up the discussions. *Pravda*, June 21, August 19, 1939.

[53] "That an effective pact of mutual assistance against aggression, a pact of an exclusively defensive character, be concluded between Great Britain, France and the U.S.S.R.; that a guarantee against attack by the aggressors be extended by Great Britain, France and the U.S.S.R. to states of central and eastern Europe, including all European countries bordering on the U.S.S.R., without

reported that the British and French were unwilling at that time to make reciprocal guarantees regarding the Baltic countries. The next Soviet comment on the progress of the negotiations took the form of a letter to *Pravda*[54] from Zhdanov, in which he expressed his personal opinion that the English and French governments did not want an equal treaty with the U.S.S.R. He pointed to repeated stalling, to excuses raised against guarantees to the Soviets' northwestern neighbors, in contrast to the rapidity with which agreements had been reached by England with Poland and Turkey. Zhdanov concluded that the other powers did not want a treaty—they merely wanted negotiations for a treaty to facilitate reaching a deal with the aggressor by deceiving their own public with false rumors of Moscow's "uncompromising" attitude.

At the end of August the Soviet non-aggression pact with Germany was signed. The first Soviet statement was made by Voroshilov[55] in connection with the breakdown of the Anglo-French-Soviet military conversations. He told the press that the deadlock had arisen over the alleged unwillingness of Poland to accept Soviet military aid. His conclusion was that "the military negotiations with England and France did not break down because the U.S.S.R. concluded a non-aggression pact with Germany. On the contrary, the U.S.S.R. concluded the pact with Germany because the military negotiations had got into a blind alley, because of insoluble differences of opinion."

On August 31 when Molotov submitted the pact for ratification to the Fourth Session of the Supreme Soviet, his speech

---

exception; that a concrete agreement be concluded by Great Britain, France and the U.S.S.R. regarding the forms and extent of the immediate and effective assistance to be given to each other and to the guaranteed states in the event of attack by aggressors." V. Molotov, *The International Situation and Soviet Foreign Policy*, Foreign Languages Publishing House, Moscow, 1939, p. 9.

[54] *Pravda*, June 29, 1939.

[55] *Pravda*, August 27, 1939.

reiterated the charges made by Zhdanov and Voroshilov. To them he added the fact that the Anglo-French military delegations, despite the gravity of the international situation, had been sent to Moscow without any power to act. His view[56] was that

"On the one hand, the British and French Governments fear aggression, and for that reason would like to have a pact of mutual assistance with the Soviet Union, inasmuch as it would strengthen them, Great Britain and France. But, on the other hand, the British and French Governments are afraid that the conclusion of a real pact of mutual assistance with the U.S.S.R. may strengthen our country, the Soviet Union, which, it appears, does not answer their purpose. It must be admitted that these fears of theirs outweighed other considerations. . . .

"The decision to conclude a pact of non-aggression between the U.S.S.R. and Germany was adopted after the military negotiations with France and Great Britain had reached an impasse owing to the insurmountable differences I have mentioned. As the negotiations had shown that the conclusion of a pact of mutual assistance was not to be expected, we could not but explore other possibilities of ensuring peace and averting the danger of a war between Germany and the U.S.S.R. If the British and French Governments refused to reckon with this, that is their lookout."

In discussing changed relations with Germany, he reminded his audience of Stalin's references in the spring to efforts by certain groups to stir up discord between the two nations and his hints that it might be possible to improve relations. Molotov also harked back to the position long held by Soviet diplomats that they were not concerned with the internal regimes of countries but stood rather for mutual non-interference; *that Soviet relations with other countries depended on their*

[56] V. Molotov, *On the Ratification of the Soviet-German Pact of Non-Aggression*, Foreign Languages Publishing House, Moscow, 1939, p. 8.

foreign policies;[57] and that in the past they had been party to agreements—trade agreements and neutrality or non-aggression pacts—with both Italy and Germany. "Differences of outlook and political systems," Molotov said, "must not and cannot be an obstacle to the establishment of good political relations between the U.S.S.R. and other non-Soviet, capitalist countries."[58]

FURTHER DIFFICULTIES WITH JAPAN

Germany's agreement with the U.S.S.R. evidently was not palatable to its anti-Comintern partner in the Far East;[59] Japan's protest to Berlin that the pact with the U.S.S.R. was incompatible with the Axis pact was followed shortly by the fall of the Hiranuma government. The reason was clear: Japan at the time was engaged in serious warfare against Soviet troops on the Mongolian-Manchurian border. Beginning in May 1939 there had been press reports of fighting along that frontier. By June the clash had assumed large dimensions with tanks and airplanes being brought into action.[60] Because of the relative unimportance of the territory under dispute, the incident appeared to Moscow primarily to be a diplomatic move. Therefore, it led the Soviets to minimize the significance of the fact that Japan had not joined Italy and Germany in their military alliance of that spring. It further coincided with Japanese pressure on Tientsin[61] and the negotiations being carried on in Europe;

[57] Cf. Litvinov's speeches of September 28 and November 28, 1936 in reference to relations with fascist states, *Against Aggression, op. cit.*

[58] V. Molotov, *op. cit.*, p. 13.

[59] The German Ambassador to Tokyo, Ott, had explained, according to the Japanese account, that the pact arose "out of Germany's dire need to ensure Soviet neutrality in the event of a conflict in Europe. The non-aggression pact was concluded as a result of overtures made by the Reich." The Japanese Ambassador to Berlin had been instructed to file a strong protest because the treaty "contravenes the spirit of the Japan-German Anti-Comintern Pact." *Japan Weekly Chronicle*, August 31, 1939, p. 242.

[60] Cf. *Japan Weekly Chronicle*, June 1, 1939, p. 650; June 8, 1939, p. 687; September 7, 1939, p. 272. Also, Soviet press for that period.

[61] It is interesting to note that some Japanese attributed the incident to the

in short it was regarded as one phase of Axis cooperation to disrupt all attempts by the non-Axis nations to reach a common understanding.

The territory under dispute lay in the Nomonhan district, east of Lake Buir. At that point the border, according to the Soviet version, lies somewhat east of the Khalka River; but according to the Japanese the river itself constitutes the frontier. To support the Russian view, *Pravda*[62] reproduced a map from the 1919 Chinese Postal Atlas and declared further that the Mongol People's Republic had always maintained frontier posts east of the river.

This was the first major incident along that border since the signing of the Soviet-Mongol mutual assistance pact, so that it was notable that the reports from Moscow consistently referred to the troops engaged in the battle as Mongol-Soviet forces pitted against the Japanese-Manchurian army.[63] Judging from newspaper accounts, the losses on both sides were considerable and bombing operations were carried on well behind the lines. On September 16, a truce was effected and a commission set up to fix the frontier. The Soviet claims that they had held firmly to their original positions were subsequently borne out by a Japanese War Office report[64] blaming the disastrous results of the battle for Japan on the superior mechanization of the opposing forces a view which had been taken earlier in a Soviet press account.[65]

During the summer months of 1939 other issues had arisen to create tension between Moscow and Tokyo. The most important of these was the dispute over the operation of the

---

exact opposite reasons. They claimed that all incidents had been synchronized with trouble arising in China between Japan and third powers. "Thus, the attitude of Soviet Russia towards Japan has been in line with that of Britain and France in this respect." Cf. *Japan Weekly Chronicle*, June 29, 1939, p. 782.

[62] *Pravda*, July 14, 1939.

[63] The Japanese took note of the same fact. Cf. *Japan Weekly Chronicle*, June 8, 1939, p. 687.

[64] *New York Times*, October 4, 1939.

[65] *Pravda*, July 14, 1939.

Sakhalin concessions. Controversy centering about the labor force had been reported in 1937 and 1938; in addition, the Japanese complained of the difficulty of obtaining permission to make certain changes in their operations and explore new territory.[66] On April 27, 1939 Japan had submitted a memorandum listing all the grievances of the concessionaires. While this remained unanswered, in the meantime a judgment had been handed down by Soviet courts in July against a Japanese coal concessionaire for failure to provide adequate supplies of consumers' goods to the workers during 1938. On July 16 Ambassador Togo handed a note to the Soviet Foreign Commissar protesting the court decision and demanding before July 18 an answer to his earlier complaints. Vice-Commissar Lozovsky refused to accept the note, regarding it as an ultimatum. However, a week later, on July 24, he presented the Japanese chargé with a long memorandum in reply to the April note. In this were listed all the acts of the concessionaires which according to Moscow contravened the contracts. These ranged from violations of safety requirements to curtailment of production; the smuggling and accumulation of very large stores of supplies while simultaneously failing to supply adequate goods for the workers; employment of 43 per cent Japanese instead of observing the 25 per cent limit set; export of oil on naval tankers; failure to pay rent for equipment, etc. In conclusion he denied that the U.S.S.R. was attempting to end the concessions although the contracts had in fact been violated in such a way as to make legitimate their denunciation. He also referred to the fact that Japan had failed to live up to its contract to insure the Chinese Eastern Railway payments and to assist in settling the payments of the Matsuo Dockyards. The latter case, a new controversy over non-fulfillment of the terms of a contract for building ships for the U.S.S.R., was to remain on the

[66] Cf. *Japan Weekly Chronicle*, March 17, 1938, p. 337; May 4, 1939, p. 526; June 1, 1939, p. 657.

books until early 1941: the C.E.R. payments, on the other hand, were settled in connection with the fisheries agreement for 1940.

While there was no report in the press of any final settlement of all these points, an agreement was reached between the oil companies and the trade union,[67] by which certain working and living conditions were improved in return for allowing the concessionaires to bring in more Japanese workers.

The ensuing lull in Soviet-Japanese relations after the truce on the Mongolian front enabled Molotov to report in his speech of October 31 that certain signs pointed to a general over-all improvement of relations and that "the development of Soviet-Japanese trade is in the interest of both countries.[68] This reference to trade came as quite a new departure inasmuch as Soviet-Japanese trade had dwindled almost to the vanishing point during the years after the bulk of the Chinese Eastern Railway payments were completed.[69] In the past Soviet raw materials such as lumber, fish, oil, etc. had been exchanged for manufactured goods, ships, chemicals, cement, etc.; commerce in such products could advantageously have been resumed. Nothing, however, developed out of the hint at that time nor even in 1940 when actual trade negotiations began.

At the close of the year, when the question of renewal of the

[67] Cf. *Pravda*, August 12, 1939.

[68] Speech to the Supreme Council on October 31, 1939. V. Molotov, *Foreign Policy of the Soviet Union*, Foreign Languages Publishing House, Moscow, 1939, p. 27.

[69] Japan's trade with U.S.S.R. was as follows, in thousand yen:

Year	*Exports*	*Imports*
1934	13,005	40,808
1935	28,319*	17,904
1936	31,350*	21,333
1937	27,968*	13,534
1938	5,183	756
1939	202	99

* Including payments on the Chinese Eastern Railway.
Source: *Oriental Economist*, November 4, 1940.

fisheries agreement came up once again, further evidence signified a return to more normal relations. In exchange for an agreement on the part of Moscow to reopen negotiations for a long-term fisheries convention, the Japanese arranged for the payment of the last installment on the Chinese Eastern Railway—the 5.9 million yen debt in arrears since March 1938. The final disposition on this point included the original amount plus an adjustment due to yen depreciation and 3 per cent interest charges. From this sum was deducted 1.3 million yen representing Manchukuo's claims against the Soviet Government. It was further agreed that these claims along with others against the U.S.S.R. and Soviet claims estimated at $590,000 for pensions due the former Soviet railroad employees were to be referred for negotiation to the representatives of the three governments in Tokyo. Finally, the U.S.S.R. consented to take out in trade two-thirds of the sum, provided the assortment and prices of goods offered were suitable.

The fisheries agreement signed on December 31 extended the existing arrangements and provided for negotiations on a long-term convention to replace them. The accompanying exchange of notes reaffirmed the 5,000,000-pood catch limit for the Soviet state fisheries; the 32.5 sen exchange rate for payments in debentures of the Kamchatka company; and the gold clause for adjustments in case of currency fluctuations.[70]

THE EFFECT OF THE EUROPEAN WAR

After September 1939 the U.S.S.R. was caught between two wars. Soviet relationship to the war in Asia was already well-defined, but in Europe new problems were raised. Although relations with Germany recently had been revised publicly by the non-aggression pact, as yet they had not been tested and Germany was now moving into Poland. On the other hand relations with the other chief belligerents—

[70] *Pravda*, January 1, 1940.

England and France—were equally uncertain. Having labelled the war "imperialist," the Soviet government professedly pursued a policy of neutrality, with corollary efforts to keep the war from spreading, to improve its own defenses, and to trade with all parties.

In the economic sphere the Soviet position was difficult. Even though the U.S.S.R. had no need of large foreign markets for surplus produce (its internal market in terms of existing purchasing power was still far from satiated) and although the government's monopoly of foreign trade facilitated shifts in the direction of trade, nevertheless to be cut off from foreign trade entirely was a serious matter. The U.S.S.R.'s generous endowment of natural resources does not include rubber, tin, and a few other essential raw materials, while its program of capital expansion required continuous imports of machine tools and other technical industrial equipment. For these reasons trade with abroad remained vital and early in the war Molotov reported he had registered a protest against the British blockade for its inclusion of consumers' goods in the contraband list.[71] Because of its geographic isolation from commercial sea lanes after the outbreak of war the Soviet Union had to concentrate on trade with its land neighbors and in fact concluded trade agreements with an imposing number of countries. Up until the extension of the American licensing system at the end of 1940 to cover almost all items of Soviet purchase, the U.S.S.R. also was able to carry on a large-scale trade across the Pacific with the United States.

The outbreak of war in Europe made no immediate change in the Soviet view of the Far East. The basic analysis stood; China was fighting a "just" war of national liberation against the Japanese imperialists and was deserving of Soviet support. Commerce between the two countries had continued to grow; according to Chinese sources the U.S.S.R. had granted about

[71] *Pravda*, October 26, 1939.

$300,000,000 in credits of China,[72] in connection with barter arrangements for the exchange of machinery and munitions for tea, minerals, and other raw materials. The largest of these credits was provided for at the time the trade treaty was signed in June, 1939[73] establishing most-favored-nation relations between the two countries and giving diplomatic status to Soviet trade representatives. Accompanying notes explained that the most-favored-nation treatment referred to by the Chinese was equivalent to that accorded under the so-called "equal treaties" negotiated with other powers since 1928. Soviet aid had been gratefully acknowledged by the Chinese on numerous occasions and they frequently remarked that it was being given without strings attached.[74] Reports indicated that neither internal friction between the Kuomintang and the Chinese Communist Party nor the new Soviet agreements with Japan caused any lessening in supplies from the U.S.S.R., which in fact remained a chief source of war materials for China.[75]

Although Soviet-Chinese relations continued unaltered by European events, the same can hardly be said of Soviet relations with Japan. As mentioned above, the signing of the Soviet-German pact at first had met with a sharp reaction in Japan. But soon afterwards a truce was reached on the Mongolian frontier; Molotov then was able to suggest in October 1939 that as a result of this first step to improve relations Moscow would look with favor on overtures for trade negotiations. Though it was announced in November that a basis for negotiations had been found and a Japanese

[72] October, 1938—$50,000,000; February, 1939—$50,000,000; August, 1939—$150,000,000; December, 1940—$50,000,000. Source: *Contemporary China*, No. 1, May 25, 1941.

[73] For text cf. *Vedomosti Verkhovnogo Soveta SSSR*, Moscow, June 15, 1940. See Appendix, p. 189.

[74] Cf. Speech of Chinese Ambassador to London. He spoke of the U.S.S.R. as "China's great neighbor who has proved also to be a good neighbor" and "has given us great material assistance by barter arrangements without any political conditions whatever." *Anglo-Russian News Bulletin*, July 25, 1940.

[75] Cf. *New York Times*, April 2, 1940.

trade delegation reached Moscow early in 1940, nothing was accomplished. As a matter of fact the tone of Molotov's March 1940[76] report was pessimistic: for the Mongol-Manchurian border commission had made no progress; obstacles were raised by the Japanese to utilization of funds derived from the last Chinese Eastern Railway payment; and there were charges of mistreatment of Soviet employees in Manchuria and Japan. At the same time Molotov further took the opportunity to counter the suggestion made not long before in the Japanese Diet that Japan should purchase the Maritime region by remarking that he was sure purchasers for southern Sakhalin could be found in the U.S.S.R.

In the late spring, however, with Japan feeling its way southward into Indo-China, taking advantage of American and British preoccupation in Europe, the Japanese press began to raise the question of improved relations with the Soviet Union as a prerequisite to the execution of other policies. Then followed reports of German mediation in such negotiations—rumors which were assiduously denied by Moscow[77] for obvious enough reasons when viewed in the light of German efforts to effect a compromise settlement of the China issue.

In August Molotov had taken note of these Japanese feelers and applauded the very real progress made toward reaching an agreement on the basis of demarcation of the Mongolian frontier. But he added:[78] "It must, however, be admitted that there is still much that is unclear in the program of the new Japanese Government, concerning the establishment of the 'new political structure. . . .' It is apparent that the southward expansion of which the Japanese papers are noisily

[76] V. Molotov, *Foreign Policy of the Soviet Government*, Foreign Languages Publishing House, Moscow, 1940.

[77] Cf. Tass, September 7, October 18, October 26, November 14, 1940.

[78] V. Molotov, "Soviet Foreign Policy," speech at the 7th session of the Supreme Soviet of the U.S.S.R., issued by *Anglo-Russian News Bulletin*, London, August 1940.

shouting is attracting the attention of leading circles of Japan to an even greater extent, particularly in view of the fact that changes which have occurred in Europe cannot but have their reverberations in the districts in which these circles of Japan are interested. But the real political aspirations of these circles are still unclear in many respects. This refers also to Soviet-Japanese relations."

Soviet commentators in this period were watching closely the jockeying for position which was taking place among the major powers in the Pacific. One wrote as follows:[79] "The world has become crowded in this century of flying and floating fortresses with their wide radius of action. The explosion of bombs over London echoes loudly not only over the Atlantic, but also over the Pacific. There, as a result of the European war, the balance of forces has shifted violently along with the change in strength and position of the imperialist powers fighting for dominance over the Pacific. Defeated France cannot resist Japan. All the strength of England is thrown into the war against Italy and Germany. In the struggle for the Pacific only Japan and the United States, in fact, now face each other. Japan is anxious to seize the 'golden opportunity' afforded by events in Europe, while the United States considering itself the 'legal' heir to the British Empire wants 'the open door' for itself in China, but it is trying to close the door to Japanese expansion to the South. Both rivals are closely following the developments of the war in Europe and at the same time are preparing feverishly for impending events."

For Moscow, the axis Tri-partite Treaty of September 27, 1940, put an end to whatever separation there may have been in the two spheres of imperialist rivalry. Pointing to the simultaneous attempts on Dakar and on Indo-China, Viktorov

[79] Ya. Viktorov, "The Pacific Ocean Front of the Second Imperialist War," *Bolshevik*, No. 17, 1940. See also, E. Zhukov, "The Fight for Supremacy in the Pacific," *Pravda*, September 16, 1940.

asserted: "The end of the war is not yet in sight, and yet the map of the world is already being redrawn; the division of the French colonial Empire is already beginning." *Pravda's* editorial comment on the pact[80] also stressed the fact that Japan had finally renounced the policy of non-intervention in European affairs, while Germany and Italy had done the same with regard to Far Eastern developments. The United States, *Pravda* held, though not formally a belligerent, was in "the same common military camp with the adversaries of Germany, Italy and Japan in both hemispheres."

On the whole the Soviets reacted to the pact calmly, both because in their view it represented only a crystalization of existing alignments and because they had been informed of it by Germany in advance. They were satisfied with Article V, which stated that the pact did not "affect the political status existing at present between each of the three participants to the agreement and the Soviet Union;" they regarded it as recognition of Soviet neutrality and reaffirmation of their non-aggression pacts with Germany and Italy. Following the pact, the trend toward gradual improvement of Soviet-Japanese relations continued. In December Japan felt constrained to explain that the anti-communist clause of the treaty with Wang Ching-wei was not directed against the Soviet Union. The Soviet reply reaffirmed its friendly relations with Chungking.[81]

On January 20, 1941, the fisheries convention was renewed and in addition to a 20 per cent rent increase the Soviets obtained a settlement of the Matsuo dockyard debt in dispute since the middle of 1938.[82] The Japanese firm concerned had broken a contract for the construction of three ships, concluded two years before; aside from refusing delivery, it had retained the advance payment of 1.6 million yen and

[80] *Pravda*, September 30, 1940.
[81] *Pravda*, December 5, 1940.
[82] Cf. *Pravda*, August 18, 1939.

declined to pay the 10 per cent forfeit for failure to carry out the contract. Failing to obtain satisfaction in the Japanese courts, Moscow had made it a question of diplomatic negotiation in the summer of 1939. The 1941 settlement met Soviet demands in full; both the down-payment and the 10 per cent forfeit were paid.

At the time of the fisheries extension no explanation was given for the failure to negotiate a long-term convention as had been provided in the *modus vivendi* for 1940. However, from 1936 on, Moscow had made its willingness to discuss that problem contingent on good relations in other spheres and the Matsuo dockyards case may have been one of the reasons for the delay. In any case the 1941 fisheries agreement again provided for the negotiation of a permanent convention; at the time of the signing of the temporary extension the appointment of the two delegations was announced.

In February 1941 Japan showed other signs of a desire to reach further settlement. It was reported from Shanghai that steps were being taken to curb White Guard activities,[83] while Thailand, now virtually Japan's satellite, established diplomatic relations with the U.S.S.R.

THE SOVIET-JAPANESE NEUTRALITY PACT

Upon Matsuoka's return from Berlin in April a neutrality pact was signed between Japan and the U.S.S.R.[84] Reviewing the history of enmity between the two countries from the Russo-Japanese war through Siberian intervention to Changkufeng and Nomonhan, *Izvestia* declared that the U.S.S.R. could not but welcome Japan's desire to end friction and recognize that the Soviet Union was no object of easy attack, that its policy could not be dictated from outside.[85] It admitted that in itself the pact did not settle all the problems outstanding between the two countries, but it reiterated the

[83] *New York Times*, February 10, 1941.
[84] See Appendix, p. 200.
[85] *Izvestia*, April 15, 1941. See Appendix p. 251.

old Soviet view that once the basic political relationships were normalized, the way was open for negotiations on fisheries, trade and other economic matters. It termed the pact an "historic reversal in Japanese-Soviet relations."

Konoye's statement on April 14 was to much the same effect.[86] The United States, however, officially took the view that no great significance should be attached to the pact since it was "descriptive of a situation which has in effect existed between the two countries for some time past."[87] *Pravda* on April 19,[88] took issue with both this attempt to minimize the agreement and the comment prevailing in England and the United States expressing disappointment at the peaceful settlement of Soviet-Japanese differences. In refuting rumors that the pact had been negotiated through German mediation, the same article traced the ten-year-old history of the idea of a pact, and brought it down to July 1940 when Japanese Ambassador Togo had first reopened the question by suggesting a neutrality pact. While the idea was accepted in principle, negotiations did not proceed at once and in October the new Japanese Ambassador Tatekawa proposed a pact similar to the Soviet-German treaty of August 1939. However, Moscow preferred an agreement along the lines of the old 1926 Soviet-German neutrality treaty. *Pravda* also revealed that in November, 1940 the U.S.S.R. had refused an invitation to join the tri-partite mutual assistance pact to make it a four-power agreement. Thus, the question had been strictly confined to Moscow and Tokyo. Matsuoka's visits in March and April, according to *Pravda*, made possible the successful conclusion of the negotiations. Not until 1944 did it become known that, at the time the pact was signed, Japan agreed to give up its concessions on Soviet Sakhalin (see below).

[86] *Tokyo Gazette*, Vol. IV, No. 12, June, 1941, pp. 488–491. For Matsuoka's statement, April 22, see *ibid.*, pp. 537–538.

[87] *Department of State Bulletin*, April 19, 1941, p. 472.

[88] For English translation, see *Moscow News*, April 24, 1941, p. 5.

Comment from both sides on the supplementary agreement respecting the territorial integrity of the Mongol People's Republic and Manchukuo referred to the necessity of eliminating this grave source of friction between Japan and the Soviet Union.[89] The Chinese government reportedly queried the Soviets as to whether the agreement constituted recognition of Manchukuo and also as to the likely effect of the pact on Soviet-Chinese trade. Soviet assurances that the new treaty in no way altered its relations to China were evidently acceptable and the subsequent course of trade tended to bear them out.[90]

The first concrete result of the neutrality pact was the Soviet-Japanese commercial convention reached in June, providing for an exchange of goods totalling 60,000,000 yen.[91] The five-year treaty was the first of its kind between the two countries, defining tariff and commercial procedures, although general principles of commercial relations had been laid out in Article IV of the 1925 Treaty. The new convention was accompanied by a one-year barter agreement. At the same time it was announced that the Soviets had released a Japanese trawler, held fourteen months for illegal entry into Soviet waters.[92] Plans also were reported for expanding the shipping service between Vladivostok and Japan and Korea.

The conclusion of a neutrality pact with Japan completed the definition by treaty of Soviet relationships in the Far East. A comparison of the texts of the respective pacts with China, Japan, and the Mongol People's Republic (see appendix) indicates to some degree the differences in Soviet

[89] The Chinese government issued a formal statement: "The Chinese government and people cannot recognize any engagements entered into between third parties which are derogatory to China's territorial and administrative integrity, and wish to state that the Soviet-Japanese declaration just announced has no binding force whatsoever on China." *China Handbook 1937–43,* Compiled by the Chinese Ministry of Information, The MacMillan Company, New York, 1943, p. 170.

[90] *New York Times,* April 14, 1941.

[91] *New York Times,* June 13, 1941.

[92] *New York Herald Tribune,* June 13, 1941

attitudes and relationships with the countries involved in the war. The Mongol Mutual Assistance Pact, already implemented in practice at Nomonhan, forms the most thoroughgoing type of mutual-aid agreement which the Soviets have ever concluded with foreign countries. The Chinese pact, promising a benevolent Soviet neutrality and guaranteeing that the U.S.S.R. will do nothing "directly or indirectly" to injure the Chinese position, has also had its practical test in trade relations between the two countries. With Japan the Soviet pact was rather strictly limited in scope, merely providing for the maintenance of formal neutrality.

VI. THE U.S.S.R. AT WAR, JUNE 1941 TO PEACE IN EUROPE

"We are all in the same boat now, and will either perish together or together triumph." Thus Litvinov in his statement on December 13, 1941 expressed the Soviet view of the Pacific war. How completely the short six months that separated Pearl Harbor from the Nazi invasion of the Soviet Union reversed the trend of relations between the U.S.S.R. and the Anglo-American powers! Right up to June 22, 1941, relations with America and Britain deteriorated. Soviet commentators saw in British warnings of an impending attack a desire to exacerbate Soviet-German relations. And London and Washington suspected that every ounce of Soviet imports was destined to aid the Nazi war machine. But on the morrow of invasion, the die was cast. A common enemy threw the erstwhile strangers together.

It was Churchill's immediate and unqualified recognition of Britain's community of interest with the Soviet Union as a fighting ally that assured coalition warfare in Europe and prevented the war from being divided, perhaps fatally, into private wars of differing "ideological content." By July 12, Great Britain and the U.S.S.R. were wartime allies—not just "associated powers"—and on August 2 the United States and the Soviet Union renewed their annual trade agreement with an exchange of notes to accelerate wartime trade under the loans being extended to the U.S.S.R.[1] In August Harry Hopkins made his flying trip to Moscow and reported back enthusiastically to President Roosevelt and Prime Minister Churchill at their Atlantic Conference. In Septem-

[1] *New York Times*, August 5, 1941.

ber, the Soviet Union, along with other anti-Axis powers in Europe, endorsed the Atlantic Charter. In October the Beaverbrook and Harriman missions to Moscow paved the way for cooperation and material aid, and November saw the extension of Lend-Lease to cover the U.S.S.R.

PEARL HARBOR

Thus the foundations of the United Nations had already been laid when Japan struck against the United States and Great Britain. The Axis, too, had coordinated its plans: Pearl Harbor coincided with the time set by Hitler for the expected capture of Moscow. Marshal Zhukov's victorious counter-attack at the gates of the city began on December 6. As Litvinov's statement explained, the two camps were lined up for a life and death struggle. Newly appointed as Ambassador to the United States, Litvinov himself arrived by plane in San Francisco from across the Pacific on December 6. A week later, at his first press conference, he said in part:[2]

" . . . During the last few days the battlefront has become considerably more extensive, spreading to all continents. It must now be plain even to those who are, politically speaking, babes or blind, that all that is now going on is the result of a vast conspiracy by a handful of international gangsters, calling themselves Axis Powers to plunder all countries, enslave their peoples. The outlines of this plot were roughed out with the creation of the so-called Anti-Comintern Pact. Against this little handful of plotters who have made of their peoples slaves and mere instruments of their will is arraigned the whole of the rest of the world. We now have, in various parts of the world, separate sectors of one great battlefield.

"In this struggle against the international gangsters the heavy end has fallen to the Soviet Union, Great Britain and the United States. We are proud and happy to count ourselves the allies of your great country. I am quite sure that

[2] *New York Times*, December 14, 1941.

complete understanding exists or will be arrived at among these three allies as to which of them should concentrate its greatest efforts and energy on which sector and that they will be ruled in this by the interests of the common cause. We are all in the same boat now, and will either perish together or together triumph over the greatest evil of our times, over the spirit of aggression, of international infamy and barbarity. And triumph we will. . . . "

From the very outset the Soviet Union reacted to the new extension of the war and predicted an Allied victory. It was but five days after Pearl Harbor that *Pravda* wrote editorially:[3] " . . . The Japanese aggressor has plunged into a very hazardous adventure, which bodes him nothing but defeat. If he counted on the possibility of 'lightning victory' he is in for a disappointment no less cruel than that suffered by bloodthirsty Hitler as a result of his bandit attack on the Soviet Union.

"Japan faces a powerful coalition formed by the united forces of the United States of America, Great Britain and China—for there can be no doubt that the outbreak of a great war in the Pacific will entail a sharp intensification of activity on the Sino-Japanese front as well. . . .

"These facts show that Japan's first successes decide nothing. In future Japan's resources will be exhausted by this war, while American resources will grow. This is the circumstance that will decide the issue of the war. Japan will indisputably suffer defeat."

Technically, the Soviet Union stood in the following relation to the Far Eastern belligerents. She had the neutrality pact of April 1941 with Japan, a non-aggression pact with China which had been supplemented by material military aid, a mutual-assistance pact with the Mongol People's Republic, a military alliance with Britain in Europe and various agree-

[3] *Information Bulletin*, Embassy of the U.S.S.R., Washington, D.C., December 13, 1941, p. 5. For full text, see Appendix, p. 254.

ments with the United States regarding military supplies. Admittedly, Soviet relations in the Far East had become complicated and delicate. For the entire first year of the Pacific phase of the war—throughout 1942—the Soviets were being driven back deeper and deeper in the West, until the Nazis reached Stalingrad and the first oil of the Caucasus in the summer of 1942. Would Japan, flushed with the early successes of its advance to the south, attack Siberia as Hitler demanded? Should forces be shifted from east to west or vice versa? How would China fare now completely cut off from Allied aid? What of the Japanese demands regarding the fisheries agreement which would expire at the end of the year? Would the Allies now be in a position to carry out their agreements to send supplies to the U.S.S.R.—and if so, when would they begin to arrive? To follow how the U.S.S.R. proceeded in this explosive situation, it is most convenient to take up Soviet wartime relations country by country.

SINO-SOVIET RELATIONS

On June 22, 1941, the new Foreign Minister of China, Dr. Quo, said:[4] "The Russo-German war has greatly clarified the whole international situation. China was in the vanguard in resisting aggression and it has always been our desire to work with our friends and with those who would make a similar stand." The sentiment was reiterated subsequently on a number of occasions. For instance, in November 1943, Generalissimo Chiang sent a message of congratulations to Kalinin, in connection with the anniversary of the Revolution: "We are confident," he said, "that, when victory is won, we shall be equally successful in our effort to build a new and lasting peace."[5] For their part, the Soviets, contrary to popular belief, were not super-cautious in expressing friend-

[4] *New York Times*, June 29, 1941.
[5] *New York Times*, November 7, 1943.

ship for China after the conclusion of the Soviet-Japanese neutrality pact.

SOVIET AID TO CHINA

Prior to Soviet involvement in the European war, it was generally recognized that the U.S.S.R. had, in practice, been one of China's most effective friends in her war against Japan. Not only had Litvinov tried to secure international support for China, but the material supplies reaching Free China from the U.S.S.R. exceeded those from other countries. In addition, the Soviets had supplied technical advisers to the Chinese army, air force and other war services. After the end of 1941, the situation with regard to the flow of supplies from Soviet sources was obscure. In October, 1941 the Soviet Embassy in Washington reported that Chungking had been notified that Moscow no longer was able to continue shipments. Yet as late as July 1942 an announcement by Wong Wen-hao, Chinese Minister of Economic Affairs,[6] reported a continuous flow of materials in trucks and carts over the road from the Soviet railhead at Alma Ata toward Chungking. While Chinese officials informally state that nothing had been received since the beginning of 1942, there has been some evidence that Soviet goods never completely ceased to come into China. The confusion may arise out of a distinction between military supplies (which undoubtedly did cease) and "civilian supplies" such as oil, trucks, etc.

At the same time two other forms of aid are known to have continued for some time longer. Certain Russian technical advisers remained in China, and the Soviet Union put its transportation system at the disposal of the Allies for transhipping goods from Iran and India across Soviet Central Asia and into China, via Chinese Turkestan (Sinkiang).[7] As a

[6] *New York Times*, July 18, 1942.

[7] *Foreign Policy Association Bulletin*, October 2, 1942; and *New York Times*, July 6, 1943.

result, consulates were opened by other powers in Urumchi (Tihwa), capital of Sinkiang.

DEVELOPMENTS IN SINKIANG

Opening the road through Sinkiang drew world attention to other developments in that little known province, about which the Soviet and Chinese Governments have never issued a detailed report. The end result of the changes that took place was the significant reduction of Soviet economic interest in China's westernmost province. Geography for centuries had determined the main flow of trade and migration across what is now the frontier of China and Russia in Central Asia. Sinkiang, separated by more than a thousand miles of semi-desert from other populated provinces of China, had always traded across its western frontier. Many of its peoples, too, only a scant ten per cent being Chinese or Chinese-speaking, are in part related to the Kirghiz and Kazakhs, Uigurs, Uzbeks and other Mohammedan peoples of Soviet Central Asia.

Sheng Shih-tsai, until the fall of 1944 Governor of Sinkiang Province, came to power in 1933 after a number of years of serious disorders which he had put down with Soviet aid.[8] In the subsequent decade the Soviets extended considerable economic and technical aid to him. Through joint enterprises, certain local industries were established—notably, in recent years, some oil wells and refineries and mills. It was generally understood that several commercial agreements had been concluded between Soviet trading organizations and the provincial authorities, with loans amounting to perhaps several million gold rubles. Trade was carried on by a special agency, Sovsintorg. Soviet technicians in every field —education, public health, agriculture, transport, manufacture—were employed as advisers.

[8] See Eleanor Lattimore, "Behind the Sinkiang Incident," *Far Eastern Survey*, May 3, 1944.

The nature of this relationship, nevertheless, was not the same as that between the Mongol People's Republic and the U.S.S.R., nor did it become a source of public diplomatic friction between the two governments. There was no question of independence or autonomy for Sinkiang, or of separate diplomatic representation there. The Soviets maintained a consulate—not an embassy, and a trade agency—not a trade representative. Indeed on occasion, the Central Chinese Government publicly reassured Sheng that it understood his arrangements with the Soviets. In fact, despite frequent assertions by foreigners to the effect that Sinkiang was becoming independent of China and affiliated with the U.S.S.R., Chen Li-fu, Chinese Minister of Mass Training and Propaganda, stated in 1937:[9] "It is natural that Sinkiang and Russia have close relations, particularly in the economic sphere, since the geographical isolation of Sinkiang from China and its proximity to Russia makes for easier communications. But no attempt is being made to 'communize' the province, which is developing along the lines of the rest of China under General Sheng, who is completely loyal to Nanking [then the capital of China—H. M.]."

Nevertheless, the effort of the Central Government to bind the provincial governments more closely to itself led in 1942 to a complete reorientation in Sinkiang.[10] Local provincial officials were replaced by Kuomintang appointees. Soviet technical assistance and economic installations were completely withdrawn, and at the same time, many of the educational and social policies developed under Sheng during the period of Soviet advisers were abandoned or reversed.

From available reports, the change was effected smoothly enough, without recriminations over removal of enterprises which were of obvious use and value to Sinkiang Province.

[9] *New York Times*, October 31, 1937.

[10] "Report from Turkestan," *Time*, October 25, 1943; "Heart of Asia," December 6, 1943; "Sinkiang," *Life*, December 13, 1943; "The Story of Sinkiang," *Amerasia*, December 15, 1944.

One incident was reported in April, 1944 when Tass carried a protest against a Chinese attack on some Kazakhs who had evidently fled from Sinkiang into Outer Mongolia, with which the Soviets have the Mutual Assistance Pact. Chungking denied the report and nothing further was seen in the press about it. Subsequently, Moslem disorders in the province were asserted by some Chinese to be Soviet-inspired and equipped.[11]

UNDERLYING ATTITUDES

In spite of the correct official relations between Chungking and Moscow, an underlying tension between them is apparent from all the personal reports which have been coming out of Free China since 1942. The situation is somewhat reminiscent of the period in American relations with the Soviet Union in 1938 and 1939 when mutual suspicions were so strong that relations between the two countries were as if in a state of suspension, although formally they continued normal. This sort of thing cannot be documented as there are no overt actions to signalize it, but it is reflected in the press of the two countries.

From the Soviet side, press treatment of China after Pearl Harbor had been confined largely to progress reports on the fighting, or articles marking Chinese historical events. Without exception, they consistently praised Chinese resistance and expressed great friendship for the Chinese people.[12] They also backed Chiang Kai-shek as leader of China's war effort. However, in 1943, for the first time, an article appeared criticizing the Chungking government for failure to mobilize completely the human and economic resources

[11] Eleanor Lattimore, "Report on Sinkiang," *Far Eastern Survey*, April 11, 1945.

[12] Cf. "Soviet Union Greets China on Anniversary of 1911 Revolution," *Moscow News*, October 10, 1942; "Soviet Public Opinion Welcomes New Treaties by Britain, U.S.A. with China," *Moscow News*, January 20, 1943; "Review of the Chinese Fronts," *Krasnaia Zvezda*, March 25, 1943; "Six Years of the Japanese-Chinese War," *Krasnaia Zvezda*, July 7, 1943.

of the country.[13] Written by Vladimir Rogov, a veteran Soviet newspaper man in China, the article was very similar to many appearing in the American press, expressing concern over the internal situation in China. In fact it was relatively mild in its charges. Rogov, for example, mentioned the difficulties between the Kuomintang and the Communists. He did not attack Chiang, nor did he say that the Communists were the saviors of China. In reply to Chinese criticism of the article, Rogov wrote:[14] "In my article I described the heroic fight which the Chinese people under the leadership of Generalissimo Chiang Kai-shek have been carrying on against the invaders under difficult conditions. I noted the decision of the Chinese people to carry this liberating war on to full victory. At the same time I especially emphasized that the most important condition for victory, the most vital question to China is real unity of all national forces in the struggle for freedom and national independence."

He went on to say that he had been criticized for mentioning the Communists and replied by quoting a Chinese newspaper as advocating "decisive measures" against the Communists which would, in his opinion, mean civil war and diversion of forces from the national liberation war against Japan.

Since that time other Soviet writers have expressed the same concern.[15] *Izvestia* also carried a lengthy report on Congressman Mike Mansfield's report to Congress on his trip to China[16] which documented many of the causes for anxiety. Yet, any over-all summary of the Soviet press since 1941—or, for that matter, since 1937—would reveal a friendly atti-

[13] Vladimir Rogov, "The Situation in China (Personal Impressions)," *Voina i Rabochii Klass*, No. 5, 1943, pp. 17–22.

[14] *Voina i Rabochii Klass*, No. 8, 1943, p. 26.

[15] Cf. I. Aleksandrov, "On the Situation in China," *Voina i Rabochii Klass*, No. 14, July 15, 1944, p. 9; B. Grigorev, "China in its Eighth Year of War," *Bolshevik*, No. 17–18, September, 1944, p. 55; V. Avarin, "China at the Present Stage of the War," *Voina i Rabochii Klass*, No. 23, December 1, 1944, p. 9; I. Aleksandrov, "On the Situation in China," *Trud*, April 5, 1945.

[16] *Izvestia*, January 31, 1945. Representative Mansfield's speech appeared in the *Congressional Record*, January 16, 1945.

tude toward China and no question whatever about her right to the full fruits of victory.

Sections of the Chinese press have for many years been critical of the Soviet Union. For a time after Pearl Harbor, the criticism was directed against Soviet neutrality in the Far East, but more recently it has reversed itself and expressed fears of Soviet "claims" in case it should come into the war. There has been no basis in the Soviet record for believing that Moscow has territorial ambitions in Manchuria, even though it may be assumed that if the Chinese government in the post-war period returns to a policy of granting foreign concessions on railroads or other economic enterprises the U.S.S.R. will seek to participate in such concessions, especially in Manchuria. Rumors are also said to be circulating in Chungking about Soviet inspiration of the 1944 Sinkiang revolts mentioned above and even of Soviet leadership of the Chinese Communists, though the latter charge is unanimously denied by all foreign observers on the spot in China. In fact, the U.S.S.R. has been reported by all to have been scrupulously strict about confining all of its dealings to the Chungking government, and sending nothing to Yenan. Chinese concern over alleged Soviet ambitions in Manchuria or Korea is more probably a reflection of worry over the possible spread of the Chinese Communists and their united front "border governments" into Manchuria. Naturally the internal tension in China between the Kuomintang and the Communists cannot but aggravate such speculation about the U.S.S.R.

Whatever may be the story behind these unofficial and undocumented frictions, the Four-Power Accord signed in Moscow November 1943 pledging the cooperation of the Big Four in building the peace, has not suffered from any Sino-Soviet friction. Although China and the Soviet Union did not sit together at Dumbarton Oaks, nor were the two represented simultaneously at any international conference prior to the denunciation of the Soviet pact with Japan, the Soviets accepted the Chinese amendments to the Dumbarton Oaks plan. At the San Francisco Conference, the Chinese and the Soviet delegates seemed to share many views in common and it was reported that Premier T. V. Soong would return to Chungking from San Francisco via Moscow. It was thought that his negotiations there might lead to a general improvement of Soviet-Chinese relations and to more active cooperation between the two countries.[17]

RELATIONS WITH JAPAN

Although the period since Pearl Harbor, or since April 1941 when the Soviet-Japanese Neutrality Pact was concluded, was relatively peaceful in terms of border incidents, and although diplomatic relations outwardly remained normal, the overtones in Soviet-Japanese relations could never have been called cordial. Little more than a month after the Nazis crossed the Soviet border, the Japanese cabinet fell and Matsuoka, whose great triumph had been the Soviet-Japanese neutrality pact, went out of the government. Although a Japanese spokesman had declared in June that Japan would "remain faithful to her treaty obligations to both parties" in the Soviet-German war,[18] very shortly afterwards Japan began to do Germany's work. Rumors were circulated that the U.S.S.R. had given the United States bases in Kamchatka and Siberia. Tokyo let it be known that it would be in an "awkward and embarrassing position" if the United States gave aid to the U.S.S.R.[19] After the Japanese Foreign Office sent a note to Moscow questioning whether these American supplies were actually being shipped on to Europe or whether Vladivostok was being converted into America's "first line of defense against Japan," Molotov and Hull both rejected

[17] *New York Herald Tribune*, May 14, 1945. On August 15 it was announced that a Treaty of Friendship and Alliance had been signed by the U.S.S.R. and China, *New York Times*, August 15, 1945. For text see Appendix p. 265.
[18] *New York Times*, June 24, 1941.
[19] *New York Sun*, June 27, 1941.

any such interpretation or any right on the part of Japan to question the freedom of the seas for such shipments.[20] By October 1941, Japan was trying to exert pressure on the Netherlands East Indies to stop supplies to the U.S.S.R.[21]

Following Pearl Harbor much the same sort of official relations continued. While in January 1942 Vice-Commissar of Foreign Affairs Lozovsky reiterated Soviet adherence to its neutrality pact with Japan,[22] critical comment in the Soviet press and in public speeches continued. To mention but a few such items, there was in January 1942 a *Pravda* editorial reply to Japanese press speculations on the defeat of the U.S.S.R., advising the Japanese not to try to "divide the skin of the unkilled bear";[23] in April 1942, *Pravda* again carried a long and important editorial on the first anniversary of the Soviet-Japanese neutrality treaty, stating in part:[24]

"Momentous and stormy events which directly concerned both signatories of the Neutrality Pact have taken place in the past year. In violation of treaties which Germany had signed, it treacherously attacked the Soviet Union. . . . On November 25, 1941 Japan took part in the prolongation of the Anti-Comintern Pact . . . On December 7, 1941, Japanese troops suddenly attacked naval bases of the United States and Great Britain and war broke out in the Pacific . . . On December 11 of last year a new Tripartite Pact was signed by Japan, Germany and Italy . . .

"Thus the Neutrality Pact between Japan and the U.S.S.R. was subjected to serious trial. At the moment when the Soviet-Japanese Neutrality Pact enters the second year of its operation, we must say that despite the extremely complicated

[20] *New York Times*, August 13, 27, 28, 1941.
[21] *New York Herald Tribune*, October 3, 1941.
[22] *New York Times*, January 14, 1942.
[23] *Pravda*, January 28, 1942.
[24] *Information Bulletin*, Embassy of the U.S.S.R., Washington, D.C., April 14, 1942. For an analysis of the Soviet press attitude toward Japan, cf. Andrew J. Grajdanzev, "Japan in Soviet Publications," *Far Eastern Survey*, November 29, 1944.

and peculiar world situation, this pact has played a positive part and preserved its validity. It has preserved its validity in the first place because the Soviet Union has never violated treaties which it has signed.

"By its consent to prolonging for one year, on definite terms, the Soviet-Japanese Fisheries Convention, the Soviet Government confirmed its readiness to maintain normal business relations with Japan, based on sober consideration of mutual economic interests. For the further existence of the Neutrality Pact it is necessary that Japan show the same attitude toward treaties as displayed by the Soviet Union . . . It is necessary that the Japanese military fascist cliques whose heads are turned by military successes realize that their prattle about an annexationist war in the north may cause damage in the first place and most of all to Japan itself . . . "

We now know that the reference to the need for Japan to observe her treaty obligations was inspired by the fact that Japan had failed to carry out its agreement regarding Sakhalin made a year before (see below).

The persistence of a critical tone in the press of both countries and their open admission of full sympathy and confidence in their own allies did not impair the careful preservation of strict diplomatic neutrality. As various agreements were concluded by the U.S.S.R. with the Allies, the wording[25] permitted the exclusion of Far Eastern war commitments, just as Japan's Axis agreements exempted it from war with the U.S.S.R.

[25] *United Nations Agreement* of January 1, 1942. "Each government pledges itself to employ its full resources, military or economic, against those members of the tripartite pact and its adherents with which such government is at war." *Anglo-Soviet Alliance*, May 26, 1942 "Article I . . . The high contracting parties mutually undertake to afford one another military and other assistance and support of all kinds in war against Germany and all those states associated with her acts of aggression in Europe." *Moscow Declaration*, November, 1943: " . . . united in their determination . . . to continue hostilities against those Axis powers with which they respectively are at war until . . . unconditional surrender."

It will be recalled that the frequency and intensity of border incidents had in the years since Japan's invasion of Manchuria been a barometer of Soviet-Japanese relations. The last large-scale "incident" had been in 1939 on the border of Outer Mongolia and had been concluded hastily after the signing of the Soviet-German pact. Moreover, at the time the Soviet-Japanese Neutrality Pact was signed, an exchange of notes had in effect extended the pact to cover the borders of Outer Mongolia and Manchuria. However, the job of "redemarcating" the borders had never been completed. Further sections of the Mongolia-Manchuria border were marked and duly agreed upon during the months just preceding Pearl Harbor. Ratification took place even later—in May 1942. Although there were one or two vague reports of border clashes in the succeeding three years, nothing of any magnitude was made public.

On the other hand, there were two or three cases in which the Soviets accused the Japanese of sinking their ships. Such protests were recorded in 1942. It is worth noting that the sinkings took place, as far as we know, up to the time when the tide of war began to turn in favor of Russia. Despite the fact that in 1943 and 1944 a growing amount of Lend-Lease materials went to the Soviet Union via the Pacific, there seem to have been few incidents to interrupt the flow in this later period.

LONG-TERM FISHERIES AGREEMENT

In the other chronic problem of Soviet-Japanese relations, the Japanese fisheries in Soviet waters, a real change took place. Since 1936, the terms under which the Japanese were permitted to exercise their fishery rights obtained at Portsmouth, had been defined in annual agreements. However, this had not been according to Japanese desires, for Japan had sought to end her annual anxiety by concluding a long-term agreement. Twice (in 1940 and 1941) the yearly agreement included provision for negotiation of a convention; yet in both 1942 and 1943 the arrangements dealt only with one year (Agreement of March 20, 1942 and March 26, 1943). Moreover, each year, the rent rate was increased and the number of lots reduced slightly. Not until March 1944 was the situation clarified with the announcement of a long-term agreement, following Japan's rendition of its concessions on Northern (Soviet) Sakhalin.

The Soviets had always found the fisheries a good bargaining point, for there was nothing Japan could do about them "short of war" and they were a profitable enterprise for the important fishing industry of Japan. It is worth recalling that the two countries were on the verge of signing a basic long-term convention in 1936 to replace the original 1928 convention when the Anti-Comintern Pact was disclosed. The Soviets immediately broke off the parleys and refused to sign. Year after year, the bargaining had gone on. At the end of 1939, the Soviets, in return for a promise to reopen negotiations on the convention, had obtained the last payments on the Chinese Eastern Railway which had been in arrears nearly two years. At the beginning of 1941, the fisheries agreement had been accompanied by a settlement of the Matsuo Dockyard debt—a dispute nearly three years old. Finally, in 1944 the long-term convention was accomplished as part of a bargain struck in 1941 when the neutrality pact was signed.

The new five-year agreements[26] extended the 1928 convention with certain changes: exclusion of 24 lots previously worked by the Japanese; right of Soviet organizations to acquire up to 10 per cent of lots auctioned each year; increase in rents by 6 per cent. It also closed off more strategic areas and included an agreement that the Japanese would not work the lots held by them on the east coast of Kamchatka and in the Olyutorsk region "until the end of the war in the Pacific."

[26] See Appendix, p. 205.

In the protocol itself, one of the most important clauses was Paragraph 2, reaffirming complete Soviet sovereignty over the fisheries: "All questions relating to the fisheries, activities of the fish industry and citizens of the U.S.S.R. are not regulated by the Fisheries Convention or the documents attached thereto, as they fall exclusively within the competence of the U.S.S.R." The clause annulled all references to these matters in the old Convention.

TERMINATION OF THE SAKHALIN CONCESSIONS

But the most significant fact about this agreement was that it was preceded by the termination of Japan's eighteen-year-old concessions on Northern Sakhalin[27] which had been due to run until 1970. These oil and coal concessions had, in the past, been regarded as relatively important to Japan, which lacked oil especially. Since 1936, there had been considerable trouble over the concessions; the Soviets were suspicious of Japanese operations in the accumulation of unnecessarily large supplies of materials, use of naval vessels in exporting oil, and violations of various other working arrangements. The Japanese complained that the Soviets did not supply the necessary labor force and were slow in granting permits for pipelines, etc. It appears that production in the Japanese concessions was, in fact, declining, although the figures given by the Japanese may be low: 1943 oil output—16,000 tons, compared with 190,000 tons in 1933; coal—5,000 tons compared with 240,000 tons peak in 1935. Soviet figures for earlier years appeared to make the peak in Japan's exports of oil from Sakhalin nearer 300,000 tons.[28]

[27] It will be recalled that the Cairo Agreement, while enumerating the areas to be returned to China also stated: "Japan also will be expelled from all other territories which she has taken by violence and greed." This would apply to Southern Sakhalin, taken at the end of the Russo-Japanese War, 1905.

[28] *New York Herald Tribune*, April 1, 1944. In 1938, *Japan Weekly Chronicle* reported (March 17, 1938, p. 337) that in 1936 the Japanese got 200,000 tons of oil from Soviet Sakhalin and had a total of 255,000,000 yen invested in the fields.

For the Soviets, these concessions had become not only a nuisance but a menace, as their location made it impossible to have "naval secrets" in the most strategic section of its coast. The successive fishery agreements had taken from Japan those fishery lots in strategic areas but this accomplished little as long as the Japanese remained on Northern Sakhalin, provided with the necessary shipping facilities to the ports opposite the mainland.

According to the Soviet release which accompanied the new agreement, the annulment had been agreed upon in April, 1941 and should have been carried out within six months of the signing of the Neutrality Pact. It now appears that the events of June 22 changed Japan's view and it was not until the autumn of 1943 that "the Japanese government recognized the necessity and timeliness of the negotiations," as *Pravda* put it in an editorial explaining that Japan had delayed on the strength of Hitler's attack.[29]

The agreement provided that all the concessions[30] and the installations should be turned over to the U.S.S.R. immediately, in return for which the Soviet Union would pay five million rubles and would deliver annually 50,000 metric tons of oil "on ordinary commercial terms over a period of five consecutive years after the cessation of the present war."[31]

FOREIGN REACTIONS

The agreement caused widespread comment abroad, favorable and unfavorable. There were those who saw in it a great triumph of Soviet diplomacy based on a realistic

[29] *Pravda*, April 1, 1944.

[30] There were only two Japanese firms involved, one for coal and one for oil. The other coal concession had been liquidated in 1937 because the concessionaire had failed to begin exploitation of the mines. For a detailed account of the concessions, cf. A. Ilin, "On the Liquidation of the Japanese Concessions on Northern Sakhalin and the Five-Year Extension of the Fisheries Convention," *Bolshevik*, No. 9, May, 1944, pp. 67–73. For text of agreement, see Appendix p. 202.

[31] *Pravda*, March 31, 1944.

appraisal by Japan of the strength behind that diplomacy.[32] Others, saw behind it the same sinister alliance that they had seen behind every step taken by the U.S.S.R. to adjust its relations with Japan whether it was the sale of the C.E.R. or the Neutrality Pact. They found the agreement to be the cause of Japan's renewed offensives in China, reasoning that this agreement had somehow or other created that atmosphere of trust which none of the earlier agreements had achieved and thereby given Japan the courage to move some of its troops south from Manchuria. Aside from the fact that there were other compelling reasons inherent in Japan's military position at the time which may have dictated the new offensive in China, there was nothing in either the Japanese or Russian press which could be labelled "cordiality," not even in the announcements accompanying the new agreement.[33]

Others thought they found a loophole in the wording on oil shipments which were to run for five years after the "cessation of the war." What war? they asked. Perhaps it referred only to the European war. Editorially, *Pravda* had answered this directly: "The Soviet Union when concluding these agreements took into account the specific circumstances facing our Allies as a result of the war in the Pacific."[34]

RELATIONS WITH THE UNITED STATES AND GREAT BRITAIN

These suspicions simply underlined the fact that the development of the war alliance with the Western powers in regard to the European war had not yet dispelled completely from the public mind, especially in the United States, the

[32] *New York Herald Tribune*, April 2, 1944—"U.S. Hails Soviet Damming of Oil Flow to Japan"; April 9, 1944, "Sakhalin Pact Defect is seen in Washington"; April 12, 1944, "Welles Calls Moscow-Tokio Pact' (Concrete Advantage to Allies)."

[33] "Soviet Press Tone Hostile to Japan—No gratitude for Surrender of Sakhalin Concessions by Tokyo is seen by Papers," *New York Times*, April 9, 1944 (dispatch of W. H. Lawrence from Moscow).

[34] *Pravda*, April 1, 1944.

suspicions carried over from pre-war years. On the other hand, great strides had been made in drawing together the governments and peoples who will ultimately be concerned with the peace of the Pacific. For the United States, the first step had been taken June 25, 1941, when the government declared that the American Neutrality Act would not be extended to the Pacific and thus left the way open for Soviet imports from this country. This trade increased each month from the time Lend-Lease was originally extended to Russia; so that by April 1943 it was reported that one-third of Lend-Lease material was going to Russia across the northern Pacific and by the end of the European War the figure may even have been higher, especially if to the seaborne imports are added the thousands of planes flown in through Alaska. Following V-E Day it was officially announced that Lend-Lease shipments to Siberia and the Soviet Far East would be continued.[35]

The supplies were, of course, carried entirely in Soviet ships, many of which were obtained here under Lend-Lease, and they were entirely non-military supplies, in the technical sense. Under the Soviet-Japanese Neutrality Pact, Soviet ships passed freely through Japanese waters to Vladivostok and other Far Eastern ports, but they were subject to Japanese inspection for contraband. The planes, likewise, were flown into Siberia by Soviet pilots. On return trips, the ships carried lumber and sometimes ores. As a result of this commerce, the American west coast and Alaska became very conscious of the fact that they are next-door neighbors to the U.S.S.R. and can profitably exchange with that neighbor in peace, as well as in war. The sea route is as short from Seattle or Portland to Vladivostok as from New York to Murmansk, and much of Russia's future seems to lie in her eastern territories. The rest of the United States gained a similar realiza-

[35] *New York Times*, June 26, 1945.

tion from the trips of Ambassador Davies, Wendell Willkie and Vice-President Wallace, via Alaska.

On the other hand, note must be taken of the various rumors or "theories" which gained currency in the United States in regard to Soviet Far Eastern policy. First was the charge that the Soviets were "helping Japan." From time to time various versions of this rumor were widespread. One took the fantastic turn that the U.S.S.R. was giving Japan rubber which it had obtained from Lend-Lease—at a time when Japan had captured the largest rubber-producing areas in the world and the Soviets were "consuming" in battle tremendous quantities of rubber. Another version was that the Soviets were giving Japan meteorological information for operations in the north Pacific—this at a time when the Japanese still occupied some of the Aleutians.

Second, was the theory that the Soviets should give the United States air bases in Siberia from which to attack Japan. This plan at one time received considerable public support largely because the American public knew little of the strategic situation in that part of the world. The United States Army itself felt it necessary to refer as follows to this fallacious scheme in one of its orientation courses:[36] "If we or the Russians were to use these bases to bomb Japan, the bases would immediately be made useless and Russia would be involved in a two-front war. Russia is engaging the main Nazi strength and a two-front war for Russia would diminish the pressure on the worried Nazis and endanger the plans of our own army."

The circulation of such rumors brought forth denials in the Soviet press and also angry comment on the sources of the rumors, particularly the Hearst Press, the *Chicago Tribune* and individual commentators who gave them currency. The other press incident in connection with the Pacific war was the "Lady Bug" article, criticizing the Americans for declaring

[36] From *War Department Record*, An official U.S. War Department Film, issued in 1943.

Manila an open city.[37] Soviet officials apologized for it, stating that it represented only the opinion of the author Zaslavsky. The existence of such currents in public opinion could of course have led back to the atmosphere of 1931–1939 when public ill-will and misunderstanding so paralyzed government action that cooperation with the Soviet Union proved impossible. During and after the San Francisco Conference the anti-Soviet campaign in the American press became a matter of concern to the Administration itself.[38]

In Britain, on the other hand, the very close feeling of comradeship with the Soviet Union engendered by the European war went further to overcome pre-war ill-will. After 1941, Soviet relations with the British Empire changed even more radically than with the United States. The twenty-year alliance became the new basis. However, this change had little or nothing to do with the Pacific arena up until the end of the war in Europe. The most important steps there, in fact, were the establishment of diplomatic relations between the U.S.S.R. and the Dominions: Canada in June 1942, Australia in October 1942, and New Zealand in April 1944. Canada had previously refused to have any dealings with Moscow and it was even illegal for any Soviet citizen to enter the country. During the war, Canada sent considerable material to the U.S.S.R. under her mutual aid agreements. Some of this also was sent via the Pacific, and Canada is showing increasing interest in post-war trade arrangements with the Soviets.

DENUNCIATION OF THE SOVIET-JAPANESE NEUTRALITY PACT

As the end of the war in Europe approached, the rest of the world became increasingly concerned over Soviet attitudes

[37] *Pravda*, December 31, 1941.

[38] Cf. Radio address of Assistant Secretary of State MacLeish on May 26, 1945 and press conference of President Truman reported in the *New York Times*, June 14, 1945.

toward the war in the Pacific. Would Moscow consider its interest in the United Nations coalition at an end? The test by many was thought to lie in the Neutrality Pact with Tokyo which would be renewed automatically if neither party denounced it one year before its expiration date, April 25, 1946.

On April 5, the following announcement was made on the Moscow radio:[39]

"At 3 o'clock this afternoon the People's Commissar for Foreign Affairs of the U.S.S.R., Molotov, received the Japanese Ambassador, Mr. Sato, and in the name of the Soviet government made the following statement to him:

"The pact of neutrality between the Soviet Union and Japan was concluded on April 13, 1941—that is, before the attack by Germany on the U.S.S.R. and before the outbreak of war between Japan on the one hand and Great Britain and the United States of America on the other.

" 'Since that time the situation has radically changed. Germany attacked the U.S.S.R. and Japan—Germany's ally —helped the latter in her war against the U.S.S.R.

" 'In addition, Japan is fighting against the United States of America and Great Britain, which are the allies of the Soviet Union. In such a situation the pact of neutrality between Japan and the U.S.S.R. has lost its meaning and the continuance of this pact has become impossible.

" 'On the strength of the aforesaid and in accordance with Article 3 of the pact mentioned, which envisages the right of denunciation one year before the expiration of the five-year period of validity of the pact, the Soviet government by the present statement announces to the Japanese government its desire to denounce the pact of April 13, 1941.'

"The Japanese Ambassador, Mr. Sato, promised to bring the declaration of the Soviet government to the attention of the Japanese government."

[39] *New York Herald Tribune*, April 6, 1945.

Soviet editorial comment strengthened this statement by reiterating the fact that the denunciation "is a direct consequence of the fact that Japan is the ally of Germany, who is waging a vile piratical war on the Soviet Union, and that she is at the same time waging war on the United States and Great Britain, who are Allies of the Soviet Union."[40]

Although the pact had one more year to run, the Soviets felt completely released from any remaining inhibitions about commenting on Japan. The V-E Day press in Moscow carried in full President Truman's and Prime Minister Churchill's statements about the war with Japan, yet to be won.

Spring 1945 can well be taken as the beginning of a new period in Soviet Far Eastern history. The denunciation of the Soviet-Japanese Neutrality Pact, victory in Europe, and the opening of the San Francisco Security Conference together marked a sharp break with the recent past and afford an opportunity to build a new future in the Far East with the participation of the U.S.S.R. Needless to say, Moscow is preparing to interest itself in this future through the United Nations Organization. From the day-to-day record of Soviet Far Eastern policies over the last decade it is perhaps possible to draw some very general conclusions regarding the projection of these policies into the future. What is at stake in the Far East for the Soviet Union is the sanctity of its own frontiers, the most compelling of all national interests. For their protection Moscow is prepared to go to any lengths. Its past performance and its statements at San Francisco reemphasize Soviet belief in collective security as the best means to this end.[41] In his speech of

[40] *Izvestia* April 7, 1945. For full text, see Appendix, p. 260.

[41] In his opening speech in San Francisco, Foreign Commissar Molotov said: "You know there are millions of people in the Soviet Union who know how to defend their motherland to the last by means of arms. At the same time the people of our Soviet country are especially devoted with all their hearts to the cause of the establishment of general peace and are willing to support as best they can the efforts of other nations to create a reliable peace and security organization of nations." *Information Bulletin, Special Supplement*, May 24, 1945, Embassy of the U.S.S.R., Washington, D. C.

November 14, 1944, Stalin set the tone which is likely to prevail:[42]

"One cannot regard as an accident such distasteful facts as the Pearl Harbor 'incident,' the loss of the Philippines and other Pacific islands, the loss of Hongkong, and Singapore, when Japan as the aggressive nation proved to be better prepared för war than Great Britain and the United States of America, which pursued a policy of peace. Nor can one regard as an accident such a distasteful fact as the loss of the Ukraine, Byelorussia and the Baltics in the very first year of the war, when Germany as the aggressive nation proved better prepared for war than the peace-loving Soviet Union. . . . " To prevent the repetition of such aggression, there is only one means, he said, "in addition to the complete disarmament of the aggressive nations: that is, to establish a special organization made up of the representatives of the peace loving nations to uphold peace and safeguard security; to put the necessary minimum of armed forces required for the averting of aggression at the disposal of the directing body of this organization, and to obligate this organization to employ these armed forces without delay if it becomes necessary to avert or stop aggression and punish the culprits."

[42] *Information Bulletin*, Embassy of the U.S.S.R., Washington, D.C., November 14, 1944.

POSTSCRIPT

On August 8, 1945 Foreign Commissar Molotov handed the following statement to Japanese Ambassador Sato for transmission to the Government of Japan.[43]

"After the defeat and capitulation of Hitlerite Germany, Japan remained the only great power which still stands for the continuation of the war.

"The demand of the three powers, the United States, Great Britain and China, of July 26 for the unconditional surrender of the Japanese armed forces was rejected by Japan. Thus the proposal made by the Japanese Government to the Soviet Union for mediation in the Far East has lost all foundation.

"Taking into account the refusal of Japan to capitulate, the Allies approached the Soviet Government with a proposal to join the war against Japanese aggression and thus shorten the duration of the war, reduce the number of casualties and contribute toward the most speedy restoration of peace.

"True to its obligation as an Ally, the Soviet Government has accepted the proposal of the Allies and has joined in the declaration of the Allied powers of July 26.

"The Soviet Government considers that this policy is the only means able to bring peace nearer, to free the people from further sacrifice and suffering and to give the Japanese people the opportunity of avoiding the danger of destruction suffered by Germany after her refusal to accept unconditional surrender.

"In view of the above, the Soviet Government declares that from tomorrow, that is from August 9, the Soviet Union will consider herself in a state of war against Japan."

[43] *Information Bulletin*, Embassy of the U.S.S.R., Washington, D.C., August 11, 1945.

APPENDIX I: DOCUMENTS

*TREATY OF PORTSMOUTH, SEPTEMBER 5, 1905**

His Majesty the Emperor of Japan on the one part, and His Majesty the Emperor of all the Russias, on the other part, animated by the desire to restore the blessings of peace to Their countries and peoples, have resolved to conclude a Treaty of Peace, and have for this purpose, named Their Plenipotentiaries, that is to say:

His Majesty the Emperor of Japan: His Excellency Baron Komura Jutaro, Jusammi, Grand Cordon of the Imperial Order of the Rising Sun, His Minister for Foreign Affairs, and His Excellency M. Takahira Kogoro, Jusammi, Grand Cordon of the Imperial Order of the Sacred Treasure, His Envoy Extraordinary and Minister Plenipotentiary to the United States of America;

and His Majesty the Emperor of all the Russias: His Excellency M. Serge Witte, His Secretary of State and President of the Committee of Ministers of the Empire of Russia, and His Excellency Baron Roman Rosen, Master of the Imperial Court of Russia and His Ambassador Extraordinary and Plenipotentiary to the United States of America.

Who, after having exchanged their full powers which were found to be in good and due form, have concluded the following articles:

Article I. There shall henceforth be peace and amity between Their Majesties the Emperor of Japan and the Emperor of all the Russias and between their respective States and subjects.

Article II. The Imperial Russian Government, acknowledging that Japan possesses in Corea paramount political, military and economic interests, engage neither to obstruct nor interfere with the measures of guidance, protection and control which the Imperial Government of Japan may find it necessary to take in Corea.

It is understood that Russian subjects in Corea shall be treated exactly in the same manner as the subjects or citizens of other foreign Powers, that is to say, they shall be placed on the same footing as the subject or citizen of the most favoured nation.

* John van A. MacMurray, *Treaties and Agreements with and Concerning China* New York, 1921, pp. 522–525, as quoted in Yakhontoff, *op. cit.*, pp. 370–374.

It is also agreed that, in order to avoid all cause of misunderstanding, the two High Contracting Parties will abstain, on the Russo-Corean frontier, from taking any military measure which may menace the security of Russian or Corean territory.

Article III. Japan and Russia mutually engage:

1. To evacuate completely and simultaneously Manchuria except the territory affected by the lease of the Liao-tung Peninsula, in conformity with the provisions of additional Article I, annexed to this Treaty and:

2. To restore entirely and completely to the exclusive administration of China all portions of Manchuria now in the occupation or under the control of the Japanese or Russian troops, with the exception of the territory above mentioned. The Imperial Government of Russia declare that they have not in Manchuria any territorial advantages or preferential or exclusive concessions in impairment of Chinese sovereignty or inconsistent with the principle of equal opportunity.

Article IV. Japan and Russia reciprocally engage not to obstruct any general measures common to all countries, which China may take for the development of the commerce and industry of Manchuria.

Article V. The Imperial Russian Government transfer and assign to the Imperial Government of Japan with the consent of the Government of China, the lease of Port Arthur, Talien and adjacent territory and territorial waters and all rights, privileges and concessions connected with or forming part of such lease and they also transfer and assign to the Imperial Government of Japan all public works and properties in the territory affected by the above mentioned lease. The two High Contracting Parties mutually engage to obtain the consent of the Chinese Government mentioned in the foregoing stipulation.

The Imperial Government of Japan on their part undertake that the proprietary rights of Russian subjects in the territory above referred to shall be perfectly respected.

Article VI. The Imperial Russian Government engage to transfer and assign to the Imperial Government of Japan, without compensation and with the consent of the Chinese Government, the railway between Chang-Chun (Kuan-cheng-tzu) and Port Arthur and all its branches, together with all rights, privileges and properties appertaining thereto in that region as well as all coal mines in the said region belonging to or worked for the benefit of the railway.

The two High Contracting Parties mutually engage to obtain the consent of the Government of China mentioned in the foregoing stipulation.

Article VII. Japan and Russia engage to exploit their respective railways in Manchuria exclusively for commercial and industrial purposes and in no wise for strategic purposes.

It is understood that that restriction does not apply to the railway in the territory affected by the lease of the Liao-tung Peninsula.

Article VIII. The Imperial Governments of Japan and Russia with a view to promote and facilitate intercourse and traffic, will, as soon as possible, conclude a separate convention for the regulation of their connecting railway services in Manchuria.

Article IX. The Imperial Russian Government cede to the Imperial Government of Japan in perpetuity and full sovereignty the Southern portion of the island of Saghalien and all islands adjacent thereto, and all public works and properties thereon. The fiftieth degree of North latitude is adopted as the northern boundary of the ceded territory. The exact alignment of such territory shall be determined in accordance with the provision of additional Article II, annexed to this treaty. Japan and Russia mutually agree not to construct in their respective possessions on the island of Saghalien or the adjacent islands any fortifications or other similar military works. They also respectively engage not to take any military measures which may impede the free navigation of the Straits of La Perouse and Tartary.

Article X. It is reserved to the Russian subjects, inhabitants of the territory ceded to Japan, to sell their real property and retire to their country; but, if they prefer to remain in the ceded territory they will be maintained and protected in the full exercise of their industries and rights of property on condition of submitting to Japanese laws and jurisdiction. Japan shall have full liberty to withdraw the right of residence in, or to deport from, such territory, any inhabitants who labour under political or administrative disability. She engages, however, that the proprietary rights of such inhabitants shall be fully respected.

Article XI. Russia engages to arrange with Japan for granting to Japanese subjects rights of fishery along the coasts of the Russian possessions in the Japan, Okhotsk and Behring Seas.

It is agreed that the foregoing engagement shall not affect rights already belonging to Russian or foreign subjects in those regions.

Article XII. The Treaty of Commerce and Navigation between

Japan and Russia having been annulled by the War, the Imperial Governments of Japan and Russia engaged to adopt as the basis of their commercial relations, pending the conclusion of a new treaty of commerce and navigation on the basis of the Treaty which was in force previous to the present war, the system of reciprocal treatment on the footing of the most favoured nation, in which are included import and export duties, customs formalities, transit and tonnage dues, and the admission and treatment of the agents, subjects and vessels of one country in the territories of the other.

Article XIII. As soon as possible after the present Treaty comes into force, all prisoners of War shall be reciprocally restored. The Imperial Governments of Japan and Russia shall each appoint a special Commissioner to take charge of prisoners. All prisoners in the hands of one Government shall be delivered to and received by the Commissioner of the other Government or by his duly authorized representative, in such convenient numbers and at such convenient ports of the delivering State as such delivering State shall notify in advance to the Commissioner of the receiving State. The Governments of Japan and Russia shall present to each other, as soon as possible after the delivery of prisoners has been completed, a statement of the direct expenditures respectively incurred by them for the care and maintenance of prisoners from the date of capture or surrender up to the time of death or delivery. Russia engages to repay to Japan, as soon as possible after the exchange of the statements as above provided, the difference between the actual amount so expended by Japan and the actual amount similarly disbursed by Russia.

Article XIV. The present Treaty shall be ratified by Their Majesties the Emperor of Japan and the Emperor of All the Russias. Such ratification shall, with as little delay as possible and in any case not later than fifty days from the date of the signature of the Treaty, be announced to the Imperial Governments of Japan and Russia respectively through the French Minister in Tokyo and the Ambassador of the United States in Saint Petersburg and from the date of the later of such announcements this Treaty shall in all its parts come into full force.

The formal exchange of the ratifications shall take place at Washington as soon as possible.*

Article XV. The present Treaty shall be signed in duplicate in both the English and French languages. The texts are in absolute

* Ratifications were exchanged at Washington, November 25, 1905.

conformity, but in case of discrepancy in interpretation, the French text shall prevail.

In witness thereof, the respective Plenipotentiaries have signed and affixed their seals to the present Tieaty of Peace.

Done at Portsmouth (New Hampshire) this fifth day of the ninth month of the thirty-eighth year of Meiji corresponding to the twenty third day of August (fifth September) one thousand nine hundred and five.

(*Signed*) JUTARO KOMURA (L.S.)
(*Signed*) K. TAKAHIRA (L.S.)
(*Signed*) SERGE WITTE (L.S.)
(*Signed*) ROSEN (L.S.)

*AGREEMENT ON GENERAL PRINCIPLES FOR THE SETTLEMENT OF THE QUESTIONS BETWEEN THE UNION OF SOVIET SOCIALIST REPUBLICS AND THE REPUBLIC OF CHINA, MAY 31, 1924**

The Union of Soviet Socialist Republics and the Republic of China desiring to reestablish normal relations with each other, have agreed to conclude an agreement on general principles for the settlement of the questions between the two countries, and have to that end named as their Plenipotentiaries, that is to say—

The Government of the Union of Soviet Socialist Republics: LEV MIKHAILOVITCH KARAKHAN,

His Excellency the President of the Republic of China: V. KYUIN WELLINGTON KOO,

Who, having communicated to each other their respective full powers, found to be in good and due form, have agreed upon the following Articles:

Article I. Immediately upon the signing of the present Agreement, the normal diplomatic and consular relations between the two Contracting Parties shall be reestablished.

The Government of the Republic of China agrees to take the necessary steps to transfer to the Government of the Union of Soviet Socialist Republics the Legation and Consular buildings formerly belonging to the Tsarist Government.

Article II. The Governments of the two Contracting Parties agree to hold, within one month after signing the present Agreement, a Conference which shall conclude and carry out detailed arrangements relative to the questions in accordance with the principles as provided in the following Articles.

Such detailed arrangements shall be completed as soon as possible and, in any case, not later than six months from the date of the opening of the Conference as provided in the preceding paragraph.

Article III. The Governments of the two Contracting Parties agree to annul at the Conference as provided in the preceding Article, all Conventions, Treaties, Agreements, Protocols, Contracts,

* As published in English in the *Russian Review* of October 15, 1925, Washington, D.C. as quoted in Yakhontoff, *op. cit.*, pp. 387–395.

etc., concluded between the Government of China and the Tsarist Government and to replace them with new treaties, agreements, etc., on the basis of equality, reciprocity and justice, as well as the spirit of the Declarations of the Soviet Government of the years of 1919 and 1920.

Article IV. The Government of the Union of Soviet Socialist Republics, in accordance with its policy and Declarations of 1919 and 1920, declares that all Treaties, Agreements, etc., concluded between the former Tsarist Government and any third party or parties affecting the sovereign rights or interests of China, are null and void.

The Governments of both Contracting Parties declare that in future neither Government will conclude any treaties or agreements which prejudice the sovereign rights or interests of either of the Contracting Parties.

Article V. The Government of the Union of Soviet Socialist Republics recognizes that Outer Mongolia is an integral part of the Republic of China and respects China's sovereignty therein.

The Government of the Union of Soviet Socialist Republics declares that as soon as the questions for the withdrawal of all the troops of the Union of Soviet Socialist Republics from Outer Mongolia,—namely, as to the time limit of the withdrawal of such troops and the measures to be adopted in the interests of the safety of the frontiers—are agreed upon on the Conference as provided in Article II of the present Agreement, it will effect the complete withdrawal of all the troops of the Union of Soviet Socialist Republics from Outer Mongolia.

Article VI. The Governments of the two Contracting Parties mutually pledge themselves not to permit within their respective territories the existence and (or) activities of any organizations, or groups whose aim is to struggle by acts of violence against the Governments of either Contracting Party.

The Governments of the two Contracting Parties further pledge themselves not to engage in propaganda directed against the political and social systems of either Contracting Party.

Article VII. The Governments of the two Contracting Parties agree to redemarcate their national boundaries at the Conference as provided in Article II of the present Agreement, and pending such redemarcation, to maintain the present boundaries.

Article VIII. The Governments of the two Contracting Parties agree to regulate at the aforementioned Conference the questions relating to the navigation of rivers, lakes, and other bodies of water which are common to their respective frontiers, on the basis of equality and reciprocity.

Article IX. The Governments of the two Contracting Parties agree to settle at the aforementioned Conference the question of the Chinese Eastern Railway in conformity with the principles as hereinafter provided:

1. The Governments of the two Contracting Parties declare that the Chinese Eastern Railway is a purely commercial enterprise.

The Governments of the two Contracting Parties mutually declare that with the exception of matters pertaining to the business operations which are under the direct control of the Chinese Eastern Railway, all other matters affecting the rights of the National and the Local Governments of the Republic of China—such as judicial matters, matters relating to civil administration, military administration, police, municipal government, taxation and landed property (with the exception of lands required by the said Railway)—shall be administered by the Chinese Authorities.

2. The Government of the Union of Soviet Socialist Republics agrees to the redemption by the Government of the Republic of China, with Chinese capital, of the Chinese Eastern Railway, as well as all appurtenant properties and the transfer to China of all shares and bonds of the said Railway.

3. The Governments of the two Contracting Parties shall settle at the Conference as provided in Article II of the present Agreement the amount and conditions governing the redemption as well as the procedure for the transfer of the Chinese Eastern Railway.

4. The Government of the Union of Soviet Socialist Republics agrees to be responsible for the entire claims of the shareholders, bondholders and creditors of the Chinese Eastern Railway incurred prior to the Revolution of March 9, 1917.

5. The Governments of the two Contracting Parties mutually agree that the future of the Chinese Eastern Railway shall be determined by the Union of Soviet Socialist Republics and the Republic of China, to the exclusion of any third party or parties.

6. The Governments of the two Contracting Parties agree to draw up an arrangement for the provisional management of the Chinese Eastern Railway pending the settlement of the questions as provided under Sec. 3 of the present article.

7. Until the various questions relating to the Chinese Eastern Railway are settled at the Conference as provided in Article II of the

present Agreement, the rights of the two Governments arising out of the Contract of August 27 (September 8), 1896, for the Construction and Operation of the Chinese Eastern Railway, which do not conflict with the present Agreement and the Agreement for the Provisional Management of the said Railway and which do not prejudice China's rights of sovereignty, shall be maintained.

Article X. The Government of the Union of Soviet Socialist Republics agrees to renounce the special rights and privileges relating to all Concessions in any part of China acquired by the Tsarist Government under various Conventions, Treaties, Agreements, etc.

Article XI. The Government of the Union of Soviet Socialist Republics agrees to renounce the Russian portion of the Boxer indemnity.

Article XII. The Government of the Union of Soviet Socialist Republics agrees to relinquish the rights of extraterritoriality and consular jurisdiction.

Article XIII. The Governments of the two Contracting Parties agree to draw up simultaneously with the conclusion of a Commercial Treaty at the Conference as provided in Article II of the present Agreement, a Customs Tariff for the two Contracting Parties in accordance with the principles of equality and reciprocity.

Article XIV. The Governments of the two Contracting Parties agree to discuss at the aforementinned Conference the questions relating to the claims for the compensation of losses.

Article XV. The present Agreement shall come into effect from the date of signature.

In witness whereof, the respective Plenipotentiaries have signed the present Agreement in duplicate in the English language and have affixed thereto their seals.

Done at the City of Peking this Thirty-first Day of May, One Thousand Nine Hundred and Twenty-Four, which is the Thirty-first day of the Fifth Month of the Thirteenth Year of the Republic of China.

L. M. KARAKHAN (*Seal*) V. K. WELLINGTON KOO (*Seal*)

DECLARATION

The Government of the Union of Soviet Socialist Republics and the Government of the Republic of China declare that immediately after the signing of the Agreement on General Principles between the Union of Soviet Socialist Republics and the Republic of China of May 31, 1924, they will reciprocally hand over to each other all the real estate and movable property owned by the former Tsarist Government and China, and found in their respective territories. For this purpose each Government will furnish the other with a list of the property to be so transferred.

In faith whereof, the respective Plenipotentiaries of the Governments of the two Contracting Parties have signed the present Declaration in duplicate in the English language and have affixed thereto their seals.

Done at the City of Peking this Thirty-First Day of May, One Thousand Nine Hundred and Twenty-Four, which is the Thirty-First Day of the Fifth Month of the Thirteenth Year of the Republic of China.

Seals.

L. KARAKHAN
V. K. WELLINGTON KOO

DECLARATION

The Government of the Union of Soviet Socialist Republics and the Government of the Republic of China hereby declare that it is understood that with regard to the buildings and landed property of the Russian Orthodox Mission belonging as it does to the Government of the Union of Soviet Socialist Republics the question of transfer or other suitable disposal of the same will be jointly determined at the Conference provided in Article II of the Agreement on General Principles between the Union of Soviet Socialist Republics and the Republic of China of May 31, 1924, in accordance with the internal laws and regulations existing in China regarding property-holding in the inland. As regards the buildings and property of the Russian Orthodox Mission belonging as it does to the Government of the Union of Soviet Socialist Republics at Peking and Patachu, the Chinese Government will take steps to immediately transfer same as soon as the Government of the Union of Soviet Socialist Republics will designate a Chinese person or organization, in accordance with the laws and regulations existing in China regarding property-holding in the inland.

Meanwhile the Government of the Republic of China will at once take measures with a view to guarding all the said buildings and property and clearing them from all persons now living there.

It is further understood that this expression of understanding has the same force and validity as a general declaration embodies in the said Agreement on General Principles.

In faith whereof, the respective Plenipotentiaries of the Governments of the two Contracting Parties have signed the present Declaration in duplicate in the English language and have affixed thereto their seals.

Done at the City of Peking this Thirty-First Day of May, One Thousand Nine Hundred and Twenty-Four, which is the Thirty-First Day of the Fifth Month of the Thirteenth Year of the Republic of China.

Seals. L. KARAKHAN
V. K. WELLINGTON KOO

DECLARATION

The Government of the Union of Soviet Socialist Republics and the Government of the Republic of China jointly declare that it is understood that with reference to Article IV of the Agreement on General Principles between the Union of Soviet Socialist Republics and the Republic of China of May 31, 1924, the Government of the Republic of China will not and does not recognize as valid any treaty, agreement, etc., concluded between Russia since the Tsarist regime and any third party or parties, affecting the sovereign rights and interests of the Republic of China. It is further understood that this expression of understanding has the same force and validity as a general declaration embodied in the said Agreement on General Principles.

In faith whereof, the respective Plenipotentiaries of the Governments of the two Contracting Parties have signed the present Declaration in duplicate in the English language and have affixed thereto their seals.

Done at the City of Peking this Thirty-First Day of May, One Thousand Nine Hundred and Twenty-Four, which is the Thirty-First Day of the Fifth Month of the Thirteenth Year of the Republic of China.

Seals. L. KARAKHAN
V. K. WELLINGTON KOO

DECLARATION

The Government of the Union of Soviet Socialist Republics and the Government of the Republic of China jointly declare that it is understood that the Government of the Republic of China will not transfer either in part or in whole to any third Power or any foreign organization the special rights and privileges renounced by the Government of the Union of Soviet Socialist Republics in Article X of the Agreement on General Principles between the Union of Soviet Socialist Republics and the Republic of China of May 31, 1924. It is further understood that this expression of understanding has the same force and validity as a general declaration embodied in the said Agreement on General Principles.

In faith whereof, etc.

Seals. L. KARAKHAN
V. K. WELLINGTON KOO

DECLARATION

The Government of the Union of Soviet Socialist Republics and the Government of the Republic of China jointly declare that it is understood that with reference to Article XI of the Agreement on General Principles between the Union of Soviet Socialist Republics and the Republic of China of May 31, 1924:

1. The Russian share of the Boxer Indemnity which the Government of the Union of Soviet Socialist Republics renounces, will after the satisfaction of all prior obligations secured thereon be entirely appropriated to create a fund for the promotion of education among the Chinese people.

2. A special Commission will be established to administer and allocate the said fund. This Commission will consist of three persons two of whom will be appointed by the Government of the Republic of China and one by the Government of the Union of Soviet Socialist Republics. Decisions of the said Commission will be taken by unanimous vote.

3. The said fund will be deposited as it accrues from time to time in a Bank to be designated by the said Commission.

It is further understood that this expression of understanding has the same force and validity as a general declaration embodied in the said Agreement of the two Contracting Parties on General Principles.

In faith whereof, etc.

Seals. L. KARAKHAN
V. K. WELLINGTON KOO

DECLARATION

The Government of the Union of Soviet Socialist Republics and the Government of the Republic of China agree that they will establish equitable provisions at the Conference as provided in Article II of the Agreement on General Principles between the Union of Soviet Socialist Republics and the Republic of China of May 31, 1924, for the regulation of the situation created for the citizens of the Government of the Union of Soviet Socialist Republics by the relinquishment of the rights of extraterritoriality and consular jurisdiction under Article XII of the aforementioned Agreement, it being understood, however, that the nationals of the Government of the Union of Soviet Socialist Republics shall be entirely amenable to Chinese jurisdiction.

In faith whereof, etc.

Seals. L. KARAKHAN
V. K. WELLINGTON KOO

DECLARATION

The Government of the Union of Soviet Socialist Republics and the Government of the Republic of China, having signed the Agreement on General Principles between the Union of Soviet Socialist Republics and the Republic of China of May 31, 1924, hereby agree, in explanation of Article V of the Agreement for the Provisional Management of the Chinese Eastern Railway of the same date, which provides for the principle of equal representation in the filling of posts by citizens of the Union of Soviet Socialist Republics and those of the Republic of China, that the application of this principle is not to be understood to mean that the present employees of Russian nationality shall be dismissed for the sole purpose of enforcing the said principle. It is further understood that access to all posts is equally open to citizens of both Contracting Parties, that no special preference shall be shown to either nationality, and that the posts shall be filled in accordance with the ability and technical as well as educational qualifications of the applicants.

In faith whereof, etc.

Seals. L. KARAKHAN
V. K. WELLINGTON KOO

NOTE OF WELLINGTON KOO TO KARAKHAN

Peking, May 31, 1924.

DEAR MR. KARAKHAN:

On behalf of my Government, I have the honor to declare that, an agreement on General Principles for the settlement of the Questions between the Republic of China and the Union of Soviet Socialist Republics having been signed between us today, the Government of the Republic of China will, in the interests of friendship between the Republic of China and the Union of Soviet Socialist Republics, discontinue the services of all the subjects of the former Russian Empire now employed in the Chinese army and police force, as they constitute by their presence or activities a menace to the safety of the Union of Soviet Socialist Republics. If you will furnish my Government with a list of such persons, the authorities concerned will be instructed to adopt the necessary action.

I have the honor to remain,

Yours faithfully,
V. K. WELLINGTON KOO

NOTE OF KARAKHAN TO WELLINGTON KOO

Peking, May 31, 1924

DEAR DR. KOO:

I have the honor to acknowledge the receipt of the following Note from you under this date:

[A repetition of Wellington Koo's note follows.]

In reply, I beg to state, on behalf of my Government, that I have taken note of the same and that I agree to the propositions as contained therein.

I have the honor to be,

Very truly yours,
L. M. KARAKHAN

*AGREEMENT FOR THE PROVISIONAL MANAGEMENT OF THE CHINESE EASTERN RAILWAY May 31, 1924**

The Union of Soviet Socialist Republics and the Republic of China mutually recognizing that, inasmuch as the Chinese Eastern Railway was built with capital furnished by the Russian Government and constructed entirely within Chinese territory, the said railway is a purely commercial enterprise and that, excepting for matters appertaining to its own business operations, all other matters which affect the rights of the Chinese National and Local Governments shall be administered by the Chinese Authorities, have agreed to conclude an Agreement for the Provisional Management of the Railway with a view of carrying on jointly the management of the said Railway until its final settlement at the Conference as provided in Article II of the Agreement on General Principles for the Settlement of the Questions between the Union of Soviet Socialist Republics and the Republic of China of May 31, 1924, and have to that end named as their Plenipotentiaries, that is to say:

The Government of the Union of Soviet Socialist Republics: LEV MIKHAILOVITCH KARAKHAN.

His Excellency the President of the Republic of China: V. KYUIN WELLINGTON KOO.

Who having communicated to each other their respective full powers found to be in good and due form, have agreed upon the following Articles:

Article I. The Railway shall establish, for discussion and decision of all matters relative to the Chinese Eastern Railway, a Board of Directors to be composed of ten persons, of whom five shall be appointed by the Government of the Union of Soviet Socialist Republics and five by the Government of China.

The Government of the Republic of China shall appoint one of the Chinese Directors as President of the Board of Directors, who shall be Director-General.

The Government of the Union of Soviet Socialist Republics

* As published in the *Russian Review* of November 1st, 1925, Washington, D.C. as quoted by Yakhontoff, *op. cit.*, pp. 395–398.

shall appoint one of the Russian Directors as Vice-President of the Board of Directors, who shall also be the Assistant Director General.

Seven persons shall constitute a quorum, and all decisions of the Board of Directors shall have the consent of not less than six persons before they can be carried out.

The Director-General and Assistant Director-General shall jointly manage the affairs of the Board of Directors, and they shall both sign all the documents of the Board.

In the absence of either the Director-General or the Assistant Director-General, their respective Governments may appoint another Director to officiate as the Director-General or the Assistant Director-General (in case of the Director-General, by one of the Chinese Directors, and in that of the Assistant Director-General, by one of the Russian Directors).

Article II. The Railway shall establish a Board of Auditors to be composed of five persons, namely, three Russian Auditors, who shall be appointed by the Government of the Union of Soviet Socialist Republics, and two Chinese Auditors, who shall be appointed by the Government of the Republic of China.

The Chairman of the Board of Auditors shall be elected from among the Chinese Auditors.

Article III. The Railway shall have a manager, who shall be a national of the Union of Soviet Socialist Republics, and two Assistant Managers, one to be a national of the Union of Soviet Socialist Republics and the other to be a national of the Republic of China.

The said officers shall be appointed by the Board of Directors and such appointments shall be confirmed by their respective Governments.

The rights and duties of the Manager and Assistant Managers shall be defined by the Board of Directors.

Article IV. The Chiefs and Assistant Chiefs of the various Departments of the Railway shall be appointed by the Board of Directors.

If the Chief of Department is a national of the Union of Soviet Socialist Republics, the Assistant Chief of the Department shall be a national of the Republic of China, and if the Chief of Department is a national of the Republic of China, the Assistant Chief of Department shall be a national of the Union of Soviet Socialist Republics.

Article V. The employment of persons in the various departments of the railway shall be in accordance with the principle of equal representation between the nationals of the Union of Soviet Socialist Republics and those of the Republic of China.

Article VI. With the exception of the estimates and budgets, as provided in Article VII, of the present agreement, all other matters, on which the Board of Directors cannot reach an agreement shall be referred for settlement to the Governments of the Contracting Parties.

Article VII. The Board of Directors shall present the estimates and budgets of the Railway to a joint meeting of the Board of Directors and the Board of Auditors for consideration and approval.

Article VIII. All the net profits of the Railway shall be held by the Board of Directors and shall not be used pending a final settlement of the question of the present Railway.

Article IX. The Board of Directors shall revise as soon as possible the statutes of the Chinese Eastern Railway Company, approved on December 4, 1896, by the Tsarist Government, in accordance with the present Agreement and the Agreement on General Principles for the Settlement of the Questions between the Union of Soviet Socialist Republics and the Republic of China of May 31, 1924, and, in any case, not later than six months from the date of the constitution of the Board of Directors.

Pending their revision, the aforesaid statutes, insofar as they do not conflict with the present Agreement on General Principles for the Settlement of the Questions between the Union of Soviet Socialist Republics and the Republic of China, and do not prejudice the rights of sovereignty of the Republic of China, shall continue to be observed.

Article X. The present Agreement shall cease to have effect as soon as the question of the Chinese Eastern Railway is finally settled at the Conference as provided in Article II of the Agreement on General Principles for the Settlement of the Questions between the Union of Soviet Socialist Republics and the Republic of China of May 31, 1924.

Article XI. The present Agreement shall come into effect from the date of signature.

In witness whereof, the respective Plenipotentiaries have signed the present agreement in duplicate in the English language and have affixed thereto their seals.

Done at the city of Peking this Thirty-First Day of May, One Thousand Nine Hundred and Twenty-Four, which is the Thirty-First Day of the Fifth Month of the Thirteenth Year of the Republic of China.

L. Karakhan
V. K. Wellington Koo

*AGREEMENT BETWEEN THE GOVERNMENT OF THE UNION OF SOVIET SOCIALIST REPUBLICS AND THE GOVERNMENT OF THE AUTONOMOUS THREE EASTERN PROVINCES OF THE REPUBLIC OF CHINA, SEPTEMBER 20, 1924**

The government of the Union of Soviet Socialist Republics and the Government of the Autonomous Three Eastern Provinces of the Republic of China desiring to promote the friendly relations and regulate the questions affecting the interests of both parties, and to that end named as Plenipotentiaries, that is to say:

The Government of the Union of Soviet Socialist Republics: NIKOLAI CYRILOVITCH KOUZNETSOFF.

The Government of the Autonomous Three Eastern Provinces: *Chen-Tsian*, *Lui-Jun-Huan*, and *Jun-Shi-Min*.

The abovementioned delegates, having communicated to each other their respective full powers found to be in good and due form, have agreed upon the following articles:

ARTICLE I

Chinese Eastern Railway. The Governments of the two Contracting Parties agree to settle the question of the Chinese Eastern Railway as hereinafter provided:

1. The Governments of the two Contracting Parties declare the Chinese Eastern Railway is a purely commercial enterprise.

The Governments of the two Contracting Parties declare that with the exception of matters pertaining to the business of operations which are under the direct control of the Chinese Eastern Railway, all other matters, affecting the rights of the National and Local Governments of the Republic of China, such as judicial matters, matters relating to civil administration, military administration,

* Translated from the Russian text, as published in the *Documents of the Narcomindiel—The Soviet-Chinese Conflict of 1929*, Moscow, 1930, as quoted by Yakhontoff, *op. Cit.*, pp. 398–404.

police, municipal government, taxation and landed property (with the exception of lands required by the Chinese Eastern Railway itself) shall be administrated by the Chinese Authorities.

2. The time limit as provided in Article XII of the Contract for the Construction and Operation of the Chinese Eastern Railway of August 27th (September 8th), 1896, shall be reduced from eighty to sixty years, at the expiraion of which the Chinese Government shall enter gratis into possession of the said Railway and its appurtenant properties.

Upon the consent of both Contracting Parties the question of a further reduction of the said time limit (that is, sixty years) may be discussed.

From the date of signing the present Agreement the Government of the Union of Soviet Socialist Republics agrees that China has the right to redeem the Chinese Eastern Railway. At the time of redemption the two Contracting Parties shall determine what the Chinese Eastern Railway had actually cost, and it shall be redeemed by China with Chinese capital at a fair price.

3. The Government of the Union of Soviet Socialist Republics agrees on a Commission to be organized by the two Contracting Parties to settle the question of the obligations of the Chinese Eastern Railway Company in accordance with the Section 4 of Article IX of the Agreement on General Principles for the Settlement of the Questions between the Union of Soviet Socialist Republics and the Republic of China, signed on May 31st, 1924 at Peking.

4. The Governments of the two Contracting Parties mutually agree that the future of the Chinese Eastern Railway shall be determined by the Union of Soviet Socialist Republics and the Republic of China to the exclusion of any third party or parties.

5. The Contract for Construction and Operation of the Chinese Eastern Railway of August 27th (September 8th), 1896, shall be completely revised, in accordance with the terms specified in this Agreement, by a Commission of the two Contracting Parties in four months from the date of signing the present Agreement.

Pending the revision, the rights of the two Governments, arising out of said Contract, which do not contradict the present Agreement, and do not prejudice China's rights of sovereignty, shall be maintained in force.

6. The Railway shall establish for discussion and decision of all matters relating to the Chinese Eastern Railway a Board of Directors to be composed of ten persons, of whom five shall be appointed by

the Union of Soviet Socialist Republics and five by the Government of China.

China shall appoint one of the Chinese Directors as President of the Board of Directors, who shall be ex officio the Director General.

The Union of Soviet Socialist Republics shall appoint one of the Russian Directors as Vice-President of the Board of Directors, who shall also be ex officio the Assistant Director General.

Seven persons shall constitute the quorum, and all decisions of the Board of Directors shall have the consent of not less than six persons before they can be carried out.

The Director General and the Assistant Director General shall jointly manage the affairs of the Board of Directors and shall both sign all the documents of the Board.

In the absence of either the Director General or the Assistant Director General, their respective Governments may appoint another Director to officiate as the Director General or the Assistant Director General (in the case of the Director General, by one of the Chinese Directors, and in that of the Assistant Director General by one of the Russian Directors).

7. The Railway shall establish a Board of Auditors, to be composed of five persons, namely, three Russian Auditors who shall be appointed by the Union of Soviet Socialist Republics and two Chinese Auditors who shall be appointed by China.

The Chairman of the Board of Auditors shall be elected from among the Chinese Auditors.

8. The Railway shall have a Manager, who shall be a citizen of the Union of Soviet Socialist Republics, and two Assistant Managers, one to be a citizen of the Union of Soviet Socialist Republics, and the other a citizen of the Republic of China.

The said officers shall be appointed by the Board of Directors and such appointments shall be confirmed by their respective Governments.

The rights and duties of the Manager and Assistant Managers shall be defined by the Board of Directors.

9. The Chiefs and Assistant Chiefs of the various Departments of the Railway shall be appointed by the Board of Directors.

If the Chief of Department is a national of the Union of Soviet Socialist Republics, the Assistant Chief of the Department shall be a national of the Republic of China, and if the Chief of Department is a national of the Republic of China, the Assistant Chief of the Department shall be a national of the Union of Soviet Socialist Republics.

10. The employment of persons in the various departments of the Railway shall be in accordance with the principle of equal representation between the nationals of the Union of Soviet Socialist Republics and those of the Republic of China.

(*Note*: In carrying out the principle of equal representation the normal course of life and activities of the Railway shall in no case be interrupted or injured, that is to say the employment of the people of both nationalities shall be based in accordance with experience, personal qualifications and fitness of the applicants.)

11. With the exception of the estimates and budgets, as provided in Section 12 of the Article I of the present Agreement, all other matters, on which the Board of Directors cannot reach an agreement, shall be referred to the Governments of the Contracting Parties for a just and amicable settlement.

12. The Board of Directors shall present the estimates and budgets of the Railway to a joint meeting of the Board of Directors and the Board of the Auditors for consideration and approval.

13. All the net profits of the Railway shall be held by the Board of Directors and shall not be used pending a final settlement, in a joint Commission, of the question of its distribution between the two Contracting Parties.

14. The Board of Directors shall make a complete revision, as soon as possible of the Statutes of the Chinese Eastern Railway Company approved on December 4th, 1896, by the Tsarist Government, in accordance with the present Agreement and, in any case, not later than four months from the date of the constitution of the Board of Directors.

Pending their revision of the aforesaid Statutes, insofar as they do not conflict with the present Agreement and do not prejudice the rights of sovereignty of the Republic of China, shall continue to be observed.

15. As soon as the conditions of the redemption by China of the Chinese Eastern Railway are settled by both Contracting Parties, or as soon as the Railway reverts to China upon the expiration of the time-limit as stipulated in Section 2 of Article I of the present Agreement all parts of this Agreement concerning the same shall cease to have any effect.

ARTICLE II

Navigation. The Governments of the two Contracting Parties agree to settle, on the basis of equality, reciprocity and the respect of each other's sovereignty the question relating to the navigation of all kinds of their vessels on those parts of the rivers, lakes and other bodies of water, which are common to their respective borders, the details of this question to be regulated in a Commission of the two Contracting Parties within two months from the date of signing of the present Agreement.

In view of the extensive freight and passenger interests of the Union of Soviet Socialist Republics on the River Sungari up to and including Harbin, and the extensive freight and passenger interests of China on the lower Amur River into the sea, both Contracting Parties agree on the basis of equality and reciprocity to take up the questions of securing the said interests in the said Commission.

ARTICLE III

Boundaries. The Governments of the two Contracting Parties agree to redemarcate their boundaries through a Commission to be organized by both Parties, and, pending such redemarcation to maintain the present boundaries.

ARTICLE IV

Tariff and Trade Agreement. The Governments of the two Contracting Parties agree to draw up a Customs Tariff and conclude a Commercial Treaty in a Commission to be organized by the said parties on the basis of equality and reciprocity.

ARTICLE V

Propaganda. The Governments of the two Contracting Parties mutually pledge themselves not to permit within their respective territories the existence and (or) activities of any organization of groups whose aim is to struggle by acts of violence against the Government of either Contracting Party.

The Governments of the Contracting Parties further pledge themselves not to engage in propaganda directed against the political and social systems of either Contracting Party.

ARTICLE VI

Commissions. The Commissions as provided in the Articles of this Agreement shall commence their work within one month from the date of signing this Agreement, and shall complete their work as soon as possible and not later than six months. This does not apply to those Commissions, whose time-limits have been specified in the respective articles of this Agreement.

ARTICLE VII

The present Agreement shall come into effect from the day of signature.

In witness whereof, the respective Plenipotentiaries have signed the present Agreement in duplicate in the Russian, Chinese and English languages, and have affixed thereto their seals.

In case of dispute the English text shall be accepted as the standard.

Done at the city of Mukden, this Twentieth day of September of One Thousand Nine Hundred and Twenty-Four, which corresponds to the Twentieth day of the Ninth month of the Thirteenth year of the Republic of China.

DECLARATION I

The Government of the Union of Soviet Socialist Republics and the Government of the Autonomous Three Eastern Provinces of the Republic of China hereby declare that immediately after the signing of the Agreement of September 20th, 1924, between the Governments of the two Contracting Parties, the Government of the Autonomous Three Eastern Provinces of the Republic of China will hand to the Government of the Union of Soviet Socialist Republics the consular buildings formerly belonging to the Tsarist Government.

In faith whereof the Plenipotentiaries of the two Contracting Parties have signed the present Declaration in duplicate in the Russian, Chinese and English languages and have affixed thereto their seals.

In case of dispute, the English text shall be accepted as standard.

Done at the city of Mukden this Twentieth day of September of One Thousand Nine Hundred and Twenty-Four, corresponding to the Twentieth day of the Ninth month of the Thirteenth year of the Republic of China.

DECLARATION II

The Government of the Union of Soviet Socialist Republics and the Government of the Autonomous Three Eastern Provinces of the Republic of China mutually declare that after the signing of the Agreement of September 20th, 1924, between the Governments of the two Contracting Parties, if there are at present any Chinese in any employ of the Government of the Union of Soviet Socialist Republics which by their presence and (or) activity constitute a menace to the interests of the Autonomous Three Eastern Provinces of the Republic of China or if there are at present in the employ of the Government of the Autonomous Three Eastern Provinces of the Republic of China former Russian subjects, which constitute by their presence and (or) activity a menace to the interests of the Union of Soviet Socialist Republics, the respective Governments shall communicate to the other Party a list of names of such persons and shall instruct the respective authorities to take measures necessary to put an end to the activities or the employment of the aforesaid persons.

In witness whereof the Plenipotentiaries of the two Parties have signed the present Declaration in duplicate in the Russian, Chinese, and English languages and have affixed thereto their seals.

In case of dispute, the English text shall be accepted as standard.

Done at the city of Mukden this Twentieth day of September of One Thousand Nine Hundred and Twenty Four, corresponding to the Twentieth day of the Ninth month of the Thirteenth year of the Republic of China.

*THE SOVIET-JAPANESE CONVENTION OF JANUARY 20, 1925**

Regarding the Basic Principles of Interrelations between the Union of Soviet Socialist Republics and Japan

The Union of Soviet Socialist Republics and Japan, desiring to firmly establish mutual good-neighborly relations and economic cooperation, decided to conclude a convention regarding the basic principles of such relations and have for this purpose appointed their representatives, namely:

The Central Executive Committee of the Union of Soviet Socialist Republics appointed: Lev Mikhailovich Karakhan, Ambassador to China.

His Majesty, the Emperor of Japan appointed:

Kenkiti Yoshizawa, Envoy Extraordinary and Minister Plenipotentiary in China, Djushia, Chevalier, First Class Order of "Holy Treasure," who upon presenting to each other their respective credentials, these being found in proper and correct form, agreed upon the following:

Article I. The high contracting parties agree that with the coming into force of the present convention diplomatic and consular relations are established between them.

Article II. The Union of Soviet Socialist Republics agrees that the Treaty concluded in Portsmouth in September 5, 1905, remains in full force.

It is agreed that all treaties, conventions and agreements outside of the above mentioned Portsmouth treaty entered into between Japan and Russia up to November 7, 1917, will be revised at the conference which is to take place subsequently between the governments of the contracting parties, and that they may be changed or cancelled as will be called for by the changed circumstances.

Article III. The governments of the high contracting parties agree that with the coming into effect of the present convention

* As published in the *Russian Relief* of April 1, 1925, Washington, D.C., as quoted in Yakhontoff, *op. cit.*, pp. 404–410.

they will take up the revision of the fishing treaty of 1907 taking into consideration those changes which might have taken place in the general conditions since the said fishing treaty was concluded.

Until such a revised treaty is concluded the government of the Union of Soviet Socialist Republics will adhere to the practice established in 1924 in regard to the leasing of fisheries to Japanese subjects.

Article IV. The governments of the high contracting parties agree that with the coming into effect of the present convention they will take up the matter of concluding a treaty regarding trade and shipping in accordance with the principles set forth below and that until such a treaty is concluded the general relations between the two countries will be regulated by these principles:

1. Citizens and subjects of each of the high contracting parties, in accordance with the laws of each country, will have the right of (a) full freedom of entry, movement and stay in the territory of the other party, and (b) constant full protection of the safety of life and property.

2. In accordance with the laws of the country, each of the high contracting parties, gives on its territory, to citizens or subjects of the other party, to the widest possible extent and on conditions of reciprocity, the right of private ownership, as well as freedom to engage in trade, shipping, mining and other peaceful occupations.

3. Without prejudice to the right of each contracting party to regulate by its own laws the system of international trade in that country, it is understood that neither of the contracting parties will apply against the other party in particular any prohibitive measures, limitations or taxation, which might act as obstacles to the development of economic or other intercourse between the two countries; and both countries propose to grant to the trade, shipping and industry of each country, insofar as possible, the privileges of the most favored country.

The governments of the high contracting parties further agree from time to time, as circumstances may demand, to enter into negotiations to conclude special agreements regarding trade and shipping for the purpose of regulating and cementing the economic relations between the two countries.

Article V. The high contracting parties solemnly confirm their desire and intention to live in peace and amity with each other, conscientiously to respect the undisputed right of each State to arrange its own life within the limits of its own jurisdiction at its own desire, to refrain and restrain all persons in their governmental service, as well as all organizations receiving any financial support from them, from any open or secret action, which may in any way whatsoever threaten the peace or safety of any part of the territory of the Union of Soviet Socialist Republics or of Japan.

It is further agreed that neither of the high contracting parties will permit on the territory under its jurisdiction the presence of:

(a) Organizations or groups claiming to be the government of any part of the territory of the other party, or

(b) Foreign subjects or citizens, in regard to whom it has been established that they actually carry on political work for these organizations or groups.

Article VI. In the interests of the development of economic relations between the two countries, and taking into consideration the needs of Japan with respect to natural resources, the Government of the Union of Soviet Socialist Republics is ready to grant to Japanese subjects, companies and associations concessions for the exploitation of mineral, timber and other natural resources in all parts of the territory of the Union of Soviet Socialist Republics.

Article VII. The present convention is subject to ratification. Such ratification by each of the high contracting parties should be notified as soon as possible through the diplomatic representatives in Peking to the government of the other party, and from the date of the last of such notifications this convention comes into full force.

The formal exchange of ratifications will take place in Peking within the shortest possible time.

In testimony whereof the respective representatives have signed the present convention in duplicate, in English, and have affixed their seals thereto.

Drawn up in Peking, this twentieth day of January, in the year one thousand nine hundred and twenty five.

(*Signed*) L. KARAKHAN.
(*Signed*) K. YOSHIZAWA.

PROTOCOL (A)

The Union of Soviet Socialist Republics and Japan, upon signing this date the convention regarding the basic principles of interrelations between them, found it desirable to regulate certain questions in connection with the above convention and through their respective representatives have agreed upon the following stipulations:

Article I. Each of the high contracting parties binds itself to turn over to the other party the immovable and movable property belonging to the embassy and consulates of that party and actually situated on the territory of the first party.

In the event that it be found that the land occupied by the former Russian government in Tokio is situated in such a way as to interfere with the plans for laying out the city of Tokio or for serving the public needs, the government of the Union of Soviet Socialist Republics will be ready to consider the proposals, which may be made by the Japanese government with the view to eliminating such difficulties.

The Government of the Union of Soviet Socialist Republics will give to the Japanese government all reasonable facilities in the choice of suitable sites and buildings for a Japanese embassy and consulates to be established on the territory of the Union of Soviet Socialist Republics.

Article II. It is agreed that all questions regarding debts to the government or subjects of Japan in connection with State loans or treasury bonds issued by the former Russian governments, namely the imperial Russian government and its successor—the Provisional government—are left for decision at subsequent negotiations between the Government of the Union of Soviet Socialist Republics and the Japanese government.

It is intended that in regulating these questions the government or subjects of Japan, all conditions being equal, will not be placed in a less favorable position than that which the Government of the Union of Soviet Socialist Republics will concede to the government or citizens of any other country on the same questions.

It is also agreed that all questions relating to claims of the government of one party against the government of the other party, or of citizens of one party to the government of the other, are left to be regulated at the subsequent negotiations between the Government of the Union of Soviet Socialist Republics and the Japanese government.

Article III. In view of the fact that the climatic conditions in Northern Sakhalin prevent immediate transportation home of the Japanese troops now stationed there, these troops will be completely evacuated from the said region by May 15, 1925.

This evacuation must commence just as soon as climatic conditions permit, and in each and all of the districts in Northern Sakhalin thus evacuated by Japanese troops will immediately afterwards be restored full sovereignty of corresponding authorities of the Union of Soviet Socialist Republics.

Details regarding the transfer of administration and winding up the occupation will be arranged in Alexandrovsk between the commander of the Japanese army of occupation and representatives of the Union of Soviet Socialist Republics.

Article IV. The high contracting parties mutually declare that at the present time there exists no treaty or agreement regarding military alliance, or any other secret agreement concluded by either of them with any third party, which might constitute a violation of or threat to the sovereignty, territorial rights or national safety of the other contracting party.

Article V. The present protocol will be considered ratified with the ratification of the convention regarding the basic principles of the interrelations between the Union of Soviet Socialist Republics and Japan as signed this date.

In witness whereof the respective representatives have signed the present protocol in duplicate, in English, and affixed their seals thereto.

Drawn up in Peking, this twentieth day of January in the year One thousand nine hundred twenty five.

(*Signed*) L. KARAKHAN.
(*Signed*) K. YOSHIZAWA.

PROTOCOL (B)

The high contracting parties have agreed upon the following basic stipulations for concession agreements to be concluded during the period of five months from the day of complete evacuation of Northern Sakhalin by Japanese troops, as provided in Article III of Protocol (A), signed this date by representatives of the Union of Soviet Socialist Republics and of Japan.

1. The government of the Union of Soviet Socialist Republics agrees to give to Japanese concerns recommended by the Japanese government concessions for the exploitation of 50 per cent of the area of every oil-field in Northern Sakhalin, mentioned in the memorandum presented to the representative of the Union of Soviet Socialist Republics on August 29, 1924. In order to ascertain the area which is to be leased to Japanese concerns for such exploitation, each of the mentioned oil-fields is to be divided into checkerboard squares, from 15 to 40 dessiatins each, the Japanese being given such a number of these squares as will represent 50 per cent of the entire area; it being understood that the squares thus to be leased to the Japanese, should not as a rule be adjacent, but should include all wells which are now being drilled or worked by the

Japanese. As regards the remaining unleased oil lands mentioned in the same memorandum, it is agreed that should the government of the Union of Soviet Socialist Republics decide to offer these lands, in full or in part, on concessions to foreigners, Japanese concerns will enjoy equal chances in regard to such concessions.

2. The government of the Union of Soviet Socialist Republics will grant to Japanese concerns recommended by the Japanese government the right, for a period from five to ten years, of carrying on exploration work on the oil-fields along the eastern shore of Northern Sakhalin over an area of one thousand square versts, which must be allotted within a year from the date of the conclusion of concession agreements, and if, as a result of such exploration work by the Japanese, oil should be located, a concession for the exploitation of 50 per cent of the oil-field area thus established will be granted to the Japanese.

3. The government of the Union of Soviet Socialist Republics agrees to grant to Japanese concerns recommended by the Japanese government concessions for the exploitation of coal deposits on the western shore of Northern Sakhalin over a definite area, which is to be established by concession contracts. The government of the Union of Soviet Socialist Republics further agrees to grant to such Japanese concerns concessions for coal mining in the Dui district over an area to be established in the concession contracts. As regards coalfields situated outside the definite area mentioned in the previous two sentences, it is also agreed that should the government of the Union of Soviet Socialist Republics decide to offer them on concession to foreigners, Japanese concerns will be given equal rights in regard to such concessions.

4. The period of the concessions for the exploitation of oil and coal fields, as set forth in the previous paragraphs, is to be established for 40 to 50 years.

5. As payment for the above mentioned concessions Japanese concessionnaires will turn over annually to the Government of the Union of Soviet Socialist Republics—in the coalfields, from 5 to 8 per cent of the gross output; in the oil-fields, from 5 to 15 per cent of the gross output. It is proposed that in the event of striking oil gushers, the payment may be increased to 45 per cent of the gross production.

The percentage of production thus to revert as payment will be finally determined in the concession contracts, it being subject to change in accordance with the scale of annual production by a method to be established in the above mentioned contracts.

6. The said Japanese concerns shall have the right to cut timber necessary for the needs of the enterprise, and to erect various structures to facilitate communication and transportation of materials and products. The details in connection therewith will be stipulated in the concession contracts.

7. In view of the above mentioned rental and taking into consideration the unfavorable conditions, in which the enterprises will be placed owing to the geographical position and other general conditions in the said regions, it is agreed that there will be a duty-free import and export of all articles, materials and products necessary for such enterprises or produced in the latter, and that the enterprises will not be subject to such taxation or limitations as would actually make profitable exploitation impossible.

8. The government of the Union of Soviet Socialist Republics will provide for the said enterprises all reasonable protection and facilities.

9. The details in connection with the aforementioned articles will be stipulated in the concession contracts.

The present protocol is to be considered ratified with the ratification of the convention regarding the basic principles of interrelations between the Union of Soviet Socialist Republics and Japan as signed this date.

In witness whereof the respective representatives have signed the present protocol in duplicate, in English, and have affixed thereto their seals.

Drawn up in Peking, this twentieth day of January in the year One thousand nine hundred and twenty five.

(*Signed*) L. KARAKHAN
(*Signed*) K. YOSHIZAWA

Upon signing this day the convention regarding the basic principles of interrelations between the Union of Soviet Socialist Republics and Japan, the undersigned representative of the Union of Soviet Socialist Republics has the honor to declare that the recognition by his government of the validity of the Portsmouth treaty of September 5, 1905, in no way signifies that the government of the Union shares with the former Tsarist government the political responsibility for the conclusion of the said treaty.

Peking, January 20, 1925.

(*Signed*) L. KARAKHAN

*KHABAROVSK PROTOCOL**

(Signed at Khabarovsk, December 22, 1929)

On December 22, 1929, M. Simanovsky, representing the Moscow Foreign Office, and Mr. Tsai Yun-sheng, representing the Chinese Republic, signed the following protocol in settlement of the Chinese Eastern Railway dispute—*North China Daily News.*

1. Preliminary conditions of the Government of the U.S.S.R. understood by both parties in full conformity with the telegram of Mr. Litvinov of November 27 and the Nikolsk-Ussuriisk protocol of December 3 as restoration of the situation existing prior to the conflict and based upon the Mukden and Peking agreements.

All outstanding questions which have arisen during the period of joint Soviet-Chinese management of the Railway are to be solved at the forthcoming conference. Accordingly the following measures are to be immediately carried out:

(a) Restoration, on basis of the old agreement of the activity of the Management of the Chinese Eastern Railway and resumption by Soviet members of the management of their duties. Henceforth the Chinese Chairman of the Management and Soviet Vice-Chairman of the Management must act only jointly in conformity with article 6 of the Soviet-Mukden agreement.

(b) Restoration of the former proportion of offices held by Soviet and Chinese citizens and reinstatement (or immediate appointment of new candidates, should such be recommended on the Soviet side) of Soviet citizens, officers, chiefs and assistant chiefs of departments.

(c) Orders and instructions on the Chinese Eastern Railway issued on behalf of Management and Administration of Chinese Eastern Railway beginning on July 10, 1929, are considered invalid unless properly confirmed by the local management and administration of the road.

RELEASE OF PRISONERS

2. All Soviet citizens without exception arrested by Chinese authorities after May 1, 1929, and in connection with the conflict

* *China Year Book, 1931*, pp. 497–498.

immediately to be released without subdivision into any categories, including Soviet citizens arrested during the search of the Harbin Consulate on May 27, 1929.

The Government of the U.S.S.R. also immediately release all Chinese citizens without exception arrested in connection with the conflict and interned Chinese soldiers and officers.

3. All workers and employees of the C.E.R. citizens of the U.S.S.R. discharged or resigned, beginning July 10, to be given the right and opportunity immediately to return to positions held prior to discharge and to receive money owing them from C.E.R.

Those discharged and resigned, who fail to utilize this right must immediately be paid full wages, pensions dues, etc. owing to them.

Vacancies may be filled only by a proper order of the lawful management and administration of the C.E.R. and all former Russian citizens non-citizens of the U.S.S.R. employed by C.E.R. during conflict must be summarily and immediately discharged.

4. Chinese authorities immediately to disarm the Russian White Guards detachments and deport from the Three Eastern Provinces their organizers and inspirers.

RESTORATION OF CONSULATES

5. Leaving open the question of resumption of full diplomatic and consular relations between U.S.S.R. and China until the Soviet-Chinese Conference, both parties consider possible and necessary the immediate restoration of Soviet Consulates in the territory of the Three Eastern Provinces and Chinese Consulates at respective points of the Soviet Far East. In view of the fact that U.S.S.R. Government declared on May 21, 1929, that "since the Chinese Authorities have proved by all their actions their clear unwillingness and inability to reckon with the generally accepted principles of International Law and customs, it on its part does not henceforth regard itself bound by these principles in relation to Chinese representation in Moscow and Chinese Consulates in Soviet Territory and that this representation and these Consulates will no longer enjoy the extraterritoriality to which International Law entitles them," and that both parties intend to restore consular relations between them on a basis conforming with the principles of International Law and customs, the Mukden Government declares that it undertakes to assure the Soviet Consulates in the territory of the Three Eastern Provinces full inviolability and all privileges to which international law and custom entitle them and will of course

refrain from any action violating this inviolability and these privileges. On its part the Government of the U.S.S.R. discontinues the special Regime established by it between May 21, 1929, and the rupture of relations for Chinese Consulates and grants these Consulates, which are to be restored by virtue of the first clause of this point, in the territory of the Soviet Far East, all privileges and the full inviolability to which international law and custom entitle them.

RESUMPTION OF COMMERCE

6. With restoration of Consulates, opportunity immediately is given for the resumption of normal activity of all Soviet business organizations existing before the conflict within the Three Eastern Provinces.

Similar opportunity is offered to restore Chinese commercial enterprises which existed within the U.S.S.R. and whose operations were discontinued in connection with the C.E.R. conflict.

The question of commercial relations between the two countries as a whole to be settled at the Soviet Chinese Conference.

7. The question of real guarantees of observance of agreements and the interests of both sides are to be solved at the forthcoming conference.

8. The Soviet-Chinese Conference to regulate all outstanding questions to be held at Moscow on January 25, 1930.

9. The peaceful situation on the frontiers of China and the U.S.S.R. to be restored immediately with the subsequent withdrawal of troops by both sides.

10. This protocol comes into force from the moment of its signature.

*PROTOCOL OF MUTUAL ASSISTANCE BETWEEN U.S.S.R. AND THE MONGOL PEOPLE'S REPUBLIC, MARCH 12, 1936**

The Governments of the Union of Soviet Socialist Republics and the Mongol People's Republic, taking into consideration the unalterable friendship existing between their countries since the liberation of the territory of the Mongol People's Republic with the support of the Red Army, in 1921, from the White Guard detachments, connected with the military forces, which invaded the territory of the Union of Soviet Socialist Republics,

and desirous to maintain peace in the Far East and to contribute to the further strengthening of the existing friendly relations between them,

have decided to formulate in the shape of the present Protocol the gentlemen's agreement which exists between them since November 27, 1934, which stipulates mutual assistance by all possible means for the cause of averting and preventing the menace of aggression, and to give to each other aid and assistance in the case of aggression on the part of any third party against the Union of Soviet Socialist Republics or the Mongol People's Republic, and to this end to sign the present Protocol.

Article 1. In the event of menace of aggression on the territory of the Union of Soviet Socialist Republics or the Mongol People's Republic on the part of a third state, the Governments of the Union of Soviet Socialist Republics and the Mongol People's Republic undertake immediately to consider jointly the situation that has arisen and to take all measures which should be necessary for the protection and security of their territories.

Article 2. The Governments of the Union of Soviet Socialist Republics and of the Mongol People's Republic undertake in the event of military aggression against one of the Contracting Parties to give each other every assistance, including military assistance.

Article 3. The Governments of the Union of Soviet Socialist Republics and of the Mongol People's Republic regard it as under-

* M. Litvinov, *Against Aggression, op. cit.*, p. 192.

stood, that the troops of one of the parties stationed by mutual agreement on the territory of the other party by way of fulfillment of the obligations set forth in Articles 1 or 2 will be withdrawn from the territory concerned immediately the necessity for it ceases—similarly to what took place in 1925 with regard to the withdrawal of Soviet troops from the territory of the Mongol People's Republic.

Article 4. The present protocol is drawn up in duplicate in the Russian and Mongolian languages, both texts being equally authentic.

It shall come into force from the date of its being signed and shall remain in force for ten years.

Done at Ulan Bator, March 12, 1936.

*TREATY OF NON-AGGRESSION BETWEEN THE U.S.S.R. AND THE REPUBLIC OF CHINA, AUGUST 21, 1937**

The Government of the Union of Soviet Socialist Republics and the National Government of the Republic of China, animated by the desire to contribute to the maintenance of general peace, to consolidate the amicable relations now existing between them on a firm and lasting basis, and to confirm in a more precise manner the obligations mutually undertaken under the Treaty for the Renunciation of War signed in Paris on August 27th, 1928, have resolved to conclude the present Treaty and have for this purpose appointed as their plenipotentiaries, that is to say:

[Here follow the names of the plenipotentiaries]

Who, having communicated their full powers, found in good and due form, have agreed upon the following Articles:

Article 1. The two High Contracting Parties solemnly reaffirm that they condemn recourse to war for the solution of international controversies and that they renounce it as an instrument of national policy in their relations with each other, and in pursuance of this pledge, they undertake to refrain from any aggression against each other either individually or jointly with one or more other Powers.

Article 2. In the event that either of the High Contracting Parties should be subjected to aggression on the part of one or more third Powers, the other High Contracting Party obligates itself not to render assistance of any kind, either directly or indirectly to such third Power or Powers at any time during the entire conflict, and also to refrain from taking any action or entering into any agreement which may be used by the aggressor or aggressors to the disadvantage of the Party subjected to aggression.

Article 3. The provisions of the present Treaty shall not be so interpreted as to affect or modify the rights and obligations arising, in respect of the High Contracting Parties, out of bilateral or multilateral treaties or agreements of which both High Contracting Parties are signatories and which were concluded prior to the entering into force of the present Treaty.

* *ibid.*, p. 168.

Article 4. The present Treaty is drawn up in duplicate in English. It comes into force on the day of signature by the abovementioned plenipotentiaries and shall remain in force for a period of five years. Either of the High Contracting Parties may notify the other, six months before the expiration of the period, of its desire to terminate the Treaty. In case both Parties fail to do so in time, the Treaty shall be considered as being automatically extended for a period of two years after the expiration of the first period. Should neither of the High Contracting Parties notify the other, six months before the expiration of the two year period, of its desire to terminate the Treaty, it shall continue in force for another period of two years, and so on successively.

In witness whereof the respective plenipotentiaries have signed the present Treaty, and have affixed thereunto their seals.

Done at Nanking, the twenty-first day of August, 1937.

[Here follow the signatures]

*TRADE TREATY BETWEEN THE U.S.S.R. AND THE REPUBLIC OF CHINA, JUNE 16, 1939**

The Government of the Union of Soviet Socialist Republics and the National Government of the Republic of China, inspired by the wish to strengthen and develop friendly relations and trade relations between both countries decided to conclude a Trade Treaty, based on principles of equality, reciprocity, and respect for each other's sovereignty, and for this purpose appointed their Plenipotentiaries, namely:

The Presidium of the Supreme Soviet of the Union of Soviet Socialist Republics:

Mikoyan, Anastas Ivanovich, People's Commissar of Foreign Trade of the Union of Soviet Socialist Republics

His Excellency, the President of the National Government of the Republic of China:

Mr. Sun-fo, Special Envoy and Plenipotentiary of the National Government of the Republic of China,

who, upon exchange of their credentials, which have been found to be in proper form and due order, agreed upon the following decisions:

ARTICLE I

The products of the soil and of industry, derived and brought from the territory of one of the Contracting Parties, shall not be subjected, upon importation into the territory of the other Party to a different or less favorable regime, as regards customs, than that which is applied or will be applied to similar products derived and imported from any third country.

In a like manner, products of the soil and industry, derived and exported from the territory of one of the Contracting Parties, destined for the territory of the other Party shall not be subjected, upon their export, to a different or less favorable regime, as regards

* *Vedomosti Verkhovnogo Soveta SSSR*, June 15, 1940. Note: This is not the official text of this treaty. It is a translation from the Russian text.

customs, than that which is applied or will be applied to similar products exported to any third country.

Therefore, under the most favorable regime, provided above in this article, which is granted or shall be granted in the future to any third country, will come the following, in particular:

a.) Customs duties, additions to them, as well as charges of all kinds on imports as well as on exports;

b.) terms of collection of the said duties, additions and charges;

c.) customs regulations;

d.) the placing of goods in warehouses; the use of customs warehouses for them; regulation of the arrival and storing of goods in customs or other public warehouses, and of their removal therefrom.

e.) methods of checking and analyzing goods; terms for allowing the importation of goods or for applying to them preferences with regard to customs charges, depending on the composition of the goods, their purity, sanitary conditions, etc.

f.) customs classification and interpretation of the tariffs to be applied.

ARTICLE II

Neither of the Contracting Parties shall set up, with regard to the products of the soil and industry of the other Party, imported into its territory, any prohibitions or limitations whatsoever not applied to similar objects originating in any third country.

Similarly, neither of the Contracting Parties shall set up, with regard to products of its own soil and industry, exported to the territory of the other Party any prohibitions or limitations whatsoever, which are not applied to like objects, exported to any third country.

However, both Contracting Parties reserve the right, for reasons of state security; public safety; public health; the protection of animals and plants; for assuring the safety of objects of art; archaeological and historical valuables; for the protection of state monopolies belonging to the Parties; or for monopolies which are under their control; also for the purpose of regulating transactions with platinum, gold and silver, or with coins or other objects produced from them—to establish at any time prohibitions and limitations for import and export, if such prohibitions or limitations are equally applied in similar circumstances to any third country.

In like manner, each of the Contracting Parties has the right to establish with regard to products of the soil and industry of the other Party imported to its territory, or with regard to products of its own soil and industry exported to the territory of the other Party, prohibitions or limitations which are necessary for fulfilling international obligations, in which both Contracting Parties are participating or will participate.

ARTICLE III

Goods imported to the territory of one of the Contracting Parties from the territory of the other Party, or exported from the territory of one Party destined for the territory of the other Party, must pass only through those ports and localities of the country where there are established customs offices. Any violation of this provision shall be considered as smuggling and shall be dealt with according to the existing laws and regulations of the country.

ARTICLE IV

As regards imposing, on the territory of one of the Contracting Parties on the goods of the other Party, internal levies which are collected on the production, processing and consumption of certain goods, no matter in whose name or for whose account such levies are collected, each of the Contracting Parties is obligated to apply such a regime, as is or will be established for its own goods of a like nature, or the most favorable regime, which is accorded or may be accorded in the future to goods of a like nature of a third country, if such a regime is more favorable to the other Party.

ARTICLE V

All vessels, which are considered under the laws and regulations of the Union of Soviet Socialist Republics, Soviet vessels; and all vessels, which are considered under the laws and regulations of the Republic of China, Chinese vessels, shall be looked upon, in everything which pertains to the application of this treaty, as Soviet or Chinese vessels respectively.

ARTICLE VI

Vessels of one of the Contracting Parties, entering the territorial waters of the other Party, are strictly forbidden to conceal their nationality by means of sailing under the flag of any other country. Upon violation of this statute the vessel together with the freight which is on it will be subject to confiscation by order of the government of the Party whose territorial waters it entered.

ARTICLE VII

Each of the Contracting Parties shall afford to the seagoing vessels of the other Party in its sea ports and territorial waters the treatment, which is afforded or will be afforded to the seagoing vessels of any third party.

This treatment shall particularly apply to the terms of entry of vessels into the sea ports and territorial waters of the other Party; their remaining in them and their departure from them; to the full use of the appliances and facilities for shipping; to trade operations pertaining to seagoing vessels, freights, passengers and baggage; to various preferences pertaining to the assignment of space at wharfs for loading and unloading; fines, duties and all kinds of dues imposed upon and collected in the name of or for the account of the government, of public authorities or of various institutions.

ARTICLE VIII

Vessels, which ply under a flag of one of the Contracting Parties and enter the ports of the other Party for the purpose of loading or partial unloading of its freight, shall have the opportunity—in accordance with the existing laws and regulations of the country—to proceed with their freight to another port of the same country or to a third country without being obliged to pay any duty or dues on its freight whatsoever, or for the part of the freight which was not unloaded, with the exception of dues for inspection, which dues shall not exceed the amounts paid under the same circumstances by vessels of any third country.

ARTICLE IX

Vessels of one of the Contracting Parties, in cases of shipwreck, storm, running aground or other similar occurrences, which take place near the shores of the other Party, shall have the opportunity to enter temporarily the nearest harbors, ports or bays of the latter for shelter or repairs. The local authorities will notify the nearest consulate of the country, to which the vessel which sustained damage belongs, and will extend the necessary aid and assistance in accordance with international practices. Such vessels shall be permitted to conduct repairs and to obtain the necessary provisions, and they shall then have the right to continue their course without being obliged to pay taxes, duties or port dues. With regard to expenses for salvage, the laws of the country in which the salvage work was conducted will be applied.

In case such vessels will be obliged to unload and sell their goods on board, they shall pay taxes, duties and dues in accordance with the laws and regulations of the country in which they find themselves.

ARTICLE X

Inland and coastal navigation in the territory of one of the Contracting Parties shall be closed to citizens, economic organizations and vessels of the other Party.

Citizens and economic organizations of both Contracting Parties shall have the right to sail and fish in the rivers, lakes and waters which are common for both countries, in accordance with the regulations, which will be issued for this purpose upon agreement of the governments of both Contracting Parties.

ARTICLE XI

In view of the fact that in accordance with the laws of the Union of Soviet Socialist Republics the monopoly of foreign trade belongs to the state, comprising one of the inalienable bases of the socialist order secured by the Constitution of the U.S.S.R., the Union of Soviet Socialist Republics shall have as part of its Embassy in China a Trade Representation, whose legal status shall be determined by resolutions attached to this Treaty. This annex is an inseparable part of the Trade Treaty.

ARTICLE XII

Chinese merchants and industrialists, physical and juridical persons, formed in accordance with the laws of the Republic of China, shall enjoy with regard to their persons and property, as favorable treatment as that enjoyed by citizens, or corresponding juridical persons of any third country, when they are carrying on their economic activity on the territory of the Union of Soviet Socialist Republics under conditions in which such activity is permitted by Soviet law.

State Economic Organizations of the Union of Soviet Socialist Republics, which enjoy the rights of a juridical person, and other Soviet juridical persons, which in accordance with Soviet laws, enjoy civil rights, as well as physical persons, citizens of the Union of Soviet Socialist Republics, shall enjoy with regard to their persons and property as favorable treatment as that enjoyed by the citizens or corresponding juridical persons of any third country when they are carrying on their economic activity on the territory of the Republic of China under conditions in which such activity is permitted by law of the Republic of China.

All commercial companies formed in accordance with the laws and regulations of one of the Contracting Parties and cooperative organizations, as well as state Economic Organizations, which enjoy the right of a juridical person, shall have the right—in accordance with the laws and regulations of the other Party—to open their branches and representations on the territory of the latter and to carry on their economic activity.

In particular, citizens, or juridical persons of either Contracting Party shall have the right, personally or through their counsel, to appear in the courts of the other Party and shall enjoy free and easy access to courts. In this respect they shall not be subjected to any other limitations than those which are stipulated or shall be stipulated by laws and regulations in effect on the territory of the said other Party and shall in any case be subject to treatment which is or may be applied to citizens and to corresponding juridical persons of any third country.

ARTICLE XIII

This Treaty is drawn up in duplicate: each in Russian, Chinese and English.

In cases of disagreement on questions of interpretation of the Treaty, the English text shall be decisive.

The Contracting Parties agree that when controversies arise, they shall turn the question over to a Conciliation Committee, which must present to them its proposals within a reasonable time. The Conciliation Committee is composed of six members—the Governments of each of the Contracting Parties to name three members.

ARTICLE XIV

This Treaty shall in the shortest possible period be ratified by the Contracting Parties in accordance with their constitutional requirements.

An exchange of ratification papers shall take place in Chungking.

ARTICLE XV

This Treaty shall come into effect immediately upon the exchange of ratification papers.

The Treaty is concluded for a period of three years. Each of the Contracting Parties may inform the other Party, three months before the expiration of this period, of its wish not to extend the Treaty. In case neither of the Contracting Parties does this in due time, the Treaty will automatically be considered as extended for a period of one year from the termination of the first period. If neither of the Contracting Parties informs the other Party three months before the expiration of the annual period of its intention not to continue the Treaty in force, the Treaty remains in force for the next yearly period, and so on in the future.

In certification of which the above-named Plenipotentiaries have signed this Treaty and affixed to it their seals.

Executed in Moscow on June 16, 1939.

MIKOYAN
SUN-FO

ANNEX

to the Trade Treaty between the Union of Soviet Socialist Republics and the Republic of China of June 16, 1939.

Regarding the juridical position of the Trade Representation of the USSR in the Republic of China.

1. The Trade Representation of the Union of Soviet Socialist Republics in China shall perform the following functions:

a) aid in the development of economic relations between the Union of Soviet Socialist Republics and the Republic of China;

b) represent the interests of the Union of Soviet Socialist Republics in the field of foreign trade;

c) regulate on behalf of the Union of Soviet Socialist Republics trade operations between the Union of Soviet Socialist Republics and the Republic of China;

d) conduct trade between the Union of Soviet Socialist Republics and the Republic of China.

The Trade Representation of the Union of Soviet Socialist Republics in China, acting as an organ, which carries out the monopoly of foreign trade of the Union of Soviet Socialist Republics, is an integral part of the Embassy of the Union of Soviet Socialist Republics in China.

The Trade Representation of the Union of Soviet Socialist Republics in China has its residence in the capital of the Republic of China.

The Trade Representative of the Union of Soviet Socialist Republics in China and his two deputies are included in the diplomatic personnel of the Embassy of the Union of Soviet Socialist Republics in China and enjoy all rights and privileges accorded members of diplomatic missions.

The Trade Representation of the Union of Soviet Socialist Republics in China shall have its branches in the cities: Tientsin, Shanghai, Hankow, Canton and Lanchow. New branches of the Trade Representation of the U.S.S.R. in China shall be established upon agreement between the said Trade Representation and the competent authorities of the National Government of the Republic of China.

The quarters of the Trade Representation of the Union of Soviet Socialist Republics in China and its branches shall enjoy extra-territoriality.

The Trade Representation of the Union of Soviet Socialist Republics in China and its branches shall have the right to use the cypher.

Officials, belonging to the personnel of the Trade Representation and of its branches—citizens of the Union of Soviet Socialist Republics—shall be absolved in China from payment of central and local taxes of any kind, as well as of any personal and material obligations.

All officials, belonging to the staff of the Trade Representation of the Union of Soviet Socialist Republics in China and to its branches, do not come under the jurisdiction of Chinese courts in matters arising out of their official relations with the Trade Representation.

The Trade Representation of the Union of Soviet Socialist Republics in China does not come under the rule of trade register. It will publish in the official organ of the Government of the Republic of China names of persons who are authorized to carry out in its name legal acts, as well as data on the extent of the rights of each such person with regard to signing trade obligations of the Trade Representation.

2. The Trade Representation of the Union of Soviet Socialist Republics in China shall act on behalf of the Government of the Union of Soviet Socialist Republics. The Government of the Union of Soviet Socialist Republics assumes full responsibility for all

trade transactions which will be concluded or guaranteed in China in the name of the Trade Representation by persons authorized thereto.

For the validity of trade transactions as concluded or guaranteed by the Trade Representation of the Union of Soviet Socialist Republics in China, it is necessary to have on the papers of transaction, or respectively on the papers of guarantee, proper signatures of persons authorized by the Government of the Union of Soviet Socialist Republics or by the People's Commissar of Foreign Trade, with the publication of the names of such persons and the scope of their powers in accordance with Section 1 of this Annex.

All trade transactions, entered into or guaranteed by the Trade Representation of the Union of Soviet Socialist Republics in China, on the territory of the Republic of China, are subordinated to the Chinese code of laws and come under the jurisdiction of Chinese courts, provided that the laws of the Republic of China or the terms of individual transactions do not stipulate otherwise.

In view of the responsibility, (established in the first paragraph of this section)—of the Government of the Union of Soviet Socialist Republics with regard to transactions concluded or guaranteed in the Republic of China by the Trade Representation of the Union of Soviet Socialist Republics in China, regulations referring to all preliminary measures of security for actions and for costs and provisional execution of decisions, orders and judgments before the final decisions of the courts as well as administrative bodies are not applicable to the claims against the said Trade Representation.

Forced execution—with regard to the Trade Representation of the Union of Soviet Socialist Republics in China—shall be applied only to those final court decisions, which became legal, on all disagreements, which arose from trade transactions, signed or guaranteed by the Trade Representation in accordance with the second paragraph of this section and only in cases where the final decision of the courts has been made and come into force.

The said final decisions shall be applied only to property, which is in the Republic of China, and to the rights of the Trade Representation with regard to transactions named in this section.

However, forced execution of court decisions, mentioned in the foregoing paragraph of this section, cannot apply to objects, which are—according to the established norms of international law—extraterritorial, as well as to objects which are necessary for performing official functions of the Trade Representation of the Union of Soviet Socialist Republics in China.

3. Responsibility for any trade transaction, entered into, without the guarantee of the Trade Representation of the Union of Soviet Socialist Republics in China, by any state Economic Organ of the Union of Soviet Socialist Republics, which has, according to the laws of the Union of Soviet Socialist Republics, the rights of an independent juridical person, is borne only by the said organ, and execution of such transactions may only be applied to its property. Neither the Government of the Union of Soviet Socialist Republics, nor its Trade Representation in China, nor any other Economic Organs of the Union of SSR bear the responsibility for such transactions.

Trade transactions, concluded in China by these Economic Organs, shall be subject to Chinese law and to the jurisdiction of Chinese courts, if this law or the individual transactions do not stipulate otherwise.

Moscow, June 16, 1939.

A. MIKOYAN SUN-FO.

MR. PLENIPOTENTIARY:

In connection with the signing on this date of the Trade Treaty between the Republic of China and the Union of Soviet Socialist Republics I have the honor, in the name of my Government, to state that the words "any third country" in Articles I, II, IV, VII, VIII and XII must be understood with regard to the Republic of China as pertaining to those countries, which signed agreements with China, beginning with the year 1928, based on principles of equality. I shall be much obliged if you will confirm this interpretation.

Accept, Mr. Plenipotentiary, assurances of my high esteem for you.

Moscow, June 16, 1939.

SUN-FO.

To: ANASTAS IVANOVICH MIKOYAN
People's Commissar for Foreign Trade of the USSR.

MR. PLENIPOTENTIARY:

I have the honor to acknowledge receipt of your note of this date of the following contents:

[see above]

In the name of the Government of the Union of Soviet Socialist Republics I have the honor to state that it is in accord with the above named interpretation.

[See above . . . assurances, etc.]

June 16, 1939, Moscow.

A. MIKOYAN.

To Mr. SUN-FO, Special Plenipotentiary and Representative of the National Government of the Republic of China.

(Ratified by the Presidium of the Supreme Soviet of the U.S.S.R., January 5, 1940. Exchange of articles of ratification took place in Chungking March 16, 1940.)

*NEUTRALITY PACT BETWEEN THE U.S.S.R. AND JAPAN, APRIL 13, 1941**

The Presidium of the Supreme Soviet of the U.S.S.R. and His Majesty the Emperor of Japan, guided by a desire to strengthen peaceful and friendly relations between the two countries, decided to conclude a pact on neutrality, for the purpose of which they appointed their representatives:

For the Presidium of the Supreme Soviet of the U.S.S.R., Viacheslav M. Molotov, Chairman of the Council of People's Commissars and People's Commissar for Foreign Affairs.

For His Majesty the Emperor of Japan, Yosuke Matsuoka, Minister of Foreign Affairs, Jusanmin, Cavalier of the Order of the Sacred Treasure, first class; and Yoshitsugu Tatekawa, Ambassador Extraordinary and Plenipotentiary in the U.S.S.R. Lieutenant General, Jusanmin, Cavalier of the Order of the Rising Sun, first class, and the Order of the Golden Kite, fourth class—who, after the exchange of their credentials, which were found in due and proper form agreed on the following:

Article 1. Both contracting parties undertake to maintain peaceful and friendly relations between them and mutually respect the territorial integrity and inviolability of the other contracting party.

Article 2. Should one of the contracting parties become the object of hostilities on the part of one or several third powers, the other contracting party will observe neutrality throughout the duration of the conflict.

Article 3. The present pact comes into force from the day of its ratification by both contracting parties and remains valid for five years. In case neither of the contracting parties denounces the pact one year before expiration of the term, it will be considered automatically prolonged for the next five years.

Article 4. The present pact is subject to ratification as soon as possible. Instruments of ratification shall be exchanged in Tokyo also as soon as possible.

In confirmation whereof the above-named representatives signed the present pact in two copies, drawn up in the Russian and Japanese languages, and affixed thereto their seals.

* Tass, April 13, 1941.

Done in Moscow, April 13, 1941, which corresponds to the 13th day of the fourth month of the 16th year of Showa.

Signed by MOLOTOV, YOSUKE MATSUOKA, YOSHITSUGU TATEKAWA.

DECLARATION

In conformity with the spirit of the neutrality pact concluded April 13, 1941, between the U.S.S.R. and Japan, the governments of the U.S.S.R. and Japan in the interests of insuring peaceful and friendly relations between the two countries, solemnly declare that the U.S.S.R. pledges to respect the territorial integrity and inviolability of Manchoukuo, and Japan pledges to respect the territorial integrity and inviolability of the Mongolian People's Republic.

Moscow, April 13, 1941, signed on behalf of the government of the U.S.S.R. by MOLOTOV; on behalf of the government of Japan by YOSUKE MATSUOKA and YOSHITSUGU TATEKAWA.

*PROTOCOL ON THE TRANSFER OF JAPANESE OIL AND COAL CONCESSIONS IN NORTHERN SAKHALIN, MARCH 30, 1944**

The Government of the Union of Soviet Socialist Republics and the Imperial Government of Japan, as a result of negotiations which had been conducted with a view to the implementation of an understanding they had reached in connection with the neutrality pact of April 13, 1941, concerning the liquidation of Japanese oil and coal concessions in Northern Sakhalin, have agreed on the following:

ARTICLE I

The Government of Japan transfers to the Union of Soviet Socialist Republics all rights to the Japanese oil and coal concessions in Northern Sakhalin in accordance with the provisions of the present Protocol and the terms of application of the Protocol appended hereto.

The concession contracts concluded between the Government of the Union of Soviet Socialist Republics, on the one hand, and Japanese concessionaires, on the other hand, concluded on December 14, 1925, as well as the supplementary contracts and agreements concluded subsequently, are annulled by the present Protocol.

ARTICLE 2

All the property (structures, equipment, materials, spare parts, provisions, etc.) in the possession of the Japanese concessionaires in Northern Sakhalin is to be turned over to the Government of the Union of Soviet Socialist Republics in its present condition insofar as nothing different is provided for by the present Protocol and the terms of application of the Protocol appended hereto.

ARTICLE 3

In connection with the provisions of the two preceding articles the Government of the Union of Soviet Socialist Republics agrees to pay to the Government of Japan the sum of five million rubles in accordance with the provisions of the terms of application of the present Protocol appended hereto.

* *Moscow News* April 1, 1944, page 2.

The Government of the Union of Soviet Socialist Republics also agrees to supply annually to the Government of Japan on the usual commercial terms 50,000 metric tons of oil extracted at the Okha oil fields in the course of five consecutive years as from the time of the termination of the present war.

ARTICLE 4

The Government of the Union of Soviet Socialist Republics guarantees to the Government of Japan unobstructed and free of duty removal from the concession territories of oil and coal stocked in stores and belonging to Japanese concessionaires, in conformity with the provisions of the terms of application of the present Protocol appended hereto.

ARTICLE 5

The present Protocol comes into force on the day of its signing.

The present Protocol has been drawn up in the Russian and Japanese languages; both texts possess equal force.

In witness whereof the undersigned duly authorized by their respective governments, have signed the present Protocol and affixed their seals to it.

Drawn up in two copies in the city of Moscow on March 30, 1944 which corresponds to the 30th day of the third month of the 19th year of Showa.

S. A. LOZOVSKY,
Delegate of the Union of Soviet Socialist Republics. Assistant People's Commissar of Foreign Affairs of the U.S.S.R.

NAOTAKE SATO
Delegate of Japan, Ambassador Extraordinary and Plenipotentiary of Japan to the Union of Soviet Socialist Republics.

ON PROCEDURE OF THE TRANSFER OF PROPERTY OF JAPANESE OIL AND COAL CONCESSIONS IN NORTHERN SAKHALIN TO THE SOVIET GOVERNMENT

March 10, 1944

In connection with the initialling on this date of the Protocol on the Transfer of Japanese oil and coal concessions in Northern Sakhalin, the Soviet party and the Japanese party have agreed on the following:

The Government of Japan will take every measure for the Japanese oil and coal concessionaires to begin turning over all the property they possess in Northern Sakhalin to the Government of the Union of Soviet Socialist Republics in five days after the initialling of the Protocol on the transfer of concessions, so that this transfer may be completed before the present Protocol is signed.

The Protocol on the transfer of all the property of the Japanese oil and coal concessions in Northern Sakhalin to the Government of the Union of Soviet Socialist Republics will be signed by representatives of both parties in Northern Sakhalin after the receipt of information that the Protocol on the transfer of concessions and the Protocol on the prolongation of the fisheries convention for five years are signed in Moscow.

Moscow, March 10, 1944.

S. A. Lozovsky,
Assistant People's Commissar of Foreign Affairs of the U.S.S.R.

N. Sato
Japanese Ambassador to Moscow.

*PROTOCOL ON LEAVING IN FORCE FISHERIES CONVENTION BETWEEN THE UNION OF SOVIET SOCIALIST REPUBLICS AND JAPAN FOR A TERM OF FIVE YEARS, MARCH 30, 1944**

The Government of the Union of Soviet Socialist Republics and the Imperial Government of Japan, as a result of negotiations they recently conducted on the subject of fisheries have agreed on the following:

ARTICLE 1

The fisheries convention between the Union of Soviet Socialist Republics and Japan, as well as all documents appended thereto which were signed on January 23, 1928 and whose term of operation after the yearly prolongation beginning with 1936, expired on December 31, 1943, shall remain in force for five years as from January 1, 1944 on the terms laid down in the present Protocol.

ARTICLE 2

All matters relating to the fishing activities of fishery-owning organizations and citizens of the Union of Soviet Socialist Republics shall not be regulated by the provisions of the fisheries convention and the documents appended thereto as being exclusively within the competence of the Union of Soviet Socialist Republics.

In conformity with the provision of the preceding paragraph, all the provisions contained in the fisheries convention and in the documents appended thereto and relating to the fishing activities of fishery-owning organizations and citizens of the Union of Soviet Socialist Republics, lose their force and henceforward shall not be applied.

ARTICLE 3

The following modifications and additions are made in Article 1 of the Protocol (A), appended to the fisheries convention:

* *Moscow News*, April 1, 1944, p. 2.

a) The provisions of the last paragraph of Article 1 of the Protocol (A) shall be modified and replaced by the following provisions:

"In addition fishing is to be forbidden to Japanese subjects as well as to other foreigners in the following bays:

"1. Avachinsky Bay—in the area within the boundary formed by a line drawn from Krutov Cape to Bechevinskaya Bay (inclusive).

"2. De-Kastri Bay within the boundary formed by a line drawn from Cape Yuzhny to Bay Krestovaya (inclusive).

"3. Sovyetskaya Gavan—in the area within the boundary formed by a line drawn from the point at 49° 26 north latitude and 140° 27 east longitude to the point at 48° 40 north latitude and 140° 11 east longitude.

"4. Bay of St. Olga and Bay of Vladimir—in the area within the boundary formed by a line drawn from the mouth of Lafula River to Cape Nakhualny.

"5. Bay of Peter the Great (including Possiet Bay)—in the area within the boundary formed by a line drawn from Opasny Island to the mouth of Tyumen-Ula River."

The bays figuring in Article 1 of the Protocol (A) with numbers 16, 27, 30 and 32 henceforward will not be mentioned with these numbers as included respectively in the above five areas.

The precise boundaries of the above-mentioned five areas barred for fishing have been fixed in notes Number 2 appended to the present Protocol, which the delegates of the Union of Soviet Socialist Republics and Japan exchanged simultaneously with the signing of the present Protocol.

b) The list of bays which constitute the exception mentioned in Article 1 of the fisheries convention, contained in Article 1 of Protocol (A) shall be supplemented by the following two names:

1. Ossor Bay
2. Northwestern part of Taui Bay.

ARTICLE 4

The lump sum of the taxes and duties provided for in notes Number 1 exchanged on January 23, 1928 and appended to the fisheries convention shall be raised and fixed at 30% of the rent of the respective fishery lots.

ARTICLE 5

The rates of special payments (share payments for the work of canneries) fixed in Section Six of Paragraph (B) of Protocol (C) appended to the fisheries convention, shall be raised and established as follows:

1. For Cartilaginous fish—25 kopeks per case;
2. For Siberian salmon, Kizbuch and Chavycha—20 kopeks per case;
3. For humpback salmon—12 kopeks per case;
4. For crabs—50 kopeks per case.

ARTICLE 6

The present Protocol comes into force on the day of its signing.

The present Protocol has been drawn up in the Russian and Japanese languages; both texts have equal forces.

In witness whereof the undersigned, duly authorized by their respective governments, have signed the present Protocol and affixed their seals to it.

Drawn up in two copies on March 30, 1944, which corresponds to the 30th day of the third month of the 19th year of Showa.

S. A. LOZOVSKY,
Delegate of the Union of Soviet Socialist Republics, Assistant People's Commissar of Foreign Affairs of the U.S.S.R.

NAOTAKE SATO
Delegate of Japan, Ambassador Extraordinary and Plenipotentiary of Japan to the Union of Soviet Socialist Republics.

*EXCHANGE OF NOTES REGARDING THE FISHERIES, MARCH 30, 1944**

(*Note of Delegate of U.S.S.R. to Delegate of Japan*)

Moscow, March 30, 1944.
MR. DELEGATE,

In connection with the signing on this date of the Protocol leaving in force for a period of five years the fisheries convention between the Union of Soviet Socialist Republics and Japan and the documents appended thereto signed on January 23, 1928, I have the honor to inform you of the following:

1. The Government of the Union of Soviet Socialist Republics agrees to renew on the former terms, unless the Protocol and the documents appended thereto contain different provisions, for a period of five years as from January 1, 1944, the operation of special contracts for the exploitation by Japanese subjects of the canneries and fishery lots attached to them, signed on November 3, 1928, together with the documents and the subsequent supplementary agreements relating to these contracts.

2. The 24 fishery lots listed below which were leased to Japanese subjects but were not exploited by them for two years in succession in 1939 and 1940, irrespective of the date of expiration of the lease terms, are to be closed and will not be put on auction in the future.

Numbers of the fishery lots:
41, 42, 269, 271, 273, 367, 497, 498, 543, 555, 556, 561, 638, 641, 1002, 1003, 1004, 1082, 1104, 1190, 1265, 1266, 1267, and 95 (crab fishing).

The lease contracts for the above listed lots, the terms of operation of which have not yet expired, are to be severed.

3. The fishery lots which by the end of 1943 were rented by Japanese subjects, with the exception of the lots listed in the preceding Articles 1 and 2, after the expiration of their lease terms will be leased by auction for the corresponding periods provided by the

* *Moscow News*, April 1, 1944, p. 2.

first section of Article 6 of Protocol (A) appended to the fisheries convention.

It is specified in this connection that the number of fishery lots which will be rented by fishing organizations and citizens of the Union of Soviet Socialist Republics on the auctions provided for in the preceding paragraphs, which will take place every year in the course of five years beginning with 1944, will not exceed 10% of the total number of lots that will be placed on auction in the respective years, and that fishing organizations and citizens of the Union of Soviet Socialist Republics have no intention to rent on auction those fishery lots on which there exist canneries.

I avail myself of the opportunity to renew, Mr. Delegate, my assurances to you of my highest esteem.

S. A. LOZOVSKY,
Delegate of the Union of Soviet Socialist Republics, Assistant People's Commissar of Foreign Affairs of the USSR.

* * *

(In the note of reply the Delegate of Japan confirms receipt of the note of the Delegate of the U.S.S.R and states that he takes note of the above communication.)

* * *

(*Note of Delegate of Japan to Delegate of U.S.S.R.*)

Moscow, March 30, 1944.
MR. DELEGATE,

On behalf of my Government I have the honor to inform you of the following:

1. Complying with the wish of the Government of the Union of Soviet Socialist Republics, the Government of Japan agrees to guarantee that all fishery lots rented by Japanese subjects and situated on the eastern coast of Kamchatka and in the Olyutorsk district will not be exploited by leaseholders before the termination of the war in the Pacific.

2. It is understood in this connection that the fact of Japanese subjects refraining from exploitation of the above-mentioned fishery lots will not serve as a pretext for the severing of contracts for the

exploitation of any fishery lots or canneries situated in the said areas.

I avail myself of the opportunity to renew, Mr. Delegate, my assurance to you of my highest esteem.

NAOTAKE SATO,
Delegate of Japan. Ambassador Extraordinary and Plenipotentiary of Japan to the U.S.S.R.

(In the note of reply the Delegate of the U.S.S.R confirms receipt of the note of the Delegate of Japan and states that he takes note of the above communication.)

TREATY OF FRIENDSHIP AND ALLIANCE BETWEEN THE U.S.S.R. AND THE CHINESE REPUBLICS, AUGUST 14, 1945

See Supplement, p. 265, for text of this Treaty as monitored from Moscow radio just as this book was going to press.

APPENDIX II: STATEMENTS

*JAPANESE INTERVENTION IN MANCHURIA**

Events of greatest importance are developing in Manchuria. Japanese military forces have occupied Chinese cities, ports and inhabited places adjacent to the South Manchurian Railway zone held by the Japanese, including the capital of Manchuria—Mukden, both of the most important Chinese ports in Manchuria, Antung and Newchuang and the Kuanchengtzu the junction point of the South Manchurian Railway and the Chinese Eastern Railway. These are the limits of the occupation known to us at present by telegraph reports; it is quite possible that this occupation has been extended also in other regions deeper in Manchuria from which reports have not yet been able to come. The Mukden government has in fact ceased to function; its troops have been disarmed, the basis of its military strength—the arsenal—has been seized and the Japanese military authorities have even taken over the administration of the largest Manchurian banks. From Japanese circles official statements are being issued that the occupation has been completed and the time for negotiations has come.

According to the official Japanese version the military occupation of Manchuria was in answer to an attack by Chinese troops and to an attempt to destroy the South Manchurian Railway, guarded by Japanese garrisons. The fact of the matter is, however, that these most recent events were preceded by a series of preparatory actions by the Japanese extending over a number of months and clearly indicating an imminent large-scale Japanese action of military character. As is well known, Japanese imperialism has been actively dissatisfied by the development of events in China proper, and the extreme dependence of the Nanking government on the influence of its English and American competitors. It is no secret also that Japan played no small role in the formation of the Canton government which is inimical to the Nanking government and unites all the opposition elements of the Kuomintang; it is not for nothing that the Minister of Foreign Affairs of that government

* *Izvestia,* September 21, 1931.

hastened to make an extended visit in Tokyo. On the other hand, Japanese military circles have not concealed their dissatisfaction with Mukden's policy of rapprochement and alliance with Nanking. However, the center of attention for Japanese activities remains as before—Manchuria. Here Japanese imperialism as a result of its successful aggressive policy of two and a half decades enjoys a position approximating a monopoly of colonial control. Based on the Kuantung "leased" territory, on the gigantic transportation and industrial combine—the South Manchurian Railway with its "concessions" and extraterritorial zone in which Japanese troops are stationed, and on the whole complex of far-reaching exclusive treaty and extra-treaty privileges, Japan is indisputably the decisive factor in Manchurian affairs. But not satisfied with this situation, Japan is attempting to extend further its sphere of influence and to make its position in that area completely firm. In recent years and months the relative quiet in Japanese-Chinese relatives in Manchuria has accumulated a multitude of unresolved incidents and questions of conflict. Several months ago it was already possible to conclude that Japanese imperialism intended to force the immediate solution of these questions in its favor.

As a matter of fact, Japanese-Chinese relations suddenly began to move quickly toward a very severe crisis. It started with a change in the management of the South Manchurian Railroad and the Korean governorship and the naming to these responsible posts of politicians of the activist school. Following this there began a series of clashes between the Chinese and the Korean immigrants with consequent continuous interference by Japanese police which operate all over the territory of Manchuria. The most serious of these clashes (the Wanpaoshan incident) caused a tremendous pogrom of Chinese in Korea, costing the lives of 140 Chinese and causing the repatriation of the majority of the 90,000 Chinese living in that Japanese colony. The activities of fascist Japanese organizations in Manchuria grew stronger and a considerable part of the Japanese press carried on an open campaign for increased pressure on China. In May, a conference of the fascist "Union of Japanese Youth in Manchuria" which opened in Dairen, passed a series of militant resolutions demanding "the upholding of Japanese rights and the taking of the most decisive measures in relation to Manchuria and Mongolia." In July, it was decided to increase the Japanese garrisons in Korea and Manchuria by one division and to organize a military air base near Dairen. At the beginning of

August, the Japanese press commented on the military action which had begun in North China to the effect that the moment had come to make decisive demands on all questions at issue. On August 4th, the Minister of War Minami, in a speech delivered at a conference of Divisional Commanders made the significant statement that, "the situation in Manchuria and Mongolia is becoming threatening." At the end of August the Japanese newspaper "Dairen Shimbun" had already demanded directly the occupation of Manchuria "in order to guarantee by this means our inviolability and to hasten negotiations on the accumulated questions." At that time the incident was already known regarding the assasination of the Japanese officer Nakamura who had been traveling in regions deep in eastern Inner-Mongolia. The tone of the Japanese press in Manchuria and in Japan proper grew correspondingly stronger. During the whole of September, the situation became more tense and in conclusion, the Japanese military command actually carried out intervention in Manchuria.

At the center of the concrete program, about which Japan is doubtless going to begin negotiations, is the question of railroad construction. Japan is seeking rights for constructing with its capital and under its control a number of new railroads in Manchuria which in conjunction with the existing Japanese-Chinese railroads will form a new Japanese trunkline parallel to the C.E.R., having its outlet in the North Korean Japanese ports, now being built quickly. This trunkline will have not only economic but tremendous military significance. On the other hand, Japan has for a long time protested against independent Chinese railway construction, being developed in a direction which might compete with the South Manchuria Railroad. In particular, it has demanded that two projected connecting lines which would strengthen the existing Chinese railroad system to offset the Japanese should not be completed. Japan is seeking the consolidation of Japanese loans extended at one time for the construction of the existing Japanese-Chinese lines and the final placement of the latter under Japanese control. Japanese capital attaches great significance to these demands, not so much because the existing system of Chinese railroads could compete to a certain extent with the South Manchurian Railway as because this Chinese railroad construction could become a convenient point for the investment of foreign, partcularly American capital, which would be able to dispute Japan's present monopoly control.

But the construction of railroads is only one of many questions in dispute. Along with this, there is the dispute on the question of the right of holding long-term leases on land in Manchuria (the Japanese obtained this right by the treaty concluded as a result of the notorious "21 Demands," but they have not been able to take advantage of it up to this time); on the question of the taxes on Japanese goods and Japanese trade; and on the question of the position of the Koreans who number up to a million in Manchuria and who are used by the Japanese imperialists both as a weapon and as an excuse, not only for its economic but its political-administrative penetration in Manchuria. And even this does not exhaust the Japanese program. It is possible, for instance, to suppose, in the negotiations which are to follow after the occupation of Mukden by armed force, special claims will be made regarding the Taonan region itself in which the above-mentioned Nakamura was killed. The point is that this region, in addition to the fact that it is very important strategically and as a railroad center, contains large unoccupied land, for the colonization of which the Chinese are seriously trying to attract American capital.

Present events in Manchuria appear thus to be a new and extremely acute stage in the development of the permanent Japanese-Chinese conflict. It would be a mistake, of course, to regard these events exclusively in the frame-work of Japanese-Chinese relations. The very fact that military force has been used on such a large scale and that the vital centers in this entire tremendous region have been occupied—an action which Japan has avoided up to this time—bears witness to the serious developments in the general situation regarding international relationships in China.

It is characteristic that neither in Geneva at the session of the League of Nations, nor in Washington has the Japanese action been met by a protest anything like that which in all probability the Chinese had hoped for. The Geneva discussion club accepted "with satisfaction" the report of the usual assurances made on this matter by the representative of Japan, while the United States State Department stated directly that it did not find anything contrary to the Kellogg Pact in the actions of the Japanese troops which had occupied Manchuria. The impression is created that Japan's action was well prepared in the sense of getting the agreement of the other imperialist powers.

For this very reason, however, the disappointment of Chinese hopes for support from the other powers does not mean that these powers in their own interests will not oppose further Japanese penetration into Manchuria. On the contrary, under the circumstances of increased aggressiveness in relation to China by the imperialist powers spurred on by this crisis, it is absolutely inevitable that there will be further and very significant sharpening of the contradictions between the imperialists whose interests conflict all the more because China, impoverished and crushed by the crisis, is much less able than before to satisfy their appetites. Japanese action in Manchuria is an event of greatest international significance, not because it inevitably is becoming the object of the usual pseudo-pacifist hide-and-seek game of the Geneva comedians but because it of necessity will be the cause of further tension in the already strained international situation. This circumstance in itself is enough to make the Soviet public and the workers of the whole Soviet Union follow with close attention the further development of events in the new Far Eastern zone of war danger which carries with it the threat of new attempts at anti-Soviet provocation to which the imperialists can resort in order to conceal their aggressive policies. As for the working people of China, this new unheard of degradation imposed on their country doubtless will reveal to them the depths of the collapse and the degree of weakness to which the country has been brought by the Kuomintang—feudal-bourgeois reaction, the shameful agent of world imperialism.

N. Pakhomov

*RESUMPTION OF SINO-SOVIET RELATIONS**

I. OFFICIAL ANNOUNCEMENT

Nanking, December 13.—The Chinese Foreign Office this morning officially announced that relations had been resumed between the Chinese and Soviet Governments as from yesterday. It was further announced that Dr. W. W. Yen and M. Litvinoff yesterday morning at Geneva exchanged brief Notes in which it was stated that "In pursuance of our recent conversations during our pleasant meetings at Geneva, I am duly authorized to inform you that being desirous of promoting, in the interests of peace, friendly relations between the two countries, the Government has decided to regard normal diplomatic and consular relations as having been formally re-established as from today."—Reuter.

II. STATEMENT BY CHINESE FOREIGN MINISTER

Nanking, December 13.—Upon the subject of the resumption of relations between China and Soviet Russia, the Chinese Foreign Minister made the following statement today:

"China always desires to maintain friendly and peaceful relations with all countries, especially with her neighbours. It is thus a source of deep satisfaction that she has now resumed diplomatic and consular relations with the Soviet Union with whom she shares one of the longest common boundaries of the world.

"The Soviet Union is now engaged in gigantic works of reconstruction and its primary concern is in promoting the well-being of its very large population by undertaking enormous economic schemes. This bears testimony to its desire to foster the welfare of its people without resorting to aggressive measures.

"The task before modern China involves a similar point of view. The preoccupation of her statesmen is with extensive plans of material and economic reconstruction, whose benefits they expect to be ultimately shared by the entire world. In prosecution of these plans, however, she is now confronted with difficulties and

* *China Year Book, 1933,* pp. 655–657.

obstacles resulting from the invasion and occupation of vast areas of her most fertile territory.

"This disruption of her work in the interests of peace through foreign military measures is indeed a serious menace, likely to produce far-reaching consequences. Any effort, therefore, made to promote mutual confidence and international cooperation is a valuable asset and should be encouraged, as the world can ill afford at the present critical period of its history to allow any forces of disorder to prevail.

"The new regime is the result of a desire shared mutually by China and Russia to usher in a period of peace and prosperity in the Far East and it is only when viewed in this light that the resumption of normal relations between these two great countries of the Pacific has an especial significance."—Reuter.

III. STATEMENT BY DR. W. W. YEN

Geneva, December 12.—The agreement for the resumption of relations is the fruit of negotiations which were commenced in the Spring when M. Litvinoff was at Geneva for the Disarmament Conference. The original Chinese suggestion was for a Pact of Non-Aggression, but this was eventually declined by the Soviet because, among other things, it was not desired to make the resumption of diplomatic relations conditional on such a Pact. The idea of a Non-Aggression Pact was thus eventually dropped by the Chinese and after several months a further negotiations plan for a resumption of relations took shape.

It is understood that the resumption of relations is viewed as in no way excluding the possibility of a future Non-Aggression Pact, or any other form of agreement, should either country so desire.

Dr. Yen, chief Chinese delegate to the League Assembly, issued the following statement today: "I am very gratified to be the instrument of China in the restoration of diplomatic and consular relations with the Soviet Union. It was my feeling when I came to Geneva as the Chinese delegate to the Disarmament Conference that normal relations should be restored between the two great nations on the shores of the Pacific in the interests of peace. That feeling was also shared by M. Litvinoff.

"For some time it was realized that resumption of relations between the two countries could no longer be delayed, and the presence of M. Litvinoff was considered an excellent opportunity to bring this about.

"The publication of the Lytton Report, in which references were made to the Soviet Union and the suggestion to invite the United States and the Soviet Union to participate in the deliberations of the Committee, made more obvious the desirability of the reestablishment of normal relations.

"The Chinese Government and the Chinese people are very sincere in their decision to cultivate friendly relations with their great neighbour, and they are convinced these feelings are reciprocated."

IV. STATEMENT BY M. LITVINOFF

M. Maxim Litvinoff, Soviet Commissar for Foreign Affairs, issued the following statement: "I have to-day exchanged Notes restoring diplomatic relations between the U.S.S.R. and China. This normal act hardly requires an explanation, but what does require one is the rupture of relations between States, or the refusal to maintain relations—phenomena which constitute an infringement on normal international life and sometimes a danger to peace.

"There is no need to dwell on the events which led to the rupture between the U.S.S.R. and China. These were not due to Soviet initiative, and I am certain that no one in China today can think that the regrettable events which led to the rupture of relations were a benefit to China.

"Beyond a doubt the beginning of the present troubles in the Far East was in no small degree due to the fact that not all the States situated on the shores of the Pacific Ocean had been maintaining diplomatic relations with one another.

"The people of the Soviet Union feel the greatest sympathy towards the Chinese people and towards their efforts to maintain independence with sovereignty, and to achieve an equality status. The Soviet Government has given repeated proofs of its friendly attitude towards China. Alone among the States it freed China from unequal treaties, extraterritoriality and other rights and privileges wrung from China by Tsarist imperialism, and agreed to transform the railway concession into a commercial concession under joint management.

"These feelings of disinterestedness and friendship guided the Soviet Government when it established relations with China in 1924. These feelings, and not temporary considerations have dictated to-day the restoration of relations.

"The Soviet Union has its hands unfettered by any secret political combinations and agreements, consequently the improvement of relations with one country is not a means of rendering worse relations with another. Only such a policy can genuinely assist in strengthening general peace. Only when all States maintain relations with each other shall we be able to speak seriously of international peace pacts and agreements, and the creation of universally recognised authoritative international organizations.

"In conclusion, I am convinced that all sincere friends of peace and international cooperation will learn with satisfaction that resumption of relations between our two great States has taken place."

*SOVIET REPLY TO THE LEAGUE OF NATIONS, MARCH 7, 1933**

The Soviet government has carefully considered the proposals contained in your letters to me of February 24 and 25, has attentively studied the documents attached to them and has come to the following conclusion:

The League of Nations' decisions as well as the report of the Committee of Nineteen, have as their premises the League of Nations Covenant, the Washington Nine-Power Treaty and the Paris Treaty (the Briand-Kellogg Pact). The U.S.S.R. is not a signatory of the first two, but adhered to the last of the pacts named. At its very inception the Soviet government proclaimed as a fundamental principle of its policy, the right of all nations to self-determination under conditions of freedom to express their will and absence of any outside pressure whatsoever. It took a determined stand against any annexations and indemnities as results of military conquests or forcible seizures. From these principles absolute respect for the territorial integrity and the political social-economic and administrative independence of all states, the inadmissibility of settling international conflicts by other than peaceful means, and, of course, the obligation strictly to observe international treaties embodying these principles, logically ensue.

The proposal of the Soviet government for universal and complete disarmament was aimed to render impossible the violation of these principles even by states which do not recognize them. Very recently the Soviet delegation to the disarmament conference submitted a proposal for international condemnation of all those pretexts whereby violation of international treaties of peace and forcible seizures of territory are usually justified.

The Treaty of Paris, like other analogous international agreements, covers only part of the above principles and proposals of the Soviet government. Inasmuch as the premises of the League of Nations' decisions on the Japanese-Chinese conflict in some measure

* *Soviet Union Review*, April, 1933, p. 94, as corrected by comparison with *League of Nations Assembly Document A. Extr. 38*, 1933 VII.

approach the principles of the peace policy of the Soviet Union, it may be stated that these premises coincide to some extent with the views of the Soviet Union.

The report of the Committee of Nineteen adopted by the Assembly of the League of Nations nevertheless contains, as regards the application of the starting points of the League's decisions which I have just indicated to the Sino-Japanese conflict, certain recommendations which are not entirely compatible with these starting points and permit of a departure therefrom on a whole series of serious questions.

The Advisory Committee set up in the same spirit by the decision of the Assembly, is an organ of the League, one of whose aims is to facilitate fulfillment by the Assembly of its obligations, and which is to make its proposals to the Assembly, upon whose decisions the U.S.S.R., which is not a member of the League, can have no influence.

Another aim of the Advisory Committee is to help coordinate the actions of members and non-members of the League. However, the majority of the States which have joined and are to join the Advisory Committee, namely, 13 out of 22, do not maintain any relations with the Soviet Union and consequently are hostile to it. Obviously such a committee would hardly be capable of fulfilling the task of coordination of actions with the Soviet Union which is unable to enter into any negotiations with the majority of these States nor individually with those whose interests are most likely to coincide with its own.

It is also permissible to doubt whether such States could really take into consideration the interests of the U.S.S.R., which are mentioned in the recommendations.

In view of the circumstances set forth, the Soviet government does not find it possible to join in the decisions of the League or to take part at the present moment in the Advisory Committee.

The Soviet government, anxious by all means possible to prevent a further extension of the military conflict and its possible development into the source of a new world conflagration, has adopted a course of strict neutrality from the very beginning of the Japanese-Chinese conflict. In accordance with the above, the Soviet government, true to its peaceful policy, will always be in accord with the actions and proposals of international organizations and individual governments aimed toward the most speedy and just settlement of the conflict and assurance of peace in the Far East.

Please accept, etc.

LITVINOV

*LITVINOV EXPLAINS PROPOSED SALE OF C.E.R., MAY 12, 1933**

It is correct that in the course of my interview with Ambassador Ota on May 2 we considered the serious situation that has recently developed on the Chinese Eastern Railway as a result of the actions of the Manchurian authorities, a situation which threatens to complicate our relations with both Manchuria and Japan. We discussed the possible means for the solution of the conflicts that have arisen, and, as one of the most radical means, I mentioned the possibility of purchase of the Chinese Eastern Railway by Manchukuo—that is to say, the sale of the road by us to the Manchurian authorities.

It is also true that the Nanking government queried the Soviet government on this matter, disputing our right to sell the Chinese Eastern Railway to anyone whomsoever outside of the Nanking government, and that Ambassador Yen gave us a memorandum to this effect.

The arguments adduced by the Nanking government do not correspond with either the formal obligations of the Soviet government nor with the actual condition of affairs. Neither the Peking nor the Mukden agreements, which grant the right to China to purchase the road before the expiration of the treaties, limit the right of the Soviet government to sell the road to anyone whomsoever, especially to the authorities which exist in Manchuria and which are actually carrying out the rights and obligations accruing to the Chinese side from the Peking and Mukden agreements.

Much more important, however, is the fact that the Nanking government and its subordinate authorities have ceased to be the actual partners of the U.S.S.R. on the Chinese Eastern Railway for more than a year and a half. They have been deprived of the possibility, for reasons beyond the control of the U.S.S.R., either to make use of their rights or fulfill their obligations under the Nanking and Mukden agreements. According to these agreements the government of China must send its representatives to share in the

* *Soviet Union Review*, June, 1933, p. 134.

management of the road. But for more than eighteen months there have been no Chinese representatives in the administration. There has also been no opportunity for the Nanking government to investigate the complaints regarding the violation by the Manchurian authorities of the rights and interests of the Chinese Eastern Railway nor to take measures guaranteeing the normal functioning of the road. The failure of the Nanking government to fulfill the obligations incumbent upon it under the Peking and Mukden agreements for a period of eighteen months, deprives it both formally and morally of the right to refer to these agreements.

During his conversations with me in Geneva regarding the restoration of diplomatic relations, Dr. Yen, present ambassador of China in Moscow, proposed that we should exchange notes confirming the inviolability of the Peking and Mukden agreements. I expressed agreement with this, but with the following reservation: "Insofar as the changing situation in Manchuria does not make the fulfillment of these agreements impossible for the Nanking government." This reservation was rejected by Nanking, apparently in recognition of the impossibility for their fulfilling at the present time the obligations undertaken according to the Peking and Mukden agreements.

It seems to me that enough has been said to prove that any possible claims of the Nanking government in the event of the sale of the road to anyone whomsoever, especially the Manchurian authorities, are entirely unfounded. As for the motives impelling us to agree to the sale of the Chinese Eastern Railway, they are as follows: In building the road to Manchuria, on foreign territory, the Tsarist government unquestionably was pursuing imperialist aims. The Soviet government has not and cannot have any such aims. After the October Revolution, the road lost the significance it had had for the people of the Russian empire as an instrument of penetration. The road was, however, built out of the hard-earned money of the peoples inhabiting the Soviet Union, and therefore the Soviet government considered and still considers itself obliged to defend the property interests of the road. It has always been prepared to sell the road to China, but the latter has not been in a position to purchase it.

Fully defending its property rights to the road, the Soviet government has transformed it into a purely commercial enterprise and, taking into consideration the fact that it crosses foreign territory has considered it just to grant to the owners of the territory, parity in the administration of the road and half of the profits. Nonetheless, the Chinese Eastern Railway was becoming a source of friction among the U.S.S.R., China and Manchuria. Everyone remembers the conflict on the Chinese Eastern Railway which arose in 1929 through no fault of the U.S.S.R. With the aim of eliminating the source of conflicts the Soviet government in 1930 carried on negotiations regarding the sale of the Chinese Eastern Railway with Mo Te Hui, representing the Mukden and Nanking governments. These negotiations were broken off as a result of the Manchurian events in the autumn of 1931. Now the question of the sale of the railroad has again arisen. In consideration of the above, we have made a proposal with regard to the sale of the road. Our proposal is still another manifestation of the desire of the Soviet government to maintain peace. I am convinced that objection could be made to this proposal only by those who for some reason are interested in aggravating Soviet-Japanese and Soviet-Manchurian relations.

*STRENGTHENING PEACE IN THE FAR EAST**

The signing of the agreement for the sale of the Chinese Eastern Railway after twenty-one months of negotiation is an important political event, both from the point of view of general developments and from the point of view of the present situation in the Far East.

The C.E.R. was an instrument of the policy of conquest of Tsarist imperialism in the Far East. It served the aim of partitioning China. The masses of Russian people had only one relationship to this policy: by their labor they had to create the means for carrying out this policy and, with their blood, to pay for its consequences. Having overthrown the Tsarist regime and destroyed the rule of the bourgeoisie, the proletariat could not simply renounce the C.E.R. In it were invested large funds belonging to the people. Moreover, they attempted to protect the C.E.R. from ruin as a result of the general war and then to give the road to the Chinese people, using it in this way as an instrument of rapprochement between two great peoples. This last aim was not realized.

Up to this time the Chinese people have not succeeded in freeing themselves from the rule of foreign imperialism and its agents—the various military cliques. The weakening of China, as a result of the defeat of the Chinese masses, made possible the alienation of Manchuria from China, the coming to power on its territory of a foreign army and the development of armed conflict, most severe in the area around the railroad. Without strong military protection, conditions for the peaceful operation of the C.E.R. could not be assured. The Soviet Union, having broken finally and irreversibly with the policy of Tsarist expansion and colonial robbery, could not attempt to insure the operation of the C.E.R. with an armed fist, for such an attempt would lead to participation in the imperialist partition of Manchuria. This fact dictated the appropriateness of selling the C.E.R. to the *de facto* authorities on Manchurian territory in order to protect, as far as possible, the people's investment in it and to avoid those conflicts which were constantly taking place around C.E.R. and which could endanger peace.

The press of the enemies of the Soviet Union and the enemies of

* *Izvestia,* March 24, 1935.

the Chinese people have been talking about our defeat in the Far East and have been trying to drive a wedge between the U.S.S.R. and the Chinese people. We understand very well the motives of such a maneuver. The enemies of the Soviet Union were hoping that the quarrel about the C.E.R. would lead to war. These hopes were frustrated, thanks to the peace policy and strength of the Soviet Union which forced those who love conquest to give up their idea of liquidating the question of the C.E.R. in ways other than by negotiation. Once war did not develop over the C.E.R., then it was necessary at least to make use of the peaceful liquidation of this question in order to try to sow dissention between the Chinese people and the Soviet Union. These efforts are in vain. Every thinking Chinese patriot knows that the U.S.S.R. would have been deeply happy if it had been possible to turn over the railroad to the representatives of the great Chinese people, friendship with whom is especially valued by the people of the U.S.S.R. But the Chinese people are not master of the situation in Manchuria and they would gain nothing if the C.E.R. became the object of a war which might have destroyed this Far Eastern railroad.

The sale of the C.E.R. became possible thanks to the firm decision of the Soviet government to do everything possible to avoid a conflict in the Far East, not dictated by the vital question of the defense of the borders and interests of the U.S.S.R. This sale became possible also thanks to the fact that the Minister of Foreign Affairs in Japan, Mr. Hirota, and the circles around him, for their part, used every means to avoid any settlement of the question other than by negotiation. We are convinced that Mr. Hirota by his policy has done real service for the cause of peace between the U.S.S.R. and Japan and the cause of general peace.

We hope that the Japanese government will do everything that depends on them in order to assure the loyal fulfillment of the agreement just concluded which has served to strengthen the relations between the U.S.S.R. and Japan. Between Japan and the U.S.S.R. there remain disagreements. Their solution will demand serious negotiations in the spirit of mutual concession and understanding of the interests of the Japanese and Soviet peoples in strengthening peace. These negotiations will have meaning and will lead to good results only if in practice, the fulfillment of the agreements on the C.E.R. day by day demonstrates the desire of the Japanese government to fulfil the agreement which has just been reached.

The cause of peace is at present undergoing a serious test in Europe. It is enough to read through the speech of the French Minister of War in the Parliamentary Commission to be convinced how seriously responsible people in the countries deeply interested in the maintenance of European peace are regarding the present situation. This is all the more reason to welcome the fact that in the Far East, which had been considered the center of the most serious war danger, it has been possible to eliminate at least one source of conflict. This was possible because Soviet policy combines a firm striving for peace with the conviction that for its maintenance it is necessary to have force which will be respected. The people of the Soviet Union will welcome the decision about the C.E.R., considering this decision a factor reinforcing peace in the Ear East. They hope that the U.S.S.R., continuing its struggle for the protection of peace, will gain its aims on all fronts where peace is in danger.

*NOTE OF M. LITVINOV IN REPLY TO CHINESE PROTEST ON THE SOVIET-MONGOL PACT, APRIL 8, 1936**

MONSIEUR CHARGE D'AFFAIRES,

On the 7th inst., You, by instruction of your Government, presented me with a copy of a note, which was handed on the same day to M. Bogomolov, Ambassador of the Union of Soviet Socialist Republics to China. This note is based upon this, that the signing on March 12 by the Government of the Union of Soviet Socialist Republics of the Protocol with the Government of the Mongolian People's Republic is supposed to be a violation of the sovereignty of China and to be in contradiction with the Chinese-Soviet Agreement of May 31, 1924, in consequence of which the Nanking Government finds it possible to declare a protest.

In reply to the said note, I have the honor to declare as follows:

The Soviet Government cannot agree with the interpretation of the Soviet-Mongolian Protocol contained in this note, and cannot, therefore, recognize the protest declared by the Chinese Government as justified. Neither the fact of the signing of the Protocol, nor its separate articles, violate to the slightest degree the sovereignty of China, do not admit nor contain any territorial pretensions whatsoever on the part of the Union of Soviet Socialist Republics in relation to China or the Mongolian People's Republic. The signing of the Protocol does not introduce any changes in the formal as well as actual relations which existed up to the present between the Union of Soviet Socialist Republics and China and between the Union of Soviet Socialist Republics and the Mongolian People's Republic.

The Union of Soviet Socialist Republics, in signing the Protocol of mutual assistance, proceeded from this, that the Soviet-Chinese Agreement of 1924 concluded in Peking did not suffer any harm and retains its force. The Soviet Government hereby again affirms that the said agreement, insofar as it relates to the Union of Soviet Socialist Republics, retains its force also for the future.

* *Moscow Daily News*, April 19, 1936.

As regards the question of the formal right to conclude an agreement with the autonomous sections of the Chinese Republics, it is sufficient to recall the conclusion of an Agreement in Mukden on Sept. 20, 1924, between the Soviet Government and the Government of the Three Eastern Provinces, which act did not call forth any protests on the part of the Government of the Chinese Republic. Furthermore, the latter even recognized the said Mukden Agreement as having full force along with the Peking Agreement.

Together with this, it should be noted that the Soviet-Mongolian Agreement is not directed against the interests of other countries, since it comes into force only in the event of the Union of Soviet Socialist Republics or the Mongolian People's Republic becoming victims of aggression and being compelled to defend their own territories.

On the basis of the aforesaid, the Soviet Government considers itself compelled to reject the protest of the Chinese Government as unfounded and at the same time expresses the profound assurance that the Government of the Chinese Republic will become convinced that the Soviet-Mongolian Protocol does not conflict with the Peking Agreement and responds to the interests of both the Mongolian and Chinese peoples.

Accept, etc.

M. LITVINOV.

*PROTEST UNDER PRESSURE FROM TOKYO**

On March 12th of this year in Ulan Bator, representatives of the U.S.S.R. and the Mongol Peoples' Republic signed a protocol of mutual assistance between the two countries, bound by many years of uninterrupted friendship, beginning in 1921 in their common struggle against the white guard bands, hirelings of the Japanese imperialists. This protocol was concluded on the request of the government of the Mongol Peoples Republic which is again threatened by the plans of conquest of Japanese imperialism.

The protocol of March 12th is a weapon for peace and for protection against aggression. It is therefore not at all surprising that the aggressive groups of Japanese imperialists, not having concealed their intentions of seizing the Mongol People's Republic, should express extreme dissatisfaction in connection with the signing of this protocol. Just as soon as the fact was made public, the suitable organs of the Japanese press began, on command from above, to demand that the Nanking government should make a protest against the signing of the Soviet-Mongol protocol, as if it violated the Peking Treaty concluded between the U.S.S.R. and China in 1924. Representatives of the Japanese military at the same time addressed the Nanking government with the same demands, threatening "to take measures" in case they were not met.

And in fact, on April 7th, the Nanking government protested against the Soviet-Mongol protocol of mutual assistance regarding it as a violation of the Peking Treaty. It is clear that the absolutely unfounded protest of the Chinese government was made under direct pressure from Japan which is posing in a completely inappropriate way as the "protector" of the interests of China—that same China against which Japanese imperialism has already for almost five years carried on military action, that same China whose territories (Manchuria, Jehol, Inner-Mongolia, North China) were unceremoniously occupied by Japanese troops.

It is not at all difficult to prove that the arguments of the Chinese government are without the least foundation. The facts which were

* *Pravda*, April 9, 1936.

stated in the reply of the Soviet government established with inescapable clarity the following three circumstances:

First, the U.S.S.R. has no territorial pretentions in relation to China or the Mongol People's Republic.

Second, the Soviet-Mongol protocol of March 12th of this year has only one aim—to reinforce the defense of both countries against aggression by a third party.

And finally, third, the Soviet Union, as before, considers that the Peking Treaty retains its force.

Let us mention briefly the origin of the Soviet-Mongol protocol of mutual assistance.

As is known the white guard general, Baron Ungern von Sternberg, financed and directed by the Japanese High Command invaded the territory of Outer Mongolia with his bands in 1921. From there, carrying out the commands of his actual master—the Japanese High Command—Ungern organized an attack on Soviet territory.

The Chinese military authorities and the Mongol government then addressed a request to the Soviet government to bring their troops on to the territory of Outer Mongolia in order to liquidate the white guard band acting under the orders of the Japanese imperialists. Units of the Red Army, along with Mongol armed forces, defeated the white guard bands of Ungern.

It is important to know that before the units of the Red Army were brought on to the territory of Mongolia, the Soviet government more than once requested the Chinese government to liquidate the white guard bands but these requests did not produce any results, for the Chinese authorities and the Peking government of that time were powerless.

On the other hand, the Peking government did not regard the presence of Soviet troops on Mongol territory as any infringement of Chinese sovereignty. The leading political and social figure of China, Sun Yat-sen, understood very well the significance of this disinterested help which the Soviet government gave to the Mongol people. In January 1923, at the time when Soviet troops were on the territory of Outer Mongolia, Sun Yat-sen together with the Soviet representative in China issued a special communique. In this document Sun Yat-sen stated directly that he "does not consider the immediate withdrawal of Russian troops from Outer Mongolia either an imperative necessity nor in accord with the real interests of China, especially taking into account the inability of the present Peking government to prevent the renewal, after such an evacuation, of intrigue and inimical action against Russia on the part of the white guards and the development of an even more serious situation than exists at present."

Now when real danger of invasion of the Mongol People's Republic by Japanese troops again has developed, the Mongol government considers that it has no basis for expecting aid from the Chinese government which is itself unable to undertake any action against the seizure of many Chinese provinces by Japan. Consequently when continuous Japanese raids on Mongol territory indicated to the government of the Mongol People's Republic that Japanese imperialism was preparing for war against the Mongol people, it turned in 1934 to the Soviet government with a proposal that the mutual obligations which both countries had taken on themselves in 1921 again be confirmed.

In that same year a verbal agreement on mutual assistance was reached by the two governments. It was of the character of a gentlemen's agreement. When the danger of military attack became even more threatening, the government of the Mongol People's Republic considered it necessary to address the Soviet government with a request for a written formulation of the existing verbal agreement on mutual assistance. The government of the Mongol People's Republic made such a request, to the government of the U.S.S.R. on January 25, 1936. This request met with agreement from the Soviet government and on March 12th a protocol of mutual assistance between the U.S.S.R. and the Mongol People's Republic was signed in Ulan Bator.

In this way, the very origin of the Soviet-Mongol protocol indicates how unfounded is the protest of the Chinese government. The reference of the Chinese government to paragraph 5 of the Peking treaty is equally unfounded. In this paragraph it is exactly and clearly stated that Soviet troops will be withdrawn from the territory of Outer Mongolia only after an agreement is reached at a special Soviet-Chinese conference on other measures to guarantee the security of the frontier.

In spite of the fact that the Soviet-Chinese conference has not taken place and the government of the U.S.S.R. consequently had the right to leave its troops on the territory of the Mongol People's Republic, it withdrew them in 1925, just as soon as the danger to the inviolability of the frontier of Outer Mongolia had passed. With just as undisputable clarity, it follows from this that as soon as a similar danger might arise the Soviet government had the full right to bring its troops into Outer Mongolia at the request of local or Chinese authorities, both for the protection of its frontiers and the frontiers of the Soviet Union, inasmuch as Outer Mongolia is a base desired by the Japanese military, which aims to seize the Mongol People's Republic and to threaten the Soviet Union. The seizure of Outer Mongolia would create a direct threat to the Soviet Pri-Baikal region, the Siberian trunkline, and to the entire Far Eastern Krai.

Consequently we see that from the formal point of view, the protest of the Chinese government is likewise unfounded. Its assertion that the Soviet-Mongol protocol violates the sovereignty of China is, to say the least, strange and incomprehensible. On the contrary, it seems indisputable that the sovereignty of China could only suffer from a violation of the frontier and the integrity of Outer Mongolia by Japanese imperialists, the more so because the Chinese government is not in a position to prevent that.

The Soviet-Mongol protocol is not directed against any country in particular, inasmuch as it comes into force only in case the U.S.S.R. or the Mongol People's Republic suffers an attack by an aggressor and are forced to protect their territories. It is laughable when the Japanese imperialists raise the cry that the Soviet-Mongol protocol is "an act of conquest" of the Mongol People's Republic by the Soviet Union. The Japanese military for a long time have specialized in the seizure of foreign territory and it is least suitable of all for it to appear in the role of the protector of the Mongol People's Republic or China.

The Chinese people know who is their enemy and who is their real disinterested friend. The protest of the Chinese government will remain in the history of Soviet-Chinese relations as an episode which took place only because the Nanking government was not strong enough to resist the pressure of the Japanese imperialists.

*AFTER THE LIBERATION OF CHIANG KAI-SHEK**

The political crisis in China caused by the action of Chang Hsueh-liang—the arrest of Chiang Kai-shek and the threat of internecine war in that country—has been settled peacefully and as far as can be seen, comparatively harmlessly. Chiang Kai-shek and Chang Hsueh-liang have arrived in Nanking. There obviously remains to be worked out a final formulation of a compromise agreement which will prevent the civil war about to break out. This solution will be greeted with relief by the friends of China throughout the world who have from the very beginning of the conflict expressed hope of its speedy, peaceful solution.

The Japanese aggressors have seen in the prospect of an internecine Chinese war a source of new hope and a potentially strong weapon for achieving their dreams of conquest and a glorious solution for the difficult situation which has been developing for them (as a result of increased resistance by China and failure of their attempts to seize Suiyuan). While the fate of internal peace in China hung by a hair Japanese imperialism exerted all its strength in order, on the one hand, to cause a clash between Nanking and Chang Hsueh-liang and, on the other, to utilize the situation to convert the Nanking government into a tool of its control. Japanese Minister of Foreign Affairs Arita in conversations with the Chinese Ambassador in Tokyo directly demanded the rejection of a compromise with Chang Hsueh-liang and the immediate expulsion of "anti-Japanese elements" from the Nanking government, asserting, with threats, that Japan would not permit a compromise solution of the conflict caused by the arrest of Chiang Kai-shek. The Japanese Ambassador Kawagaoe repeated the same demands and threats in Nanking. Even the Japanese agent Prince Te Wang, nominally heading a Japanese-Mongol band which invaded Suiyuan and was defeated by Chinese troops, involved himself in this game by announcing (to the amusement of the whole world) his "loyalty" to the Nanking government and his "anxiety" over the arrest of Chiang Kai-shek and his willingness to delay the seizure of Suiyuan in order that the Nanking government might carry out a punitive expedition against

* *Izvestia*, December 27, 1936.

Chang Hsueh-liang, unhindered. It cannot be doubted, on the other hand, that if the provocateurs and the Japanese espionage agents could in general exert any influence on the course of events in Sian, this influence would not in any way have been directed in the interest of peace and the personal safety of the head of the government arrested in Suiyuan. To the many disappointments of the Japanese military, doubtless must be added the circumstance that Chiang Kai-shek returned to Nanking alive and unharmed.

The Japanese imperialists were not able to conceal their dissatisfaction and anxiety caused by the peaceful outcome of the conflict. The Japanese press only expressed the hope that Chiang Kai-shek's position had been undermined by the Sian events. The Japanese government, according to newspaper reports, took a clearly threatening position although, as usual, written in the code cf its formula (this time—"careful observation" instead of "waiting") in which anything you please can be concealed. The Japanese military have expressed themselves openly and have directly threatened China "with serious consequences." It is clear that Japan's hopes have suffered a serious blow, but it is no less clear that Japanese imperialism is using all means—from threats to provocations and direct force—in order to bring about a new conflict in China and to interfere with its real unification.

The exact conditions on which the compromise with Chang Hsueh-liang was reached are not yet known, just as the immediate concrete development of events in Nanking is also not known. But several lessons can be drawn from this episode, the first of which consists in the fact that despite the disruptive work which the Japanese imperialists and their agents in China are carrying on, the country has advanced significantly in the matter of national unification and in creating the prerequisites for successful struggle for its independence. The outcome of the present conflict confirms and reinforces the similar conclusion which could already be drawn on the basis of the failure of the uprising of the southern generals this summer and its peaceful liquidation.

The second lesson consists of the fact that the success of the Nanking government as the central organizing force in China was based in both cases precisely on those tendencies to be noted in its policies during the last year; that is, the tendency to move in the direction of making peace with public opinion in China, readiness to take more decisive steps to oppose the external enemy and the ability—although only in prospect and with many hesitations and failures—to be included in the powerful movement, now inspiring that country, demanding the unification of all forces for defense against Japanese imperialism.

Finally, the third and most important lesson consists in the fact that the attempts to attack Nanking and to create the danger of civil war—attempts objectively favoring the Japanese aggressors—were in general possible only to the extent that the Nanking government continued to show hesitation and to make concessions to Japanese imperialism which infringed the independence and integrity of China and to reject the offers of cooperation from other anti-Japanese forces in China. This, and only this, made the government vulnerable to some extent and permitted its opponents to conceal themselves in anti-Japanese slogans and in a program of a united front which enjoyed the support of the broad masses of the population of China.

The salvation of that country is the real unification of all its human resources without exception which are prepared for the joint defense of China against the foreign aggressor.

(*Signed*) VIGILIS.

*SECURITY IN THE PACIFIC**

The opening of the British Empire Conference—the meeting of the English government with the governments of the Dominions—has caused some disillusionment to reactionaries, isolationists, enemies of the collective organization of peace and those who favor making deals with the aggressors at the expense of others. They gambled on the "provincialism" of the Dominions, counting on the fact that, not being directly interested in European affairs, the latter would come out against the principle of collective security. However they were mistaken for it appeared that many of the Dominions understand very well the dependence of their own security on the organization of peace and see the general base for British Imperial policy precisely in efforts directed toward that organization. "The Patriots" who advocated the policy of cowardly retreat before the aggressors were especially unpleasantly surprised by the speech made by the Australian Prime Minister Lyons at the opening of the Conference. Lyons stated that the cornerstone of Empire policy is precisely the principle of the League of Nations. If, unfortunately, these principles do not succeed in being applied fully in actuality, nevertheless the policy of the Empire should be constructed, in the opinion of the Australian government, on the readiness of the nations forming that Empire to take part in joint actions directed toward the support of international law and order. Lyons said in part, "The Australian government notes the tendency of governments to conclude agreements in the form of regional pacts affecting areas in which they are directly interested. Australia would welcome a regional agreement and pact of non-aggression among the countries of Pacific in the spirit of the principle of the League of Nations. In the creation of such a pact we are prepared to cooperate with all other countries of the Pacific." [Retranslated from the Russian]

The Far East as part of the Pacific Ocean basin is one of the two most important focuses of war danger at the present time. For nearly six years aggressive Japanese imperialism has been carrying

* *Izvestia,* May 21, 1937.

on uninterruptedly "a small war" in China, seizing extensive Chinese territories; at the same time feverishly preparing for "a big war" on land, on sea and in the air, and threatening the security not only of its immediate neighbors but of all the countries in the Pacific. Here as in Europe, the preservation of peace demands its collective organization as the only possible way to stop the aggressor and ensure the security of peaceful countries. The Australian project for a regional pact is therefore a step in the right direction and deserves the support of all.

The conclusion of a regional pact, in accordance with the Australian project, would serve the interests of all countries of the Pacific, each of which is threatened separately at present. It would be in the interests of Australia and New Zealand which constantly feel the threat of Japanese aggression; in the interests of China, whose very existence as a state is under the damoclean sword of that aggression; in the interests of western countries—England, France and Holland, whose possessions in the Pacific are whetting the growing appetite of the Japanese imperialists, in the interests of the United States whose Far Eastern policy is built on the principle of the Open Door and support for the sovereignty of China and its territorial integrity which is being violated by Japan. It would answer the interests of the Soviet Union because these interests are only in the guarantee of peace. It would correspond, finally, to the interests of Japan itself: the militarists insolently deceive the Japanese people, convincing them that someone or other is preparing to encroach upon Japan, and the conclusion of such a pact guaranteeing Japan the same security as the other Pacific countries would put an end to this deceit. There is no need to prove that collective security in the Pacific area would play a tremendous, perhaps decisive, role also in the protection of peace in Europe, and would be a powerful factor in preventing the terrible war which the Fascist aggressors are preparing for mankind.

It is self-evident that the Japanese imperialists will bayonet this project, for the conclusion of such a pact would to a considerable extent paralyze Japanese aggression. However the pact could nevertheless be concluded if the great powers would actively support it, if they would show a real desire and readiness to create a collective system and if Japan were presented with a choice between participation in this regional agreement or complete isolation. The policy of organization of peace in the Pacific basin fully corresponds with the hopes of the peaceful elements in Japan itself who would thus obtain a method of curbing the extremist militarists. For the success of this policy, however, first of all it is necessary that the powers should not refuse in advance to participate in a real struggle for peace in the Pacific, that they should not prefer to seek agreement with the aggressor and should not retreat before his impudent demands.

The fact that this project has been advanced remains a very positive factor, for it bears witness to the fact that the idea of collective organization of peace—the only way to guarantee that peace—burns in the consciousness of peoples and swells the ranks of its advocates. The proposal of the Australian government will have great international political significance, especially if it receives proper support from the great powers.

(*Signed*) VIG.

*THE SIGNIFICANCE OF EVENTS IN NORTH CHINA**

The news coming out of North China indicates that extremely important events are developing in the Far East. The entire circumstances surrounding the conflict in North China bear this out. It is a question of a new, important stage in the imperialist struggle in eastern Asia and in the Pacific Ocean, of an essentially new step in the aggression of Japanese imperialism, striving to enslave the Chinese people.

It is not difficult to note the general lines of resemblance between the events of July, 1937 and the events of September, 1931 when Japan began the occupation of Manchuria. The present conflict, just as Japan's predatory acts in Manchuria arose, as if accidentally, in connection with an incident which was almost incomprehensible to the outside world. In 1937, as in 1931, immediately after the "sudden" incident there was a feverish fuss and fury among the Japanese military in their attempt to exaggerate the importance of the incident which had taken place and their demands on China. In an action paralleling this, just as in September, 1931, Japanese diplomacy has gone through various maneuvers in order to create the impression in Europe and America that this was just a matter of an insignificant local conflict. In other words, now, just as six years ago, Japan is exerting decisive pressure on China, trying to intimidate it, and at the same time is putting the foreign powers off guard by reassuring reports. At the same time, now, as in 1931 the Japanese military from the very moment of the "local incident" has been sending troops to the continent, creating an atmosphere of war psychosis in Japan itself.

This instructive analogy between July, 1937 and September, 1931 only underlines those aspects of the events which are taking place which causes informed observers to conclude that the events in North China herald the beginning of the long and basically-prepared second step in the conquest of China by the Japanese imperialists. In 1931, the Japanese militarists proclaimed the necessity for establishing in Manchuria Japan's "first life line of defense." The phraseology of the Japanese military has long been familiar to the

* *Izvestia*, July 22, 1937.

world. In speaking of "life line of defense" they have in view the first step of their attack.

In undertaking to realize their further plans for conquest, the Japanese militarists have not taken any trouble in thinking up some kind of new methods or means for covering up their aggressive plans. The Japanese military, as is known, are not particularly distinguished by their ingenuity. Their plans and their motivations generally simply reflect their primitiveness. But, why should the Japanese imperialists invent new methods of expansion in 1937, if the methods used in 1931 were successful? For this very reason, in assessing the significance of the threatening events in North China, it is extremely useful to recall what were the circumstances that helped to bring about the success of Japanese aggression in 1931.

There is no doubt whatever that Japan succeeded in carrying out her plans in Manchuria only as a result of the passivity of the western powers. Moreover, open acquiescence on the part of England played no small part in the success of the Japanese conquest in 1931–32. Certain English politicians having misjudged the correlation of forces in the Far East evidently presupposed that Japanese aggression in Manchuria would unfold in an entirely different direction than toward North and Central China. It will do no harm to recall that English acquiescence at one time went so far that it was England which disrupted the diplomatic attack of the Secretary of State of the United States, Stimson, who was trying to oppose Japanese aggression through the mechanism of the Nine-Power Treaty.

Against the background of 1931–32, it is especially lamentable and alarming that in her attitude to the present conflict England is again adopting the position of 1931. And now, as then, the English Conservative Press is trying to play down the significance of the events in China, to create the impression that it is a question of an incident not affecting the interests of third countries. In other words, the London Conservative newspapers are supporting that version which is necessary to the Japanese militarist for concealing their widely conceived military operations.

But the position, occupied up to the present moment by the English government in connection with the war in North China is reminiscent not only of the Far Eastern experience of 1931. The English Conservatives are repeating, in their application to the Far East, their favorite methods which have brought British policy to failure not only in the Far East, but also in Africa and in western

Europe. The Conservative politicians, obviously, are influenced by threats of bluff and blackmail, irrespective of whether they are fabricated in the Far East or in Central Europe. Some English politicians, obviously, are prepared to believe the aggressors' blatantly lying promises to localize international conflict, regardless of whether these false promises are given in regard to the coast of the Pacific Ocean or the Mediterranean.

As is known, in 1931 Japan assured the powers, particularly England, that its aggression would be limited to Manchuria. Japan did not keep these promises at all. Having seized Manchuria, Japan occupied Jehol, invaded North China, established a puppet government in Hopei, organized the Hopei-Chahar political council, subservient to Tokyo, and brought under its control six districts of Chahar. Now Japan is attempting to complete the occupation of North China, to seize Peiping by military force, preparing the further military penetration of Central China, and perhaps, South China. The activities of the Japanese authorities in Formosa and the southern Islands of Japan make it possible even to assume the existence of concrete plans for conquest extending further than South China. In any case, it is known that a division each is prepared to be sent into Shantung and Shanghai.

Such then are the circumstances which bespeak the futility of counting on the agreement of Japanese militarists to localize the expansion being started by them. Japan will refrain from carrying out its plans of conquest only in case several reliable governments refrain from acquiescing in those plans. It is necessary to have in mind that the position of Japan and the situation in China are not at all such that the Japanese militarists could regard military operation in North China as a pleasure stroll. No matter how primitive the political conceptions of the Japanese military, they cannot but take into account the fact that Japan is not in a position to carry through a policy of conquest against the whole world.

Several years ago the Japanese government advanced the thesis that China as a whole should be placed under the protectorate of Japan. In the notorious "unofficial statement" of the Japanese Minister of Foreign Affairs made in April 1934 and in the official commentary on it Japan stated that all attempts by foreign powers to support China, to advance loans, to act in cooperation or protect their interests in China would call for "positive measures" on the part of Japan even to the extent of use of armed forces. The impossibility of realizing such a maximum program for Japanese imperialism became apparent in practice very quickly. It was exactly for this reason that Japanese diplomacy began its pilgrimage to London and attempted in the spring of this year to reach an agreement with England on a division of spheres of influence in China; however the proposals made by Japan at that time were obviously of such cynical character that they caused embarrassment even among English conservative circles. Through the mouth of Lord Cranborne the British government in May of this year denied the proposal that England was preparing to cease to respect the sovereign rights of China.

Does it then follow that now one should assume that England's ignoring of the deep significance of present events in North China means that England no longer respects the sovereignty of China? This would also mean that England renounces its own interests in China. This would mean also that London is incorrectly evaluating the relation of forces in the Far East.

Up to this point we have been speaking of those aspects in which the events of July, 1937 resembled September, 1931. There are, however, also very real lines of difference. Not mentioning such a decisive factor as the extraordinary growth of power of the Soviet Union, it is necessary to refer to two important circumstances. In the last six years the movement of the Chinese people against the Japanese invaders has grown enormously, and the Japanese rear, exhausted and disorganized by six years of adventurist policy, has become very much weakened. The rising prices and the growth of the strike movement in Japan, new financial difficulties and a number of other factors indicate that the new stage of the policy of conquest in China is developing under circumstances of great instability in the internal situation of Japan. At the same time the first days of the new conflict in North China already bear witness to the growth of firmness and opposition on the part of China, to the increase of national consciousness, and to the people's indignation against the invaders.

Specifically, these circumstances give special significance to the question of the further tactics of the powers. Several years ago the position taken by England in fact decided the question in favor of Japan. Now again the decisive moment is approaching which forces the foreign governments, especially England to take a definite position. The conflict in North China and the relationship of the powers to it can become a most important factor in the international situation.

*PACT OF NON-AGGRESSION BETWEEN THE U.S.S.R. AND CHINA**

The conclusion of the Treaty of Non-Aggression between the U.S.S.R. and China published in today's paper undoubtedly calls forth very real satisfaction and sympathy among the peoples of the U.S.S.R. and the Chinese people. The pacts of non-aggression concluded by the Soviet Union in accordance with the principles of its peace policy and with the methods used by the U.S.S.R. in the struggle for peace have always represented active instruments of peace. In all respects this is also the characteristic of the pact of non-aggression between the U.S.S.R. and China.

The Treaty of Non-Aggression between the Soviet Union and the Chinese Republic is in complete accord both with the character of Soviet-Chinese relations and with the role of the U.S.S.R., the indefatigable and consistent fighter for peace on all sectors of international relations. From the time when normal diplomatic relations between the U.S.S.R. and the Chinese Republic were reestablished in 1932 the way was open for further rapprochement between both countries. In 1933, Litvinov, speaking before the session of the Central Executive Committee of the U.S.S.R., said that the Soviet Union had accepted the suggestion of the Chinese Government for concluding a pact of non-aggression and that a draft of such a pact had been given to the Chinese Government for consideration. Litvinov pointed out in this connection that "strictly adhering to the policies of non-interference in the internal affairs of China, we are following its fight for independence and national unity with the greatest sympathy."

Is it necessary to say that this attitude remains in full force at the present moment when China is straining all its efforts to defend its independence and to secure its national unity? The position of the Soviet Union, long well known to the Chinese people, finds its documentary expression in the obligation now undertaken by the Soviet Union not to attack China and not to render any direct or indirect support to a power or powers attacking the Chinese

* *Izvestia*, August 30, 1937.

Republic. We note, at the same time, as a real factor for peace the analogous obligations assumed by China in relation to the U.S.S.R. regarding non-aggression and not rendering aid or support to the aggressor.

The negotiations for the treaty which has just been signed have been carried on for more than a year. Several factors in the internal and external policies of China prevented the conclusion of a treaty of non-aggression with the U.S.S.R. but recently a number of factors have impelled the Chinese government to take a more active interest in the question of completing the long negotiations with the Soviet Union. Not an unimportant role was played in this by the wide growth of sympathy for the Soviet Union among the masses of Chinese people. The Chinese people have always seen in the Soviet government a friend and these feelings have been especially clearly reflected in the days of trial that have now overtaken the Chinese Republic. These trials, connected with the general deterioration of the international situation, are impelling the Chinese Government to take steps to strengthen their relations with the peace-loving nations, particularly with the U.S.S.R. It is altogether natural that under these circumstances China's interest in concluding, as quickly as possible, the treaty of non-aggression with the U.S.S.R. should have increased, as a result of which the negotiations were completed and the pact of non-aggression was signed in Nanking.

The conclusion of the treaty of non-aggression with China is a new indication of the unchanging peace-loving policy of the U.S.S.R. The principle of the indivisibility of peace pronounced by the Soviet Union not only means a theoretical statement of the fact that breaking of peace in any sector of international relations brings a threat of war in the most varied places. The principle of the indivisibility of peace also means that the Soviet Union is actively interested in the preservation of peace on all sectors of international relations—in the West and in the East, in Europe and in Asia; consequently the U.S.S.R. is following with special attention the Far Eastern crisis which is threatening the general peace, and by signing the pact of non-aggression is emphasizing its friendly relations with China.

*LITVINOV'S SPEECH AT THE OPENING OF THE BRUSSELS CONFERENCE**

Having come here on the invitation of signatories to the Washington Treaty, and in view of the decisions of the League of Nations, I can subscribe to the characterization of the Far Eastern events which has been given here by the powers that sent the invitation and particularly by the esteemed representative of the United States. There is no need for me to make a special declaration here, the more so since the problem confronting the conference has already been under discussion in Geneva, where the proposal to convene this conference arose and where everything the situr ation demands was said.

The Soviet Government has had repeated occasion to express itself both on the general question of struggle against aggression, as an international phenomenon, and also concerning individual cases when this aggression was actively manifested. All these utterances have always been inspired exclusively by its devotion to the idea of peace. This idea undoubtedly inspires, with very few exceptions, the governments of the other powers as well, and this gives them all a common platform and a common point of departure. Divergencies between them begin only when the question arises of a transition from the general idea to the question of the most effective methods of preserving peace or restoring it where it is found to have been violated.

At any rate the first inevitable step for the adoption of any methods is a joint discussion of the problem at international conferences or in other organizations. In some cases the very fact of the convening of a conference for a joint discussion is in itself a certain act having a definite moral value. That is why, on behalf of the Soviet Government, I welcome this conference and express gratitude to the Belgian government and M. Spaak, its foreign minister, for the trouble they have taken in bringing about this conference, and for the reception accorded the delegations.

"Recent years have enriched international life with highly

* *Moscow Daily News*, November 4, 1937.

valuable experience, and this experience compels us to turn our attention to those dangerous gulfs and pitfalls which lie in the path of international conferences. The said experience teaches us that international conferences, committees and other organizations called upon to serve a definite purpose, particularly in cases of prolonged existence, are sometimes prone to forget their direct purpose, their serviceable role, and begin to live their own life, guided by their own interests. They begin to concern themselves chiefly with preserving their existence, with morally gratifying the initiators and organizers of these conferences, with their own outward successes which do not always coincide with the successes of the cause for which the conference was called to life. Moreover, there sometimes arises even a divergence between these various interests; there even comes a moment when the conference or committee, which should strive to eliminate and overcome aggressive phenomena, themselves imperceptibly become the tool of the aggressor, who uses them as a screen and an aid for his aggressive actions.

This happens when international organizations come into contact with the aggressors themselves in attempts to get them to change their position. In the process of negotiations connected with consistent concessions to the aggressor it is possible to overstep the line on which persons, undoubtedly inspired by the best intentions, slip, without noticing it themselves, into the viewpoint of the aggressor, commence to speak in his language, actually justifying and encouraging his actions.

When it is a question of an aggressive assault by one state against another, given a certain success of such assault, there is nothing so easy for the international organization, in order to achieve success, as to say to the aggressor: 'keep the booty you have seized by violence, and peace be with you,' and to the victim of aggression—'love your aggressor and do not resist evil.' However, this can be an outward success for the conference but not a triumph of peace, not a triumph of peace-loving countries. Such successes can merely give rise to further cases of aggression and create a need for new conferences, and so on ad infinitum. The encouragement and multiplication of aggression is facilitated also by the circumstance that with the deviation on the part of international organizations from the straight path, as I have pointed out above, friction between peaceful countries, which leads to discord between them and which in its turn, is deftly utilized by the aggressor, is inevitable. Yet the unity of peaceful countries is particularly essential at a time when the aggressive countries are uniting more and more and rallying together, creating a menace to an even greater number of states.

Deeming it necessary to warn against those dangers which any conference might encounter under present conditions, I express the wish that the Brussels conference and the proposal which we shall probably hear from the powers which have issued the invitation might be successful. I am confident that the new conference will avoid the dangers I have pointed out and that the proposals will pursue the aim not only of restoring peace in the Far East but of restoring a just peace, a peace which will not unleash but will leash aggression in the future in other parts of the world as well.

*THE BERLIN PACT OF TRIPARTITE ALLIANCE**

A pact of military alliance between Germany, Italy and Japan was concluded in Berlin on September 27. There is no need to dwell upon the contents of this pact, as its text has been published in the press. The pact does not represent anything particularly unexpected for the Soviet Union, both because it constitutes in effect the embodiment of relations already formed between Germany, Italy and Japan on the one hand, and Britain and the United States of America on the other hand, and because the Soviet Government had been informed by the German Government about the impending conclusion of a tripartite pact before it was published.

Proceeding to the significance of this pact, one should note in the first place that it signifies the advent of a new phase of the war, more extensive than that prior to the conclusion of the pact. Whereas until latterly the war has been confined to Europe and northern Africa in the West, and to China in the East, with these two spheres being separated from each other, now an end is being put to this separation, for henceforward Japan renounces the policy of non-intervention in European affairs, while Germany and Italy in their turn renounce the policy of non-intervention in Far Eastern affairs. This undoubtedly means the further intensification of the war and the expansion of its realm. Comrade Molotov was right when he said in his speech at the last session of the Supreme Soviet of the U.S.S.R. that there had arisen "the danger of further extension and fanning of the war and its transformation into a world imperialist war."

What was the reason for the appearance of this pact, what stimulated it?

Undoubtedly it was stimulated in the first place by the recent intensification and extension of military cooperation between Britain and the United States of America. This refers to the continuously increasing military assistance rendered by the United States of America to Britain; the transfer of British naval bases in the Western Hemisphere to the United States of America; the joining of the war efforts of Britain, Canada and Australia with those of the

* *Pravda*, September 30, 1940.

United States of America, and the inclusion of South-American countries into the sphere of influence of the United States of America; Britain's consent to transfer her Far Eastern and Australian bases to the United States of America. Of course, the U.S.A. has not yet formally joined the war on the side of Britain against Germany, Italy and Japan. But this is not so important since in fact the U.S.A. is in the one common military camp with the military adversaries of Germany, Italy and Japan in both hemispheres.

One of the important features of the pact is that it openly recognizes the spheres of influence of its signatories and the division of these spheres between them with the undertaking of mutual defense of these spheres of influence against attempts on the part of other states, and certainly, in the first place, on the part of Britain and the United States of America which collaborates with her. Under this pact "the great Eastern Asiatic sphere" is allotted to Japan, and "Europe" to Germany and Italy. Whether the signatories of the pact will succeed in realizing in practice such a division of spheres of influence is a different question. Undoubtedly the realization of such a plan will depend on the real correlation of forces of the belligerents, on the progress and issue of the present war which is growing more and more acute.

Another important feature of the pact is the reservation it contains with regard to the Soviet Union. The pact says:

"Germany, Italy and Japan declare that the present agreement in no way affects the political status existing at present between each of the three participants in the agreement and the Soviet Union."

This reservation should be understood, in the first place, as respect on the part of the signatories of the pact for the position of neutrality which the Soviet Union has adhered to since the very first days of the war.

Further, it should be understood as confirmation of the strength and significance of the non-aggression pact between the U.S.S.R. and Germany and the non-aggression pact between the U.S.S.R. and Italy.

True to its policy of peace and neutrality, the Soviet Union on its part can confirm that, insofar as it will depend on the Soviet Union, this policy remains and will remain unchanged.

*THE HISTORIC REVERSAL IN THE RELATIONS BETWEEN THE U.S.S.R. AND JAPAN**

The visit in Moscow of the Minister of Foreign Affairs of Japan, Yusuke Matsuoka, and the negotiations which he carried on with the Chairman of the Sovnarkom of U.S.S.R. and Peoples Commissar of Foreign Affairs, V. M. Molotov resulted in the conclusion of a pact of neutrality between the Soviet Union and Japan. This pact has great significance for the normalization and regularization of Soviet-Japanese relations as a whole. Its significance is increased if one takes into account the fact that it was signed in the heat of the second imperialist war, the end of which is not yet in sight and which, on the contrary, continues spreading more and more and drawing into its orbit more and more peoples.

In the course of several decades, relations between the two countries have been far from satisfactory. Beginning with the Russo-Japanese war, when the organizationally weak, politically near-sighted and anti-popular Russian Tsarism sent the heroic Russian soldiers and sailors to an undeserved defeat, and ending with the most recent years, not a few deplorable pages have been written in the history of the relations between the two powers. Various Japanese government officials have not understood the meaning of the Great October Socialist Revolution, have not understood the depth of the changes which have taken place, have not understood all the tremendous differences between Tsarist Russia with its oppressive regime and the great powerful Union of Soviet Socialist Republics. As a result, there was Japanese Intervention in the Soviet Far East during the years of the Civil War; there was the endless series of border incidents up to the famous events at Lake Hasan and at Khalkin-gol; but these very events helped various military and political figures in Japan understand their mistake and understand that the U.S.S.R. is not a suitable object for any kind of aggression, that the U.S.S.R. carries on its own policies and does not permit anyone ever to subject it to a foreign will, and that consequently it was essential to take a step in the direction of establishing friendly relations with the Soviet Union.

* *Izvestia*, April 15, 1941.

It is understandable that the U.S.S.R. could only welcome this desire to liquidate the atmosphere of enmity and to start on the road of friendly relations between the two countries.

In this sense the conclusion of a pact of neutrality between the U.S.S.R. and Japan is a historic reversal in the relations between these countries for it brings to an end the old unfriendly relations which had become traditional and paves the way to new good-neighborly and friendly relations between the U.S.S.R. and Japan.

It is necessary to realize that the present Japanese government from the very beginning showed an understanding of the whole importance of peaceful and good-neighborly relations between Japan and the Soviet Union. And the head of that government, the Prime Minister of Japan, Prince Konoye, (particularly in his statement published by us today) and his Minister of Foreign Affairs, Matsuoka, more than once have stressed their desire to establish friendly relations with the Soviet Union. The Soviet government, the basis of whose relations with all its neighbors is its peace policy, naturally could not but value this desire. As a result of this mutual understanding, the pact of neutrality between the Soviet Union and Japan was signed in Moscow April 13.

The signing of the treaty obviously still does not settle all the various problems of Soviet-Japanese relations, but it opens a direct road to their regularization. At the same time it is well known what difficulties usually accompany the negotiations, let us say, on the Fisheries Convention, the trade treaty, or various kinds of economic questions. There can be no doubt that a considerable share in these difficulties must be attributed to the fact that the basic political relationships between the Soviet Union and Japan were not regularized.

The signing, along with the Soviet-Japanese pact, of a declaration of mutual respect for the territorial integrity and inviolability of the Mongol People's Republic and Manchukuo will put an end to the small border conflicts which have disturbed the peace and created anxiety. This, even more, reinforces the important prerequisites provided by the pact for solving the general economic problems confronting the U.S.S.R. and Japan.

In this way the documents signed on April 13 in Moscow not only assist in strengthening peace, but also open the way to real good-neighbor friendly relations between the two great peoples of both countries. The historic paths of development of both the Soviet Union and Japan demand such relations. Enmity between these two powers can only serve as an obstacle to the realization of the tasks each one has set for itself. It is not by chance that at various historical stages various third countries have tried to support and stir up this enmity. Having passed through a multitude of difficult experiences, Soviet-Japanese relations are now entering a new phase which promises to bear good fruit.

The people of the Soviet Union warmly support any act of its government directed toward the reinforcement of peace. There can be no doubt that they will greet with full satisfaction this new peace-loving step—the conclusion of the pact of neutrality between the Soviet Union and Japan.

*WAR IN THE PACIFIC**

December 7, 1941 will go down in history as the date of the outbreak of a great war in the Pacific. On this date Japanese naval and air forces treacherously and without warning attacked American possessions in the Pacific.

On December 8 the British possessions—Malaya and Hongkong—became the objects of similar treacherous attacks. Military operations were thus begun not only against the United States but also against Great Britain.

These military operations began precisely one hour before the Japanese Ambassador in the United States, Nomura, and the special Japanese envoy who had come to Washington to conduct negotiations, Kurusu, handed to the United States Government the Japanese reply to Secretary of State Cordell Hull's memorandum of November 26. Although this reply rejected American proposals, it did not contain either threat or warning that military operations would follow.

The fact that the Hawaiian Islands, the Philippines, Guam, Hongkong and Malaya, situated at great distances from Japan and in different parts of the Pacific, were attacked almost simultaneously testified that the aggression had been carefully prepared beforehand. The negotiations which the Japanese representatives were conducting in Washington were manifestly intended to camouflage preparations for this treacherous attack. Japan resorted to a method with which the Soviet people is familiar from its experience of war against blood-thirsty Hitler, who in the same treacherous, piratical way attacked the Soviet Union.

Thus it is perfectly obvious that in this instance Japan is the undoubted aggressor, while the United States and Great Britain have become objects of a premeditated and prepared aggression.

The suddenness of the premeditated attack gained certain temporary successes for the Japanese armed forces. The Americans suffered serious losses. They lost a number of aircraft and warships. Great Britain suffered similar losses. A not inconsiderable number of noncombatants became victims of aggression.

* *Pravda,* December 12, 1941.

Military operations are continuing on a constantly growing scale. The Japanese have made several attempts to land troops in the Philippines, where they have encountered strong resistance, and to seize Guam, Wake and Midway Islands. Violent fighting is in progress in Malaya and at Hongkong, where the advance of Japanese troops has been checked.

Such is the balance of the first days of war in the Pacific, which have clearly demonstrated that the Japanese aggressor designed to strike simultaneous blows at the most important strategic centers of the British Empire. But Japan's initial successes can by no means predetermine either the further course of military events or, still less, the outcome of the war. The fact that Germany and Italy have also declared war on the United States does not alter the situation.

The Japanese aggressor has plunged into a very hazardous adventure, which bodes him nothing but defeat. If he counted on the possibility of "lightning victory," he is in for a disappointment no less cruel than that suffered by blood-thirsty Hitler as a result of his bandit attack on the Soviet Union.

Japan faces a powerful coalition formed by the united forces of the United States of America, Great Britain and China—for there can be no doubt that the outbreak of a great war in the Pacific will entail a sharp intensification of activity on the Sino-Japanese front as well.

The suddenness of Japan's treacherous attack on the United States and Great Britain enabled the Japanese armed forces to achieve certain insignificant, temporary successes. But it should not be forgotten that Great Britain is fully mobilized, that China has never ceased its struggle against Japan, and that in the United States Japan's attack was by no means completely unexpected.

Most Americans long ago realized the formidable danger threatening the whole world in connection with the predatory war launched by Hitler and his "allies." Without being formally at war with Hitlerite Germany, the United States firmly took its place in the anti-Hitler front, giving large-scale assistance to the powers fighting against Nazi tyranny. The United States made use of the breathing space afforded it by the aggressors to develop its war industry. If this development has been insufficiently rapid, there is no doubt that the United States—as shown by measures already outlined by President Roosevelt—will make up for lost time and will throw the war production machinery of the United States into high gear.

The war in the Pacific will undoubtedly be long drawn out. In a modern war of motors and resources it is production potential, resources of manpower, and resources of materials that, in the final accounting, decide the issue. In this respect the United States possesses tremendous superiority over Japan.

In comparison with the United States, Japan is poor in resources of raw materials. The Japanese production machine cannot even be compared with that of America. Suffice it to point out that the American steel industry has a production capacity of nearly 90,000,-000 tons a year, double the capacity of Germany, Italy and the countries occupied by the Nazis, and 13 times the capacity of the Japanese steel industry, which barely reaches 7,000,000 tons a year.

As for resources of manpower, no comparison is even possible, since Japan faces a united front of the United States, Great Britain and China.

These facts show that Japan's first successes decide nothing. In future Japan's resources will be exhausted by this war, while American resources will grow. This is the circumstance that will decide the issue of the war. Japan will indisputably suffer defeat

*SOVIET-JAPANESE AGREEMENTS ON LIQUIDATION OF JAPANESE CONCESSIONS IN NORTHERN SAKHALIN AND ON PROLONGATION OF FISHERIES CONVENTION BETWEEN THE USSR AND JAPAN WITH AMENDMENTS MADE IN CONVENTION**

As a result of negotiations which took place in recent months between S. A. Lozovsky, Assistant People's Commissar of Foreign Affairs of the USSR, on the one hand, and Mr. N. Sato, Ambassador Extraordinary and Plenipotentiary of Japan to the USSR on the other hand, the "Protocol on the Transfer of Japanese Oil and Coal Concessions in Northern Sakhalin to the Soviet Union" which is published today was signed in Moscow on March 30, 1944. Below is also published the agreement "On the Procedure of the Transfer of the Property of Japanese Oil and Coal Concessions in Northern Sakhalin to the Soviet Government" signed by delegates of both parties on March 10. In addition to the above-mentioned protocol, the "Terms of Application of the Protocol" were signed on March 30. This document fixes the details referring to the implementation of the provisions of the protocol concerning the transfer to the Government of the USSR of the rights and property of Japanese concessions in Northern Sakhalin, establishes the terms for the evacuation to Japan of the workers and employees of the oil and coal concession enterprises who are Japanese subjects, etc.

In 1925 the Soviet Government granted to Japan oil and coal concessions in Northern Sakhalin. The Soviet-Japanese agreements on these concessions were signed for a period of 45 years and the terms of operation of these concession agreements was to expire in 1970.

In the spring of 1941, during the negotiations for the conclusion of the Soviet-Japanese neutrality pact, the Soviet Government raised before the Japanese Government the question of the liquidation of these Japanese concessions. On April 13, 1941, simultaneously with the signing of the neutrality pact, Mr. Matsuoka,

* *Moscow News*, April 1, 1944, page 2.

then the Japanese Minister for Foreign Affairs gave to the Soviet Government a pledge in writing to settle the matter of the liquidation of the concessions in Northern Sakhalin within several months. On May 31, 1941, Mr. Matsuoka confirmed this pledge by a new statement conveyed to the Soviet Government through Mr. Tatekawa, the Japanese Ambassador to Moscow. At that time the Japanese party undertook to settle the matter of the liquidation of the concessions not later than six months of the date of the signing of the neutrality pact. This undertaking of the Japanese party was not fulfilled. And only as a result of the negotiations which concluded on March 30 there has been signed a Soviet-Japanese agreement on the liquidation of the Japanese concessions in Northern Sakhalin and on the transfer to the Soviet Union of all the property of these concessions on the terms fixed in the agreement. Thus, as a result of the present agreement, the Japanese concessions in Northern Sakhalin are liquidated 26 years before the expiration of the term of operation of the concession agreements.

Simultaneously with this is published the Soviet-Japanese Protocol signed on March 30 on the prolongation for five years of the fisheries convention of 1928 and the notes relating to the protocol, which provide for the modification of the terms of Japanese fishing in the Far Eastern waters of the U.S.S.R.

The new Soviet-Japanese agreement on the fishing convention provides for the following:

a) the withdrawal of 24 fishery lots rented by Japanese fishery owners, which had not been exploited by them for two years in succession;

b) the right of Soviet organizations to rent on auction annually 10% of the fishery lots placed on auction;

c) an increase of rent and other payments in gold made by Japanese fishery owners by 6% as compared to 1943.

Modifying the fisheries convention of 1928, under which fishing activities of Soviet organizations and Soviet citizens were subject to a number of substantial restrictions, the Soviet-Japanese agreement of March 30 abolishes all these restrictions. This agreement deletes from the fisheries convention all matters relating to the fishing activities of Soviet organizations and Soviet citizens as being exclusively within the competence of organs of the Soviet state.

The present Soviet-Japanese agreement also lays down that, pending the termination of the present war, Japanese subjects and other foreigners are forbidden to fish in certain sea areas in the Far East established by the Soviet Government in July 1941.

Besides, in accordance with the wishes of the Government of the U.S.S.R., the Japanese Government undertook to guarantee that all fishery lots situated on the eastern coast of Kamchatka and in Olyutorsk district and rented by Japanese subjects will not be exploited by Japanese leaseholders before the termination of the war in the Pacific.

On March 30 the Japanese Government informed the Government of the U.S.S.R. of its decision to close the Japanese Consulate General in the town of Alexandrovsk and the Japanese Vice-Consulate in the town of Okha in Northern Sakhalin.

On the same day the Soviet Government informed the Japanese Government of its decision to close the Soviet consulates in the towns of Hakodate and Tsuruga in Japan.

*DENUNCIATION OF SOVIET-JAPANESE NEUTRALITY PACT**

On April 13, 1941—that is, prior to Germany's attack on the USSR and before the outbreak of war between Japan, on the one hand, and United States and Great Britain on the other—a pact of neutrality was signed in Moscow between the Soviet Union and Japan. The conclusion of this pact marked the culmination of a definite stage in the development of Soviet-Japanese relations. For more than two decades, beginning with the great October Socialist Revolution and the formation of the Soviet State, these relations had been of a most unsatisfactory character.

The Japanese intervention in the Far East, during which Japanese troops landed in Vladivostok and occupied the Maritime Province; Japan's occupation of northern Sakhalin; the numerous frontier clashes, and lastly, the memorable events at Lake Changkufeng and the Nomanhan River in 1938 and 1939, are only a few of the facts indicating that over the course of many years Japan's leading circles pursued an aggressive policy toward the Soviet Union which time and again led to sharp conflicts between the two countries.

It required some considerable time before Japan's leading circles arrived at the conclusion that the establishment of formal relations with their neighbor, the Soviet Union, was essential, and renounced the policy of military provocation and adventures toward the USSR.

The conclusion of the Neutrality Pact between the USSR and Japan on April 13, 1941, testified to the failure of this policy of Japan's leading circles, who in the end were forced to adopt a course of regulating relations with the Soviet Union. The Neutrality Pact of April 13, 1941, played a beneficial role by removing a number of causes for misunderstanding and conflict with Japan, which were fraught with danger especially at the time when Germany was betraying her ambitions for new imperialist aggrandizement and for domination in Europe.

On June 22, 1941, intoxicated with her easy successes in western Europe, Germany treacherously attacked the Soviet Union. Hav-

* *Izvestia*, April 7, 1945.

ing launched into a military adventure in the east, Germany reckoned on just as easy successes in her way in the Soviet Union, confident as she was of her military might and backed as she was by the vast resources of nearly the whole of western Europe which she had seized.

Germany's temporary successes in the early months of war in the Soviet Union, which were due to the suddenness and surprise of the German fascists' dastardly attack, turned the heads, as we know, of many Japanese politicians who were ready to put their stakes on Hitler. But the rebuff which the Red Army administered to the insolent invader at the walls of Moscow and on a number of other sectors of our front, had a sobering effect on the Japanese hotheads.

However, the idea had already matured in the minds of Japan's leading political and military circles that it was necessary to take advantage of the "golden opportunity"—as the more frank of the Japanese military expressed it—to set about realizing their cherished imperialist schemes in the region of the southern seas. The subsequent course of events in the Pacific, beginning with the Japanese attack on Pearl Harbor on December 7, 1941, and the opening of hostilities between the United States and Great Britain on the one hand, and Japan on the other, is general knowledge.

In the Soviet Union's period of greatest trial, Japan continued to strengthen her cooperation with Germany, which was not only of supreme political significance, but also of substantial assistance to Germany in her war on the Soviet Union.

In the course of this war which was forced upon the Soviet Union by Germany, a radical demarcation of forces took place, which led to the formation of the Anglo-Soviet-American coalition. At the same time Japan was and still is at war with the Allies of the U.S.S.R. —the United States of America and Great Britain.

Thus, since the Neutrality Pact was concluded on April 13, 1941, the situation has undergone a radical change. Regarding this change, the statement made on April 5 by People's Commissar of Foreign Affairs of the U.S.S.R. V. M. Molotov to Japanese Ambassador N. Sato, says: "Germany attacked the U.S.S.R., while Japan—Germany's ally—is helping the latter in her war against the U.S.S.R. Moreover, Japan is at war with the United States and Great Britain, who are the Soviet Union's Allies."

All through this war, even when it was quite evident that the German gamble was doomed to complete failure, Japan continued in every way to strengthen her alliance with Germany and support

German piratical imperialism. The Soviet Government recognized that "under these circumstances, the Neutrality Pact between Japan and the U.S.S.R. has lost its meaning, and the prolongation of this pact has become impossible."

Consequently, the Soviet Government on April 5 informed the Japanese government of its desire to denounce the pact with Japan.

The statement, as we know, refers to Article III of the Neutrality Pact. It is specified in the pact that it is to remain in force for five years from the day of its ratification. Article III provides that unless either of the parties denounces the pact one year before its expiration, it automatically remains in force for another five years. Precisely at the present juncture the parties much decide whether, in accordance with Article III, the pact is to be prolonged for another five years or whether to denounce it. As we know, the Soviet Government decided to express its wish to the Japanese government to denounce the pact.

The Soviet Government's denunciation of the pact with Japan is a direct consequence of the fact that Japan is the ally of Germany, who is waging a vile piratical war on the Soviet Union, and that she is at the same time waging war on the United States and Great Britain, who are Allies of the Soviet Union.

APPENDIX III: SOVIET FAR EASTERN TRADE STATISTICS

Soviet trade statistics are difficult to use for purposes of comparison because records were kept in different types of ruble values at different periods and for different countries. For instance, for Sinkiang the figures through 1933 were compiled in internal rubles (*chervonets*). After that period, they were computed in gold rubles. In the case of Mongolia, until 1935 the figures were in goods rubles. Moreover, trade figures for all countries were compiled at first in internal rubles (*chervonets*) and subsequently, compiled in gold rubles, and finally, in 1936, the gold ruble was revalued. Therefore, the following tables, so far as possible, have all been converted to 1936 gold rubles. However, there is no fixed rate of exchange between the *chervonets* and the gold ruble or between the goods ruble and the gold ruble.

Soviet statistical handbooks are sometimes careless in adding these various kinds of rubles together. Consequently, great care must be exercised in using any figures giving percentage of total trade. This is why many Soviet sources show the trade with these small bordering countries in the East as a very large proportion of total foreign trade. This is a statistical error. For instance, the *chervonets* figure for Soviet exports to Sinkiang in 1932 is 15,698,000 whereas the gold ruble figure is 3,618,000. Nevertheless, in many later comparisons the *chervonets* figure is listed with the subsequent gold ruble figure. As a result, trade with Sinkiang is made to appear four times larger than it was in comparison with those countries whose trade figures were compiled entirely in gold rubles.[1]

[1]Cf. *Strany Vostoka*, Vol. 2, Moscow, 1936.

SOVIET TRADE WITH CHINA, EXCEPT SINKIANG; WESTERN CHINA (SINKIANG); MONGOLIA; TANNU TUVA; AND JAPAN

Figures are in thousands of 1936 gold rubles unless otherwise noted. Source: *Foreign Trade of the U.S.S.R. for 20 yrs. 1918–1937*; *Statistical Handbook* (in Russian) edited by C. N. Bakulin and D. D. Mishustin, Moscow, 1939.

	CHINA (except Sinkiang)		WESTERN CHINA (Sinkiang)		MONGOLIA		TANNU TUVA		JAPAN	
	Export[5]	*Import*	*Export*[4]	*Import*	*Export*[2]	*Import*	*Export*	*Import*	*Export*[3]	*Import*
1913	126,148[1]	331,347[1]			11,778	36,805			6,171	21,217
1918		25,794								
1919		13								
1920										66
1921 (Jan-Sept)		285								
1921/22		298								
1922/23		74								
1923/24	18,637	39,205	1,809*	9,627*	6,601*	8,620*	1,016*	622*	64,745	11,125
1924/25	28,146	54,789	11,752*	19,084*	12,128*	15,694*	1,625*	955*	55,289	11,730
1925/26	48,767	97,565	26,700*	38,233*	16,118*	16,386*	2,794*	911*	55,753	11,265
1926/27	37,283	86,242	44,816*	45,088*	20,293*	33,319*	2,519*	2,448*	79,484	15,842
1927/28	60,593	139,148	46,634*	59,112*	33,511*	53,007*	6,023*	5,729*	71,565	23,735
1928 (Oct–Dec)	17,682	19,903	17,524*	11,725*	9,040*	19,657*	950*	911*	14,375	5,707
1929	30,450	79,383	71,814*	71,985*	44,001*	66,909*	11,125*	5,676*	84,407	36,218
1930	54,719	36,932	70,193*	70,225*	78,047*	86,483*	9,163*	4,016*	70,190	73,514
1931	48,460	30,358	61,119*	44,729*	163,562*	126,289*	11,616*	3,920*	86,798	55,486
1932	35,417	25,789	68,757*	53,896*	181,310*	84,438*	19,219*	9,597*	44,234	20,963
1933	31,409	11,559	47,549*	82,440*	168,902*	75,638*	24,068*	7,564*	39,963	32,189
1934	9,001	15,067	20,717	26,039	196,250*	90,057*	30,875*	8,843*	25,325	30,244
1935	2,229	15,501	26,495	19,929	50,953	34,650	11,839	5,747	24,068	47,615
1936	573	12,791	36,145	25,671	50,433	32,120	6,171	5,193	27,679	61,968
1937	623	14,958	34,753	25,774	65,822	33,694	6,507	3,150	11,743	54,375
1938 (11 Mos.)†	736	19,620	38,363	32,507	59,282	30,464	5,458	2,321	5,883	16,875

[1] Including Sinkiang.

[2] The principal products exported to the Mongol People's Republic were: sugar, flour, meal, tea, canned goods, oil products, cotton, textiles, silk textiles, linen and other types of clothing, metal and electrical products, and in most recent years—automobile products. The chief imports were live cattle, hides, raw furs, sheep and goat skins, wool, hair, leather goods.

[3] The principal products exported to Japan were: fish, timber, oil cake, anthracite and hard coal, oil products. The chief imports were: chemical products, textiles, tea, leather goods, cement, metal products, machines and parts, ships.

[4] The principal products exported to Sinkiang were: cotton goods, shoes, matches, sugar and industrial equipment. The chief imports were: wool, raw hides, sausage casings, horse hair, cattle, fur, and cotton.

[5] The principal products exported to China were: textiles, oil, coal, fish and lumber. The chief imports were: tea, vegetable fats and oils, tungsten and antimony.

* Not comparable to figures for other years or other countries. These figures are in "goods rubles or *chervonets*.."

† *Statistika Vneshnei Torgovli S.S.S.R.* No. 11, 1938.

SUPPLEMENT

*TREATY OF FRIENDSHIP AND ALLIANCE BETWEEN THE U.S.S.R. AND THE CHINESE REPUBLIC, AUGUST 14, 1945**

The Presidium of the Supreme Council of the Union of Soviet Socialist Republics and the President of the National Government of the Chinese Republic,

desiring to strengthen the friendly relations existing between the Soviet Union and the Chinese Republic by means of an alliance of good neighborliness following military cooperation,

having decided to render each other assistance in the struggle against aggression on the part of enemies of the United Nations in this world war and cooperation in the war against Japan until its unconditional surrender,

expressing unswerving desire to cooperate in upholding peace and security for the good of the peoples of both countries and all freedom-loving nations,

acting in accordance with the principles affirmed in the common Declaration of the United Nations on the First of January, 1942, the Declaration of the Four Powers signed in Moscow on October 30, 1943 and in formation of the International Organization of the United Nations,

have decided to conclude with this aim the present treaty and have appointed as their plenipotentiaries:

The Presidium of the Supreme Council of the Union of Soviet Socialist Republics: Vyacheslav Mikhailovich Molotov, People's Commissar for Foreign Affairs of the Soviet Union;

The President of the National Government of the Chinese Republic: Wang Shih-chieh, Minister for Foreign Affairs of the Chinese Republic.

These, after the exchange of their credentials in complete and due form, have agreed as below:

* *New York Times*, August 27, 1945. This is the text as monitored from the Moscow radio.

ARTICLE I

The high contracting parties have agreed together with the United Nations to wage war against Japan until final victory. The high contracting parties have promised to give each other all indispensable military and other assistance and support in this war.

ARTICLE II

The high contracting parties have pledged themselves not to enter into separate negotiations with Japan and not to conclude a peace agreement or armistice without mutual agreement with either the present Japanese Government or with any other Government or organ in power in Japan which will not clearly repudiate all aggressive intentions.

ARTICLE III

The high contracting powers have pledged themselves after the conclusion of the war against Japan to undertake mutually all existing measures in order to make it impossible to repeat the aggression and breach of peace by Japan. If one of the high contracting powers finds herself involved in military operations against Japan as a result of the aggression and breach of peace by Japan, the other high contracting party will give military and other assistance and support with the means at its disposal. This article remains in force until such time as, following the demand of the two high contracting parties, the responsibility shall be laid on the Organization of the United Nations for the prevention of further aggression on the part of Japan.

ARTICLE IV

Each of the high contracting parties pledges itself not to conclude any alliance whatsoever and not to take part in any coalition whatsoever directed against the other contracting party.

ARTICLE V

The high contracting parties, taking into consideration the interests of security and economic development of both parties, agree to work together in close and friendly cooperation after the conclusion of peace and to act according to the principles of mutual respect for their sovereignty and territorial entity and noninterference in the internal affairs of both contracting parties.

ARTICLE VI

The high contracting parties agree to give each other all possible economic assistance in the post-war period with a view to lightening and speeding up the national rehabilitation of both countries in order to make their contribution to the prosperity of the world.

ARTICLE VII

Nothing in this treaty should be interpreted in a way which would prejudice the rights and duties of both high contracting parties as members of the Organization of the United Nations.

ARTICLE VIII

The above treaty shall be ratified within the shortest possible time. The exchange of ratification documents will take place in Chungking as soon as possible.

The treaty comes into force immediately upon ratification and remains in force for a period of thirty years. Unless one of the high contracting parties should make one year before expiration of the treaty a declaration of its desire to denounce the agreement, the agreement will remain valid for an unlimited period. Each of the high contracting parties can terminate this agreement by giving one year's notice to the other high contracting party.

In confirmation of the above the plenipotentiaries have signed and sealed this treaty.

Drawn up in Moscow on the 14th of August 1945 which corresponds to the 14th day of August of the thirty-fourth year of the Chinese Republic, in two copies, each in the Russian and Chinese languages, both texts being equally valid.

As plenipotentiary of the Presidium of the Supreme Council of the Union of Soviet Socialist Republics

MOLOTOV

As plenipotentiary of the National Government of the Chinese Republic

WANG SHIH-CHIEH

AGREEMENT BETWEEN THE UNION OF SOVIET SOCIALIST REPUBLICS AND THE CHINESE REPUBLIC ON THE CHANGCHUN RAILWAY

August 14, 1945

The Presidium of the Supreme Council of the Union of Soviet Socialist Republics and the President of the National Government of the Chinese Republic, desiring to strengthen friendly relations and economic ties between the two countries on a basis of full equality and rights and interests of both parties, have agreed as to the following:

ARTICLE I

After expulsion of the Japanese armed forces from the Three Eastern Provinces of China the main trunk lines of the Chinese Eastern Railway and the South Manchuria Railway leading from the station of Manchuria [Manchouli] to the station of Pogranichnaya and from Harbin to Dalny [Dairen] and Port Arthur shall be joined into one railway system under the name of the Chinese Changchun Railway. This railway system will become the joint property of the Soviet Union and the Chinese Republic and will be jointly exploited by them. Only that land and those branch lines will be the joint property and will be jointly exploited which have been constructed by the Chinese Eastern Railway line in the period of Russian and joint Soviet and Chinese administration as well as the South Manchuria Railway during the period of Russian administration, which are intended for the direct requirements of these railways as well as subsidiary undertakings servicing these railways and constructed in the periods of time mentioned above.

All other railways and subsidiary undertakings will be the full property of the Chinese Government. The joint exploitation of the above-mentioned railways will be carried out by one single administration under Chinese sovereignty as a purely commercial transport undertaking.

ARTICLE II

The contracting parties agree that the rights of common property of the above railway line belong to both parties equally and must not be transferred by either in full or in part.

ARTICLE III

The contracting parties with the aim of joint exploitation of the above railway, agree to set up a Sino-Soviet company of the Chinese Changchun Railway Company. An administration of ten members is being constituted for this company, five of them being appointed by the Chinese and five by the Russians. The administration will have its seat in the town of Changchun.

ARTICLE IV

The Chinese Government out of the members of the administration of the Chinese citizens appoints a chairman of administration and assistant chairman of administration.

The Soviet Government out of the Soviet citizens members of the administration appoints a deputy chairman of administration and a deputy assistant chairman of administration.

In decisions concerning administration, the chairman's vote counts as two. The legal quorum of administration is seven people.

All important questions which the administration agrees to defer must be handed over to the decision of the Governments of the contracting parties for just and friendly solution.

ARTICLE V

A commission of revision will be attached to the administration consisting of six members, of which three are appointed by the Chinese Government and three by the Soviet Government. The president of the revision committee will be elected from among the Soviet members. The deputy chairman will be elected from among the Chinese members. The chairman's vote counts as two. The quorum of the commission is five members.

ARTICLE VI

For current matters the administration will appoint a managing director of the Chinese Changchun Railway from among the Soviet members and a deputy managing director from among the Chinese members.

ARTICLE VII

The revision commission will appoint a chief controller and his deputy. The chief controller will be appointed from among the Chinese citizens and the deputy chief controller from among the Soviet citizens.

ARTICLE VIII

The directors and deputy directors of services and departments of the railway as well as station masters of the more important stations are to be appointed by the administration. The managing director has the right to suggest candidates for these posts. Single members of the administration can also suggest candidates, following the consent of the managing director of the railway.

Should the chief of a service or department be a Chinese citizen, the deputy chief must be a Soviet citizen. Should the chief of a service or department be a Soviet citizen, his deputy must be a Chinese citizen. Chiefs of services and departments will be appointed from among Soviet and Chinese citizens on a 50–50 basis.

ARTICLE IX

The Chinese Government has the responsibility of guarding the railway. For the guarding of the railway premises, equipment and other installations and in order that goods in transit should not be liable to destruction or loss or theft the Chinese Government will set up and control a railway police force. The railway police must at the same time maintain normal order on the railway. As to the duties of the police in carrying out the requirements of this article, these will be drawn up by the Chinese Government after consultation with the Soviet Government.

ARTICLE X

Only in a period of war against Japan can the railway be used for the transport of Soviet troops. The Soviet Government has the right to transport on this railway by transit without customs inspection military equipment in sealed carriages guarded by the railway police force, and the Soviet Union will not have its own armed escort.

ARTICLE XI

Goods transported on the railway by transit from one Soviet station to another and also from Soviet territory to the port of Dalny [Dairen] and Port Arthur or *vice versa* will not be subject to customs or any other duties by Chinese authorities. Such goods on arrival in Chinese territory are liable to customs examination.

ARTICLE XII

The Chinese Government pledges to supply the railway with coal according to a special agreement.

ARTICLE XIII

The railway line is subject to taxes in the same way as other Chinese State railways.

ARTICLE XIV

The contracting parties have agreed to supply the Chinese Changchun Railway administration with working capital in sums agreed upon in the Statutes of the Railway. Profits and loss from the exploitation of the line shall be divided between the two parties.

ARTICLE XV

The contracting parties within one month from the signing of the above agreement will appoint three representatives each, who, in Changchun, will work out a statute on the joint exploitation of the road. This statute must be drawn up within two months and will then be submitted to confirmation by both Governments.

ARTICLE XVI

The property which will go over to joint possession of the Union of Soviet Socialist Republics and the Chinese Republic and will be liable to joint exploitation according to Article I of the present agreement must be defined by a commission which must consist of three representatives of each Government.

This commission must be set up in Changchun within one month of the signature of the present agreement. This commission must end its work within three months of the beginning of joint exploitation of the railway and present its findings for confirmation by both Governments.

ARTICLE XVII

The present agreement has been concluded for a period of thirty years. After expiration of this period the Chinese Changchun Railway with all its property will revert to the full possession of the Chinese Government at free cost.

ARTICLE XVIII

The present agreement comes into force from the day of ratification.

Drawn up in Moscow the 14th of August, 1945, which corresponds to the 14th of August of the thirty-fourth year of the Chinese Republic, in two copies, each in the Russian and Chinese languages, both texts being equally valid.

MOLOTOV, for the Soviet Union;
WANG SHIH-CHIEH, for the Chinese Republic.

SOVIET-CHINESE AGREEMENT ON PORT ARTHUR

August 14, 1945

Both contracting parties, in accordance with the Soviet-Chinese Treaty of Friendship and Alliance, and as a supplementary section to it, have agreed upon the following:

1. With the aim of strengthening the security of China and the U.S.S.R. and the preventing of aggression again by Japan, the Government of the Chinese Republic agrees to joint utilization by both of the contracting parties of Port Arthur as a naval base.

2. The exact frontiers of the area of the naval base noted in the point above are defined in the description and map appended.

3. The contracting parties have agreed to turn Port Arthur into a purely naval base at the disposal of the battleships and merchant ships of China and the U.S.S.R. alone. A Chinese-Soviet military commission will be established on questions of the joint use of the above-named naval base. It is to consist of two Chinese and three Soviet representatives. The chairman of the commission is appointed by the Soviet side and the vice chairman by the Chinese side.

4. The defense of the above-noted naval base is given the Government of the U.S.S.R. by the Chinese Government. The Government of the U.S.S.R., with the aim of the defense of the naval base, establishes the necessary equipment, and the cost is borne by the Government of the U.S.S.R.

5. Civil administration in the given area belongs to China, and in making appointments for responsible leading posts the Chinese Government shall take into account the interests of the U.S.S.R. in the given area. The civil administration in the town of Port Arthur is appointed and dismissed by the Chinese Government by agreement with the Soviet military command.

Suggestions which the Soviet military command in this area makes to the Chinese civil administration with the aim of securing defense will be carried out by the Chinese administration. In disputable cases the question will be put for examination and decision by a Chinese-Soviet military commission.

6. The Government of the U.S.S.R. has a right to maintain in the area noted in Point 2 its Army, Naval and Air Forces and determine their location.

7. The Soviet Government has also the task of establishing the maintenance of lighthouses, signals and other equipment necessary for the security of navigation in the given area.

8. When the agreement comes to an end all the equipment and public property put up by the U.S.S.R. in the given area is handed over without compensation and becomes the property of the Chinese Government.

9. The period of the present agreement is for thirty years. The agreement comes into force from the day of its ratification. The plenipotentiaries signed the above agreement and put their seals upon it.

Done in Moscow August 14, 1945, which is equivalent to August 14 of the thirty-fourth year of the Chinese Republic.

In two copies each in the Russian and Chinese languages and both texts have equal validity.

On behalf of the Presidium of the Supreme Soviet of the Union of Soviet Socialist Republics, MOLOTOV;

On behalf of the President of the National Government of the Chinese Republic, WANG SHIH-CHIEH.

SOVIET-CHINESE AGREEMENT ON PORT DAIREN

August 14, 1945

In view of the fact that the Treaty of Friendship and Alliance has been concluded between the Union of Soviet Socialist Republics and the Chinese Republic, also of the fact that the Union of Soviet Socialist Republics has guaranteed respect for Chinese sovereignty of the Three Eastern Provinces as an inseparable part of China, in order to insure the interests of the Union of Soviet Socialist Republics in Dairen as an import and export port of commodities, the Chinese Republic hereby expresses its consent:

1. to proclaim Dairen a free port open to trade and shipping of all countries;

2. to set aside for leasing to the U.S.S.R. piers and warehouses in the said free port on the basis of separate agreement.

3. Administration in Dairen will be exercised by China.

The chief of the port shall be appointed from among Soviet citizens by the manager of the Chinese Changchun Railway by agreement with the Mayor of the town of Dairen. The assistant chief of the port shall be appointed in the above way from among Chinese citizens.

During peacetime Dairen shall not be included in the sphere of operations of regulations on the naval base contained in the agreement on Port Arthur of August 14, 1945, and will become subject to the military regime established in this port only in event of war with Japan. Goods coming from abroad to this free port and transported over the Chinese Changchun Railway directly to the U.S.S.R., also goods coming from the U.S.S.R. over the above railways through the free port for export, or materials and equipment for the port installation coming from the U.S.S.R. are exempted from customs duties.

The above goods must be transmitted in sealed cars. Chinese import duties shall be levied on goods entering China through the free port. Goods exported from other parts of China to the free port are subject to export duties during the period while such continued to be levied in China.

The present agreement has been concluded for a term of thirty years. The present agreement comes into force as from the day of its ratification.

In testimony of which plenipotentiaries signed the present agreement and have fixed their seals thereto.

Done in Moscow August 14, 1945, which corresponds to August 14 of the thirty-fourth year of the Chinese Republic. In two copies each in Russian and Chinese languages, both texts having equal force.

Signed on the authorization of the Supreme Soviet of the U.S.S.R., MOLOTOV;

On the authorization of the Presidium of the National Government of the Chinese Republic, WANG SHIH-CHIEH.

SOVIET-CHINESE AGREEMENT ON THE THREE EASTERN PROVINCES

August 14, 1945

Agreement on relations between the Soviet commander-in-chief and the Chinese administration after the entry of Soviet troops into the territory of the Three Eastern Provinces of China in connection with the present joint war against Japan:

Relations between the Soviet commander-in-chief and the Chinese administration should correspond to the spirit of friendship and allied relations existing between the two countries.

Agreed on the following:

1. After the entry of Soviet troops as a result of hostilities into the territory of the Three Eastern Provinces of China, supreme authority and responsibility in the zone of hostilities in all questions relating to the prosecution of the war for the period necessary for operations shall rest with the commander-in-chief of the Soviet armed forces.

2. Representatives of the National Government of the Chinese Republic and the personnel shall be appointed for the restored territories who shall: (a) establish and direct in accordance with Chinese laws the administration on the territory cleared of the enemy; (b) render assistance in establishing cooperation in the restored territories between the Chinese armed forces both regular and irregular and the Soviet armed forces; (c) insure active collaboration between the Chinese administration and the Soviet commander-in-chief and in particular issue instructions to local organs to this effect being guided by the requirements and wishes of the Soviet commander-in-chief.

3. To insure contact between the Soviet commander-in-chief and the representatives of the National Government of the Chinese Republic a Chinese military mission will be appointed with the headquarters of the Soviet commander-in-chief.

4. In the zones under the supreme authority of the Soviet commander-in-chief the administration of the National Government of the Chinese Republic for the restored territory shall maintain contact with the Soviet commander-in-chief, through the representative of the National Government of the Chinese Republic.

5. As soon as any part of the restored territory ceases to be a zone of direct hostilities the National Government of the Chinese Republic shall assume full authority as regards civilian affairs and shall render the Soviet commander-in-chief every assistance and support through its civil and military organ.

6. All persons belonging to the Soviet armed forces on Chinese territory shall be under the jurisdiction of the Soviet commander-in-chief. All Chinese nationals both civilian and military, shall be under Chinese jurisdiction. This jurisdiction shall also extend to the civilian population on Chinese territory, even in the event of crimes and offenses against the Soviet armed forces, with the exception of crimes and offenses committed in the zone of hostilities which are subject to jurisdiction of the Soviet commander-in-chief. In disputable cases questions shall be decided in agreement between the Soviet commander-in-chief and the representative of the National Government of the Chinese Republic.

7. A separate agreement shall be concluded concerning financial questions involved in the entry of Soviet troops to the territory of the Three Eastern Provinces of China.

8. The present agreement comes into force immediately upon ratification of the Treaty of Friendship and Alliance between the U.S.S.R. and China signed on this date. Done in Moscow on

August 14, 1945, which corresponds to August 14 of the thirty-fourth year of the Chinese Republic.

In two copies, each in Russian and Chinese languages, both the texts having equal force.

For the Presidium of the Supreme Council of the U.S.S.R., MOLOTOV;

For the President of the National Government of the Chinese Republic, WANG SHIH-CHIEH.

EXCHANGE OF NOTES REGARDING SOVIET AID TO THE CENTRAL GOVERNMENT OF CHINA AND CHINESE SOVEREIGNTY OVER MANCHURIA AND SINKIANG

August 14, 1945

Honorable Mr. Minister, in connection with the signing on this date of the Treaty of Friendship and Alliance between China and the U.S.S.R. I have the honor of placing on record that the following provisions are understood by both contracting parties in the following way:

1. In accordance with the spirit of the above treaty and for the implementation of its general ideas and purposes the Soviet Government is ready to render China moral support and assistance with military equipment and other material resources, this support and assistance given fully to the National Government as the Central Government of China.

2. In the course of negotiations on the ports of Dairen and Port Arthur, also on the joint operation of the Chinese Changchun Railway, the Soviet Government regarded the Three Eastern Provinces as part of China and again confirmed its respect for China's full sovereignty over the Three Eastern Provinces and recognition of their territorial and administrative integrity.

3. As to latest events in Sinkiang, the Soviet Government confirms that, as stated in Article V of the Treaty of Friendship and Alliance, it has no intention to interfere with China's internal affairs. In the event that you, Mr. Minister, confirm your agreement with such understanding of the above points, the present note and your answer to it shall constitute a part of the above Treaty of Friendship and Alliance. Accept, Mr. Minister, the assurances of my very high respect.

MOLOTOV

In his note of reply Minister of Foreign Affairs of China Wang Shih-chieh declared his complete agreement with such understanding of the above stated points.

EXCHANGE OF NOTES REGARDING OUTER MONGOLIA

August 14, 1945

MR. PEOPLE'S COMMISSAR:

In view of the desire for independence repeatedly expressed by the people of Outer Mongolia, the Chinese Government declares that after Japan's defeat, if a plebiscite of the people of Outer Mongolia confirms this desire, the Chinese Government will recognize the independence of Outer Mongolia in her existing boundaries.

The above statement will be binding after the ratification of the Treaty of Friendship and Alliance signed by the Chinese Republic and the U.S.S.R. on August 14, 1945.

I beg you, Mr. People's Commissar, to accept the assurances of my very high respect.

WANG SHIH-CHIEH

The note from People's Commissar of Foreign Affairs of the U.S.S.R. Molotov to Minister of Foreign Affairs of the Chinese Republic Wang Shih-chieh.

MR. MINISTER:

Hereby I confirm receipt of your note in which you state that "in view of the desire for independence repeatedly expressed by the people of Outer Mongolia the Chinese Government declares after Japan's defeat, if a plebiscite of peoples of Outer Mongolia confirms this desire, the Chinese Government will recognize the independence of Outer Mongolia in her existing boundaries. The above statement will be binding after the ratification of the Treaty of Friendship and Alliance signed by the Chinese Republic and the U.S.S.R. on August 14, 1945."

The Soviet Government, with satisfaction, has taken note of the above note of the Government of the Chinese Republic and declares on its part that it will respect the state of independence and territorial integrity of the Mongolian Peoples Republic. I beg you, Mr. Minister, to accept the assurances of my very high respect.

MOLOTOV

INDEX